Whistling Dixie

Whistling Dixie

RONALD REAGAN,
THE WHITE SOUTH, AND
THE TRANSFORMATION OF
THE REPUBLICAN PARTY

Jonathan Bartho

University Press of Kansas

Jonathan Bartho, "Reagan's Southern Comfort: The 'Boll Weevil' Democrats in the 'Reagan Revolution' of 1981," *Journal of Policy History* 32, no. 2 (2020): 214–238. Reproduced with permission.

Published by the University Press of Kansas (Lawrence, Kansas 66045), which was organized by the Kansas Board of Regents and is operated and funded by Emporia State University, Fort Hays State University, Kansas State University, Pittsburg State University, the University of Kansas, and Wichita State University.

This book will be made open access within three years of publication thanks to Path to Open, a program developed in partnership between JSTOR, the American Council of Learned Societies (ACLS), University of Michigan Press, and the University of North Carolina Press to bring about equitable access and impact for the entire scholarly community, including authors, researchers, libraries, and university presses around the world. Learn more at https://about.jstor.org/path-to-open/.

Library of Congress Cataloging-in-Publication Data

Names: Bartho, Jonathan, author.
Title: Whistling Dixie : Ronald Reagan, the white South, and the
    transformation of the Republican Party / Jonathan Bartho.
Other titles: Ronald Reagan, the white South, and the transformation of the
    Republican Party
Description: Lawrence, Kansas : University Press of Kansas, 2024. |
    Includes bibliographical references and index.
Identifiers: LCCN 2023037204 (print) | LCCN 2023037205 (ebook)
    ISBN 9780700636495 (cloth)
    ISBN 9780700636501 (ebook)
Subjects: LCSH: Reagan, Ronald. | Southern States—Politics and government.
    | United States—Politics and government—1981–1989. | Republican Party
    (U.S. : 1854–) | BISAC: HISTORY / United States / 20th Century |
    POLITICAL SCIENCE / Political Ideologies / Conservatism & Liberalism
Classification: LCC E877.2 .B378 2024 (print) | LCC E877.2 (ebook) | DDC
    973.927—dc23/eng/20240117
LC record available at https://lccn.loc.gov/2023037204.
LC ebook record available at https://lccn.loc.gov/2023037205.

British Library Cataloguing-in-Publication Data is available.

Printed in the United States of America

The paper used in this publication is acid free and meets the minimum requirements of the American National Standard for Permanence of Paper for Printed Library Materials Z39.48-1992.

For my parents, Sandra and Peter

Contents

Acknowledgments

I am hugely indebted to many people for their support and encouragement during the research and writing of this book. The assistance of numerous archivists at a range of US libraries enabled me to source important primary material, but I am particularly grateful to the archival staff at the Ronald Reagan Presidential Library, the Jesse Helms Center, and the Hoover Institution for their help and generosity.

I am also very grateful to David Farber and Sean Cunningham for their insightful comments and valuable recommendations when reviewing an early draft of this manuscript, and to Robert Mason and Alex Goodall for their very helpful advice and guidance on pursuing the publication of a monograph. In addition, I have been lucky to make numerous friends during my academic life at Canterbury Christ Church University and University College London who have provided encouragement, or sometimes a much-needed distraction, when my research and writing has hit a difficult patch. I am indebted to them for their friendship and support.

In working on this book, my biggest debt is undoubtedly to Professor Iwan Morgan. His wisdom, patience, and seemingly limitless knowledge of US history has been invaluable in guiding me through the research of what has occasionally felt like a dauntingly complex subject. He has been very generous with his time, reading drafts, helping me to clarify my thinking, and offering advice when it was required. I could not have wished for a better mentor in the study of US political history.

Finally, I am especially thankful to my parents, Sandra and Peter. I am profoundly grateful for their unwavering love and support, not simply during my time working on this book but throughout my life. Without them, I would never have made it this far.

Prologue

On the evening of 21 March 1975, Ronald Reagan was in the heart of the conservative South. He had been invited by the Chamber of Commerce in Cullman, Alabama, to be the star attraction at its annual banquet. An audience of more than 1,600 packed into a high school auditorium to hear him deliver his now familiar refrain, arguing for individual liberty and free markets in the face of creeping government bureaucracy. To loud and repeated applause, he declared that "profit, property and freedom are inseparable." "We're faced with the choice of a free market, which has blessed us beyond measure, or the deadly dullness of socialism."[1] The event was, in short, like thousands of others Reagan had addressed since the 1950s on what he drolly called "the mashed potato circuit."

For all its familiarity, Reagan's visit to Cullman was still highly significant. It represented a huge event for this small city located fifty miles north of Birmingham—over 10 percent of Cullman's population saw Reagan's Chamber of Commerce speech. The rapturous welcome he received was emblematic of the affection and admiration millions of white southern conservatives had for a man who had been appearing and speaking across the region for two decades. Also notable was the man who introduced him: Alabama's Democratic governor George Wallace, a politician who had epitomized the resentment and rage of the white South in the face of the dramatic social change of the mid-1960s. Even a decade after the height of the civil rights struggle, Wallace remained a deeply controversial figure. Nonetheless, when he had asked for the opportunity to appear alongside Reagan in Cullman, Reagan and his advisors agreed. Wallace hailed Reagan as an "excellent governor" and told him, "You are among friends here in Alabama."[2]

Since his first visit to the South in the mid-1950s, white audiences from Texas to Virginia had responded enthusiastically to Reagan's condemnations of big government and warnings about the threat of socialism. Reagan may have been adamant that he abhorred racial prejudice—he found any accusation of racism genuinely upsetting—but white southerners had undoubtedly interpreted his anti-statist rhetoric as support for their own fights against federal desegregation efforts. Over the coming decade and a half, Ronald Reagan would do more than any previous Republican—even Richard Nixon, who won every southern state in 1972—to persuade white southerners to abandon their Democratic allegiances and make a new political home in the GOP. By the time Reagan left the White House, the white South was solidly Republican at the presidential level and would follow suit in congressional and state elections within a decade.

Despite this, the priorities of Reagan and his southern supporters were rarely in step with each other. Little noted by the media at the time, Reagan's appearance in Cullman represented a meeting of two distinct strands of American conservatism: the economically-focused, small-government ideology which was ascendant on the right of the Republican Party—and which by 1980 would be regularly labelled "Reaganite conservatism" or "Reaganism"—and the southern conservative tradition, which in the mid-1970s still clung to its Democratic loyalties and retained its predispositions towards racial, social, and cultural issues. Reagan's presidential campaigns and political career would bring these strands of American conservatism together under the GOP banner, but they would never truly merge. Indeed, tensions between them would cause frequent headaches for the Reagan White House. This book examines those stresses, and considers how the Reagan administration handled—or, more typically, struggled to handle—the sometimes bitter political and economic disputes that developed, what they meant for Reagan's presidency and legislative agenda, and the lasting impact they ultimately had on the Republican Party and the broader American political landscape.

The differences between Reaganism and southern conservatism were visible even during Reagan's visit to Cullman in March 1975. The fact that he and Wallace were sharing a platform had prompted some in the South to hope that the two might unite for a conservative third-party campaign in 1976. Though Wallace appeared open to the idea, saying "nothing is inconceivable," Reagan was quick to dismiss it at a press conference prior to his Chamber of Commerce speech. While claiming Wallace would be a "formidable" opponent for Republicans, he observed, "I never sensed that he had the same libertarian approach to government that I do."[3] Reagan's response suggested he was acutely aware of the potential for friction between his own agenda and the economic and cultural instincts of conservative southerners.

Even before he reached the White House, Reagan blinded himself to the racial aspects of southern conservatism that surfaced during his campaigns in the region, while his southern supporters struggled to accept Reagan's more libertarian inclinations and displays of political pragmatism. Once he became president, his relationship with southerners in the GOP—as well as those conservative southern Democrats whom Reagan hoped to attract to the Republican Party—became more fractious, as they determinedly pursued their own political priorities even when they were at variance with Reagan's agenda. His emphasis on free markets, budget cutting, and supply-side tax cuts ran counter to southern conservatives' determination to preserve regional industries and federal subsidies. Similarly, while Reagan's advisers were careful to keep him rhetorically in tune with his southern supporters on issues of religion and morality, his neglect of their social agenda provoked widespread discontent. At times during Reagan's presidency, these tensions led to congressional battles between Reaganites and southerners within the GOP, and at other times to the emergence of cross-party southern conservative alliances which united to thwart the aims of the Reagan White House.

As this book also illustrates, the difficulties faced by the Reagan administration in handling the demands of the conservative South foreshadowed the future direction of the Republican Party. Reagan's relationship with southern conservatives was crucial to the South's conversion into a reliably Republican region and, concurrently, to the increasing "southernization" of the GOP. A fault line developed in the party, which grew ever deeper after Reagan left office and as the Republican grip on the white South tightened. Towards the end of the twentieth century, Southern conservatives existed in an uneasy and sometimes turbulent alliance with Reaganites, who now formed the mainstream of the party. During the 2010s, southern conservatives went on to form the core of an economically populist, culturally and racially conservative insurgency which pushed the Republican Party in a more disruptive, anti-intellectual, and intolerant direction, increasingly focused on tapping into the insecurities and resentments of white voters. By examining the tensions and clashes between Reaganites and southern conservatives during the 1980s, this book chronicles the earliest stages of that transformation.

The ingrained conservatism of the white South—deeply rooted in regional history and memory—underwent a significant reconfiguration in the years after the Second World War. In the two decades following the war's end, increased federal involvement in the region instigated widespread economic change and prompted the biggest upheaval in the southern way of life for generations, creating opportunities for African Americans to challenge the South's oppressive Jim Crow laws. This in turn gave rise to a political and social backlash, as whites struggled to retain power in the region and to make sense of tectonic shifts in the southern status quo. Added to the mix was a nationwide resurgence in evangelical Christianity that was at its most intense in the South and was inspired by southern pastors such as Billy Graham and W. A. Criswell. By the early-1960s, these developments had combined to forge a contemporary southern conservatism marked by economic populism, fears of racial equality, and a determination to advance the priorities of white southerners through the vehicle of evangelical Christianity.

Prior to the war, much of southern society was unchanged since the end of Reconstruction. The region remained largely rural and economically reliant on agriculture. For African Americans, Jim Crow laws meant that racism, casual cruelty, and the persistent threat of violence were facts of daily life. Conservative southern Democrats continued to dominate regional and local politics, and white southerners retained an iron grip over social and economic structures. Though the New Deal saw an infusion of federal spending in the South, this failed to change the widespread view—expressed by President Franklin D. Roosevelt in 1938—that the region was "the nation's No. 1 economic problem."[4] Yet by the end of the 1930s it was also clear that even conservative southerners were starting to adapt to the greater levels of federal investment brought by the New Deal. This investment would increase sharply when the United States entered the war.

Wartime federal spending initially came to the South in the form of military camps and airbases. However, as US involvement in the conflict deepened, the southern states also became home to hundreds of factories, plants, and installations for the construction and testing of military equipment. Matthew Lassiter has written of the transformation that came to Marietta in Cobb County, Georgia, when "local business leaders convinced federal officials to convert Marietta's small municipal airport into a massive B-29 bomber plant." The impact on what had been a chiefly agricultural area was dramatic: the plant led to the creation of industrial jobs for almost one hundred thousand people, to the paving of local roads and the construction of thousands of new homes, effectively transforming Marietta into a suburb of nearby Atlanta.[5] There were parallel stories across the South, as wartime spending comfortably eclipsed even the federal investment brought to the region by the New Deal.

In total, the South received approximately $9 billion in federal investment during the war. More consequential than the funding itself was the change in political culture that it triggered. In those parts of the South that saw the impact of federal largesse, the economic priorities of politicians and business leaders shifted dramatically. From being suspicious of big business and instinctively antagonistic to outside—and particularly federal—involvement in their region's economy, southern conservatives now embarked on a headlong rush to attract external investment and industry to the South. In Cobb County, Lassiter notes, local boosters "turned the success story of the Bell Bomber Plant into a broader crusade for economic development" as soon as the war ended.[6]

Cheap labor and an almost complete absence of union activity were already major selling points to companies looking to invest in the South, but intense competition between southern states meant that industrial subsidization policies quickly became commonplace. Mississippi, one of the poorest states in the United States, was an early adopter, with the aim of reducing the state's dependence on agriculture. The Balance Agriculture with Industry Program (BAWI), first established during the Great Depression but resurrected after World War II, encompassed a variety of methods to encourage investment in Mississippi, and was the first state-sponsored economic development program in the entire United States. Tax exemptions, bonds, worker training, and subsidized rents were all crucial in drawing companies down from the northern Rustbelt and convincing them to build industrial plants and facilities. Paper mills, textile factories, and shipyards were constructed thanks to millions of dollars of state assistance, triggering a belated (and still comparatively limited) industrial revolution in one of the most agrarian states in the South. In the late 1940s and 1950s, numerous other southern states adopted the same approach, most notably Alabama, Arkansas, Kentucky, and Tennessee.[7]

The widespread acceptance of state-funded economic development among the southern political class—most of whom regarded socialism as an eighth deadly sin—represented a remarkable turnaround. But along with it came another, perhaps even more surprising, aspect of the new southern conservative approach to economics: a steadfast resolve to bring federal government spending to the South and, once it arrived, to see that it remained in place. Federal subsidies, grants, and investment accounted for 14 percent of southern state revenues in 1940. The figure had risen to 20 percent by the mid-1950s. At the same time as encouraging private industry to come south, and even as they decried federal interference in other areas of southern life, local and state level politicians across the region were competing enthusiastically to attract as much federal money as they possibly could. By 1960, 25 percent of all federal expenditure went to the South.[8]

This federal spending came from two principal sources. The first was the federal government's effort to bring economic development to the South through national programs and projects that originated in the New Deal. Road and transport construction programs, agricultural subsidies, and large-scale development projects which covered huge swathes of the region—such as the Rural Electrification Administration and the Tennessee Valley Authority—had all been established in the 1930s and were expanded further in the postwar period. By 1960, for example, almost a quarter of the South's funding for highway construction came from the federal government. Similarly, the TVA, originally created to alleviate rural poverty in the Tennessee Valley during the Great Depression, became ever more economically and politically entrenched during 1940s and 1950s, shifting its focus from the war on poverty to the fight to attract industry to the South. Throughout this period, the TVA management gradually allied itself with southern political elites and strengthened its ties to the growing military-industrial complex, ultimately becoming a key channel through which federal money—particularly defense spending—was directed towards the South.[9]

Indeed, the second major source of federal spending in the South was an extraordinarily rapid increase in the construction and expansion of US defense and aerospace facilities. Many, like the Bell Bomber Plant in Marietta (taken over by Lockheed in 1951), were built and run by defense contractors.[10] In addition to these, however, 60 percent of new bases constructed by the US Army during the war were in the South and the region received 40 percent of all federal spending on new military facilities.[11] At the end of the war, rising alarm at the global spread of communism persuaded the federal government to maintain large-scale investment in national defense, and by the early 1960s the South was home to myriad new army, air, and naval bases, shipyards, and military training and testing centers. Among these were some of the United States' largest Cold War defense facilities, including Fort Hood in Texas, Fort Benning in Georgia, the US Marine Corps training base at Camp Lejeune in North Carolina, and vast nuclear weapons development sites like Oak Ridge in Tennessee and the Savannah River Plant, which covered hundreds of square miles of rural South Carolina. During World War II and the early years of the Cold War the South became firmly established, in Bruce Schulman's phrase, as "the nation's boot camp."[12]

"Our economy is the federal government," wrote William Faulkner in 1956 of the economic transformation of his home state. "We no longer till in Mississippi cotton fields, but in Washington corridors and Congressional committee rooms."[13] His latter observation was especially perceptive. Much of the federal money the South received in the postwar period—be it military spending, agricultural subsidies, or new highways and power stations—was diverted southwards by powerful Democratic senators and congressmen. Representatives such as Mendel Rivers from South Carolina and Georgia's Carl Vinson became notorious in Washington for using their committee assignments to procure military facilities for their districts. Together, Vinson and Senator Richard Russell were notably effective, bringing fifteen military installations to Georgia and making defense the state's largest industry by 1960.[14] Other southern Democrats were equally adept at using their congressional seniority to protect their region's economic interests. Agricultural subcommittees, particularly those which shaped the federal subsidy programs for the South's most important crops—tobacco, cotton, sugar, and peanuts—were heavily populated by southerners. Southern infrastructure projects such as highway, port, and airport construction likewise had numerous dedicated advocates in the corridors and committee rooms of Washington. By the early 1960s, the region's reliance on federal money was such that when Southern Democrats campaigned against Republican presidential candidate Barry Goldwater in 1964, media reports claimed their principal strategy was to warn southern voters "incessantly" that a Goldwater administration "would shut off the Federal spigots."[15]

While the industrialization and federal investment of the postwar years certainly brought the South closer to rest of the nation in terms of overall prosperity, the region itself became ever more divided between areas of economic success and areas of economic decline. Subsequently, in the early 1970s, the South came to be linked with the Southwest in the popular imagination as part of the "Sunbelt"—the concept created by Kevin Phillips in *The Emerging Republican Majority* in 1969 as shorthand for a region stretching from California to Florida that experienced an economic and population boom in the mid-twentieth century, along with a concurrent increase in national political influence.[16] In economic terms, cities like Atlanta, Dallas, Houston, and Miami were indeed analogous to Los Angeles, San Diego, or Phoenix when viewed as islands in a flourishing Sunbelt archipelago. But aside from these islands of urban and suburban prosperity, the Sunbelt label simply did not apply to most of the postwar South. The South was still America's poorest region, and the affluence of its biggest cities did not spread far. Anyone travelling beyond the suburbs of Atlanta, for example, would have found persistent and widespread poverty across rural Georgia. Newly established textile mills and manufacturing plants brought a measure of economic stability to local towns, but much of the rural South saw rising unemployment—a consequence of the increasing mechanization of agriculture—and population decline. By 1960, over ten million southerners, most of them black, lived outside the South. Millions of others left rural communities in search of work in southern cities.[17]

American involvement in World War II brought not only economic transformation to the South, but social turmoil. At the end of the war, veterans returned home demanding jobs and drastic changes to southern society. By far the most powerful demands for change came from returning black veterans who, having fought and defeated fascism abroad, were no longer prepared to tolerate the structures of racial segregation and white supremacy upon which southern politics and society were based. As Stephen Lawson writes, "The war loosened some of the old chains of subservience imposed by the southern caste system and freed blacks in hundreds of locales throughout Dixie to join together to overthrow Jim Crow."[18] Across the South, "many black GIs had barely taken the time to remove their uniforms before they marched to local courthouses to register to vote."[19] The resolve of these black veterans, for whom service overseas had been their first experience outside the segregated South, combined with shifts in the southern economy and mass migration across the region to create new opportunities for African Americans to overturn the status quo. Black efforts at voter registration in the South in the immediate postwar years gave birth to the civil rights movement which, within two decades, would radically alter the southern way of life.

For African Americans, resurgent southern liberals, and urban business leaders seeking a reformed southern political agenda to supplement the region's economic transformation, the late 1940s provided a glimmer of optimism. In 1948, President Harry S. Truman's administration ended segregation in the US armed forces, and the national Democratic Party voted to include a civil rights plank in its presidential election platform. Though these initiatives offered hope to opponents of the South's racist old order, they did much to forge the sense of mistrust and betrayal that white conservative southerners harbored towards the Democratic Party leadership for decades to come. While the South's political establishment had accepted, even embraced, changes to the southern economy, most conservative southerners were virulently opposed to any change that undermined racial segregation. Angered by their party's platform, a group of leading southern Democrats formed the breakaway States' Rights Democratic Party, widely known as the "Dixiecrats." With South Carolina governor Strom Thurmond as their presidential candidate, the Dixiecrats won Mississippi, Alabama, Louisiana, and South Carolina in the 1948 election, breaking the Democratic domination of the South for the first time since 1928.[20]

White southerners responded to black demands for civil rights with a mixture of fear, confusion, anger, and brutality. The angry defiance of the Dixiecrat revolt was mirrored at the local level, as the white supremacism of the conservative South inexorably reasserted itself. Already largely excluded from the benefits of the region's industrialization, black southerners were now faced with deception and intimidation when they attempted to register to vote. Examples of white resistance ranged from literacy and constitutional tests which were impossible to pass, to threats of violence and lynching. Such threats might come from local police, from a newly renascent Ku Klux Klan, or from unapologetically racist demagogues such as Mississippi senator Theodore Bilbo, whose preferred method of preventing black southerners from voting was to "do it the night before the election. I don't have to tell you more than that."[21]

But for most southern whites, the prospect of black progress and equality led to widespread disorientation. White southerners were "a confused and conflicted people, at times divided within and against themselves."[22] Ultimately this uncertainty had a unifying effect, as whites clung to the ingrained southern conservative attitudes they had known for generations: belief in law and order, pride in their region's history and identity, a conviction that segregation was good for both blacks and whites, and a fear that racial equality and civil rights would lead to black political control. The Supreme Court's 1954 ruling in *Brown v. Board of Education*, that racial segregation in schools was unconstitutional, proved to be the great cause around which white southerners could rally—be they committed segregationists or those merely fearful of social upheaval. It was the impulse to resist the *Brown* decision, more than any other factor, that acted to bring together the varied elements of white southern society into a united front of resistance. The socioeconomic convulsions that permeated the South in the late 1940s and early 1950s served to bolster the socially and racially conservative instincts of most white southerners, reinforcing their faith in the established political order.

A vital factor in this process was the perceived threat of communism. Anti-communism took root in the South in the 1930s, and in the postwar years the term "communist" was associated with any entity that appeared to endanger the region's status quo. In the late 1940s, accusations of communist influence played a crucial role in the efforts of southern political and business leaders to defeat Operation Dixie— an organized campaign by the Congress of Industrial Organizations (CIO) to unionize southern workers.[23] Anti-communism likewise became one of the most important elements in the defense of southern white supremacy, weaponized on countless occasions to undermine civil rights campaigners, the federal government, and Supreme Court justices, or used to justify the intimidation of black southerners. In 1951, a KKK leader declared that a spate of cross burnings in the South was part of the Klan's ongoing "fight against Communism."[24] Following the *Brown* decision, segregationists variously described the Supreme Court as "communist infiltrated," as "lending help, aid and support to the cause of Communism," or as being a leading force in the "establishment of the Communist Conspiracy in the United States." Such language was particularly useful when addressing southern audiences. For the many whites in the South who were enraged by *Brown* but unfamiliar with the legal niceties involved, being told that the Supreme Court was a haven of communist sympathy was both easy to comprehend and profoundly convincing.[25]

Southern anti-communism was, therefore, rather different to the Cold War fears permeating the rest of American society during the 1950s. To most whites in the South, it comprised just one aspect of a broader context of resistance, a way of rationalizing their anxiety about the changes happening around them and vindicating their opposition to the idea of racial equality. For their political leaders, anti-communist rhetoric played a variety of important roles in the fight against integration. As well as uniting white southern society, it was also a method of nationalizing issues that were predominantly regional. By

defining the civil rights movement as subversive and under communist influence, the southern establishment could claim that resistance
to desegregation was merely a part of the wider Cold War struggle—
emphasizing their patriotism while simultaneously attempting to remove race from the civil rights debate. When Martin Luther King
emerged as the talismanic leader of the black freedom struggle, he was
decried as a communist agitator, with supposed evidence being discovered of his attendance at a "Communist training school" and contacts
with other communists in Washington.[26]

Ultimately, the concept of anti-communism became so racialized
in the South during the postwar period, to a far greater extent than in
the rest of the nation, that the notions of communism and racial integration became almost interchangeable. For ordinary white southerners, whose certainties were being challenged on an almost daily basis,
anti-communism helped them comprehend the turbulence and rapid
social change they were experiencing and acted to assuage doubts
about the rightness of segregationist cause. At the political level, anti-
communism's rhetorical malleability—the way it could be shaped to
both national and regional contexts—made it hugely popular with segregationists. As Jason Sokol has observed, to southern whites in every
stratum of society, anti-communism became "a force they could mold
to their needs, fears and confusions."[27]

As the civil rights campaign gathered pace following the *Brown*
decision, white southerners' resentment, fear, and hostility to change
only intensified. Determined to preserve racial segregation and white
political control, a network of so-called White Citizens' Councils was
created in towns and cities across the South. Described as "a kind of
uptown Ku Klux Klan" by liberal Mississippi newspaperman Hodding
Carter, citizens' councils formed a key component of what came to be
known as "massive resistance," acting as a bridge between segregationist politicians and grassroots white supremacists and serving to further
unite white opposition to integration.[28] These groups of middle-class
whites—including lawyers, doctors, businessmen, and newspaper
publishers—organized resistance to black voter registration at the local level, produced racist literature, enforced segregation in businesses
and schools, and often implicitly encouraged violence and intimida-

tion.[29] The Citizens' Councils were also, in historian Anthony Badger's phrase, "determined to impose conformity to white supremacy." The rare white southerners who openly sympathized with black civil rights would find themselves threatened and silenced. In the wake of *Brown*, segregationist sentiment and propaganda acquired such force that even previously moderate politicians like Alabama senators Lister Hill and John Sparkman "ran for cover" and joined Citizens' Councils.[30]

Throughout the 1950s and early 1960s, the rhetoric of "states' rights" performed a similar role to that of anti-communism. By reviving the nineteenth-century notion of the primacy of states' rights, postwar segregationists were able to vehemently resist changes to the South's racial status quo without directly discussing race itself. Many southern politicians—most notably South Carolina governor, and later senator, Strom Thurmond—became expert at denouncing civil rights legislation, Supreme Court decisions, and federal actions on the grounds they went beyond the limits of the Constitution. The "Southern Manifesto," signed by almost all southern senators and congressmen in March 1956, was the most prominent example. Drafted by Thurmond and Georgia senator Richard Russell, the document was formally titled "The Declaration of Constitutional Principles" and attacked the *Brown* decision as "contrary to the Constitution" and an example of "naked judicial power."[31] Such language, along with Thurmond's description of a 1957 civil rights bill as "legislation that exceeds the bounds of the Constitution," was a commonly heard refrain, one that attempted to make southern opposition to black rights and integration more palatable to audiences outside the South.[32]

Though white supporters of civil rights comprised only a small segment of southern society, most white southerners were also not committed members of Citizens' Councils or the KKK. Instead, they had varied and often ambiguous views on what constituted racial progress. As with anti-communism, the notion of states' rights was employed to reassure southern audiences that opposition to segregation was part of their region's anti-statist tradition at a time when the rest of the United States increasingly viewed the South as irretrievably bigoted. "Segregationists in the 1950s and 1960s drew upon a venerable tradition of southerners opposed to federal power," argues George Lewis, "including John C. Calhoun, Thomas Jefferson, and James Madison." Instead of undermining the Constitution, by adopting the rhetoric of states' rights conservative southerners could claim they were defending it. Paying public reverence to such figures from the South's past "helped resisters to legitimize their adherence to states' rights."[33]

For millions of white southerners throughout the 1950s and early 1960s, everyday life came to be filled with confusion and nervousness, as societal foundations they had known for generations steadily crumbled around them. As demands for black equality and civil rights increased, they clung to their conservative values and traditions, encouraged to do so by segregationist politicians and organizations determined to maintain white political and economic power. For most southern whites, anti-communism and states' rights were little more than abstract notions, but they were vital in unifying a population fearful that their society was on the verge of being turned upside down. A black southerner observed to the writer Robert Penn Warren in 1956, "A lot of people down here just don't like change. It's not merely desegregation they're against so much, it's just the fact of any change. They feel some emotional tie to the way things are."[34] It was this fear of change, with an inherited belief in white supremacy at its core, that reinforced the racial and cultural conservatism of the white South in the postwar era.

At the same time, the social upheaval enveloping the white South led to the region becoming a crucible for the resurgence of evangelical Christianity, the rapid spread of which would ultimately have enormous political implications. Across the United States, the postwar years saw an evangelical revival spearheaded by Southern Baptist pastor, and North Carolina native, Billy Graham. While Graham shared several views typical of his fellow southerners—he was an ardent Cold Warrior and believed the Garden of Eden was a place with "no union dues, no labor leaders, no snakes, no disease"—his evangelicalism was conspicuously moderate on racial issues.[35] Graham largely avoided visits to the Deep South during the height of massive resistance and was holding desegregated services and advocating racial harmony even before landmark events such as *Brown*. This moderation enabled his appeal to spread outside the South, making him a national and international figure and enabling his brand of "New Evangelical" Christianity to become mainstream during the 1950s.[36] From the very start of his administration, President Dwight D. Eisenhower publicly embraced the Christian revival, believing that American religious faith provided a vital contrast to atheistic communism in the Cold War propaganda battle. Eisenhower personally led a prayer at his inauguration and was baptized ten days into his presidency. His administration would later add the words "under God" to the pledge of allegiance and "In God We Trust" to US currency. Billy Graham was a regular and welcome visitor to the White House, becoming a trusted consultant to both Eisenhower and Vice President Richard Nixon on a host of issues, including civil rights.[37]

Graham's rise to prominence also epitomized the importance of the South in what he described as "the greatest religious revival in American history." By 1961, the number of active church members across the United States had risen to 60 percent of the population, some 112 million Americans. Hundreds of millions of dollars were being spent on new churches.[38] This evangelical zeal was especially potent among white southerners. The region's biggest religious organization, the Southern Baptist Convention (SBC), almost doubled its membership between 1946 and 1961, from around six million to over ten million.[39]

Many conservative southerners viewed Billy Graham's racial moderation with mistrust and skepticism, however. Alongside Graham's mainstream New Evangelicalism, the region's more traditional fundamentalist evangelical churches were also rapidly expanding. On race, divisions between moderate and conservative religious leaders were widespread. For many whites, the South's racial structures were not merely just, but divinely sanctioned. There was a widening divide between those southern church leaders who supported integration and millions of white fundamentalist evangelicals who cleaved to southern traditions in times of turmoil. As Jason Sokol has noted, in contrast to Graham's support for integration, preachers and congregations across the South "imbued the pre-civil rights racial order with elements of timelessness and righteousness that only religion could impart."[40] Southern evangelical organizations that had openly supported the *Brown* decision, including the SBC and the Southern Presbyterian

Church, were deluged with angry correspondence from churchgoers and ministers opposed to integration. Segregationist sentiments were most widely voiced at the grassroots level, but some prominent fundamentalist leaders such as W. A. Criswell in Texas, Billy James Hargis in Arkansas, and Bob Jones Sr. (and his son, Bob Jones Jr.) in South Carolina, maintained their outspoken opposition to racial integration.[41]

It was W. A. Criswell, the intense, fire-and-brimstone pastor of the First Baptist Church in Dallas—which included Billy Graham as a member—who became the most prominent evangelical advocate for southern segregation during the 1950s. A speech he delivered in South Carolina in 1956 was worthy of the most ardent white supremacist. Criswell denounced Supreme Court justices as "a bunch of infidels, dying from the neck up" while civil rights campaigners were "two-by scathing, good-for-nothing fellows who are trying to upset all of the things that we love as good old Southern people and as good old Southern Baptists." Fellow evangelicals who supported integration did not escape Criswell's wrath. They were, he declared, "just as blasphemous and unbiblical as they can be." Following the speech, Billy Graham distanced himself from Criswell, saying, "My Pastor and I have never seen eye to eye on the race question."[42]

Leading the largest Southern Baptist congregation in the United States made Criswell an influential part of the Dallas establishment and a formidable figure in the wider Southern Baptist church. Segregation was not the only issue on which he and other fundamentalist evangelicals were becoming increasingly politically outspoken. Criswell was vociferously anti-communist (a struggle that he, like most white southerners, regularly combined with resistance to integration) and condemned socialism and liberalism with equal passion. The way to defeat communism, he argued, was through strength in both Christian faith and national defense—he even called for military training for all American citizens. Criswell also deplored the teaching of evolution and believed that American society was in rapid moral and spiritual decline. The United States, he claimed, was becoming an "amorphous society that has no morality, that gives itself to drunkenness and drugs, to debauchery and lack of personal responsibility, that is filthy and dirty and whose language is unspeakable and unacceptable."[43] While

Billy Graham was remaining avowedly neutral on most issues, despite his regular visits to the White House, W. A. Criswell's rhetoric and political engagement was blazing a trail that would be followed by later generations of conservative Southern Baptists. After several decades in which they had been discouraged by their leadership from direct involvement with politics, Criswell was leading fundamentalist evangelicals on a path that would eventually turn them into a potent electoral force.

In the late 1950s, the differences between mainstream New Evangelicals and conservative fundamentalists deepened, particularly over race and integration. Mainstream evangelicals, including the SBC's leadership, became increasingly uneasy about the loud segregationist pronouncements coming from their southern fundamentalist brethren. In return, fundamentalists decried Billy Graham not only for supporting civil rights but also for his willingness to work with church leaders and politicians who did not subscribe to the doctrine of biblical inerrancy. While Graham and other mainstream evangelical leaders courted moderate Republicans like Eisenhower and Nixon—Graham even became friendly with John F. Kennedy, despite initially being opposed to the idea of a Catholic president—fundamentalists allied themselves to southern conservatives such as Strom Thurmond.[44] With their fears about the creeping secularization of America seemingly validated by legal threats to bible readings and prayer in schools, fundamentalists also began to formulate ways of increasing their political influence and seizing control of evangelical organizations. At the same time, in Lynchburg, Virginia, the founder of the Thomas Road Baptist Church, Jerry Falwell, was among a younger generation of pastors starting to move the fundamentalist agenda away from race and onto new topics such as abortion and homosexuality.[45]

Beginning in the late 1940s, the broader religious revival in the United States was a response to the social and spiritual disruption produced by twenty years of war and economic depression. It saw mainstream evangelical leaders engaging positively with demands for change. At the local level across the South, however, the revival was more commonly led by fundamentalist pastors seeking to preserve rather than reform the southern way of life. "Their theology was intentionally and self-consciously reactionary," Paul Harvey has observed, "a rearguard response that ultimately would falter."[46] From the pulpit, fundamentalist ministers adopted the same defenses of segregation as the South's political establishment, and by the early 1960s were seeking to expand this political engagement further, increasingly preaching a deeply conservative gospel on a range of social and cultural issues. Theirs was a peculiarly southern response to changing times in the region: defensive of southern customs and traditions, suspicious of liberalism, and fueled by a belief that Washington had abandoned American values and encouraged a decline in morality.

As a result of the economic and social turbulence of the South's postwar years, what had emerged by the early-1960s was a southern brand of conservatism that retained its ancestral hostility towards the federal government, but now combined it with a determination to safeguard the enormous sums of federal money pouring into the region. Leading southern conservatives, while fighting a losing battle to preserve racial segregation, were formulating new, broader discourses designed to curb the growing political and economic power of African Americans and to play on fears of black equality to unify the white electorate. At the same time, a fervent revival of fundamentalist evangelical Baptism, which reinforced the religious and cultural conservatism of the South, was fused with a determination to maintain the region's political leverage and increasingly to impose its values on the wider nation—all while declaring a commitment to individual liberty. To outsiders, postwar southern conservatism was variously intolerant, paradoxical, and often downright contradictory. Ultimately, as the growth of southern power in the Republican Party would subsequently demonstrate, it was about furthering the economic, political, and cultural priorities of the white conservative South.

While there are clear similarities in political style and areas of overlap in foreign policy, the DNA of southern conservatism is very different to that of Reaganite conservatism. The development of Reaganism represents the confluence of two largely distinct stories: the evolution of Ronald Reagan's own political philosophy and the emergence of an ideological strain of anti-statist conservatism on the right of the Republican Party during the 1950s. Only when Reagan became a national political figure in the mid-1960s did these narratives truly merge.

Ironically, the roots of what eventually became Reaganite conservatism emerged in the Republican Party at a time when Reagan himself was still a loyal Democrat. In the years immediately following the Second World War, Republicans were split between supporters of the governor of New York, Thomas Dewey, and those backing Ohio senator Robert Taft. Internal conflict between the followers of these two men—Deweyites and Taftites—defined the GOP from the mid-1940s to the early 1950s. Initially, differences between the two factions were motivated more by power and personality than ideology. However, the two sides gradually came to identify with the labels given to them by voters and the media. As Michael Bowen observes, "as the public views of 'liberalism' and 'conservatism' began to crystallize, party insiders began to fight explicitly over ideological identity and frame their intraparty debates accordingly."[47]

In the eyes of the Taftite wing, Dewey represented the eastern, "liberal" party elite—too expedient and accommodating of the New Deal to offer real opposition to an increasingly tired Democratic administration. Conversely, to his critics Robert Taft's career was defined by hostility to the New Deal and his persona was too dour and confrontational to be a viable presidential candidate.[48] Taft's conservatism was characteristic of the Midwest. From his perspective, geography was as important as ideology in the GOP's factional conflict. In political terms, Taft regarded the East Coast with deep suspicion, believing eastern Republicans were under the sway of international financiers.[49] His steadfast opposition to global free trade and support for protectionist tariffs made him the archetype of a midwestern Republican, and his priorities lay in representing the interests of small and medium-sized businesses like those in his home state of Ohio. Taft's mistrust of trade agreements and foreign entanglements was such that many in the party viewed him as an old-fashioned isolationist.

Ronald Reagan's views on free trade may have run directly counter to those of Taft, but in his approach to domestic affairs Taft's conservatism—and particularly his rhetoric—contained the seeds of Reaganism. As Reagan would do twenty years later, Taft and his conservative allies liked to depict labor unions and Democratic leaders as socialists attempting to constrain American liberty and enterprise. As the most influential Republican on Capitol Hill, his agenda combined budget and tax cutting with a dogged determination to reduce the power of centralized government after years of New Deal expansion. After entering the Senate in 1939, Taft quickly became a protagonist in *ad hoc* alliances formed between Republicans and southern Democrats to repel the more liberal elements of the New Deal, particularly when it came to welfare and labor policies. Postwar, he would play a leading role in forging similar GOP-southern Democrat coalitions to resist Harry Truman's Fair Deal and combat the rising militancy of labor unions. Indeed, the 1947 Taft-Hartley Act—which outlawed various union practices, restricted closed shops, and placed significant limitations on union power—was enthusiastically supported by conservative southerners.[50] Subsequently, the notion of a "right to work" would become a key principle of conservative politics throughout the twentieth century. Both Taft-Hartley and the Republican Party's other big legislative achievement of the period, a tax cutting bill in 1948, were forced through after vetoes by President Truman were overridden.[51] Nonetheless, both were products of Taft's hard work and congressional expertise.

These successes gave Republicans hope for the 1948 elections. However, having prevailed over Robert Taft in the Republican nomination battle, Thomas Dewey suffered a shock defeat to President Harry Truman in the presidential race, while the GOP also lost control of the House of Representatives and experienced heavy defeats in the Senate elections.[52] Dewey's humiliating failure increased the power of the Taftites and made Taft himself the presumptive favorite to be Republican presidential candidate in 1952. Again, conservatives would be frustrated. This time the Deweyites persuaded an American national hero, General Dwight D. Eisenhower, to run for the GOP nomination, aware that he appealed to American voters in a way none of their own potential candidates could match. After a bitterly contested Republican convention, Taft lost the nomination battle for a second time. When Eisenhower won the November presidential election, Taft's presidential ambitions were over. Recriminations between midwestern and eastern

Republicans were so bitter that reconciliation appeared impossible. The divide in the party widened ever further.[53]

Less than a year later, in July 1953, Robert Taft's early death deprived conservative Republicans of the man who had led them for over a decade. His legacy was such that for years conservative Republicans still considered themselves Taftites. There was no obvious replacement. The men who succeeded Taft in guiding Republican conservatism during the mid-1950s had little of his ability, eminence, or expertise. Without a dominant leader, the GOP right found itself increasingly side-lined and severely weakened in its struggle for control of the party. While the Republican image and party machinery were dominated by President Eisenhower and his allies, the Taftite wing began to reinvent itself based on conservative ideas and principles.[54] Not until the end of the decade did another leader emerge, a man who would help transform the perception of Republican conservatism from stern midwestern traditionalism to a dynamic creed rooted in the West and Southwest: Arizona senator Barry Goldwater.

For Ronald Reagan, 1948 marked the last time he would support a Democratic presidential candidate. A moderately successful Hollywood actor, Reagan made campaign appearances on behalf of President Truman and was, in his own later description, a "near-hopeless hemophiliac liberal."[55] But over the next decade, he would embark on a philosophical and political migration. His fervent anti-communism led to a deep disenchantment with liberalism and then on to an embrace of anti-statism and free market economics. While Reagan's transformation was reflective of broader national trends—a similar journey was undertaken by countless Americans in the mid-twentieth century—it was guided chiefly by personal experiences.

In the immediate postwar years, the change in Reagan's philosophy was driven by a conviction that "America faced no more insidious or evil threat than that of Communism."[56] His fear of communist subversion in the United States was reinforced by his experiences in Hollywood during the Red Scare of the late 1940s and early 1950s. So profound were his concerns that he informed the FBI of acquaintances he suspected of having communist sympathies and appeared as a friendly witness before the House Committee on Un-American Activities (HUAC) in 1947. As president of the Screen Actors Guild (SAG), Reagan did little to resist purges of suspected communists in Hollywood.[57] By the early 1950s, he was certain that communism posed an existential threat to liberty in the United States. For Reagan, the Cold War was a struggle between good and evil, between American democracy and communist totalitarianism. A belief that his fellow liberals were not sufficiently committed to fighting communism precipitated his turn away from liberalism and instilled in him an incipient conservative mistrust of centralized power.

Underlining Reagan's skepticism of big government was his resentment at the amount of tax he was paying. His movie earnings placed him in the top marginal tax bracket and when the Truman administration announced its intention to close tax loopholes, he faced further financial pain. These experiences instilled in him an aversion to high taxes that would go on to become a fundamental element of his political character. It was the tax issue that first drove Reagan to break with the Democrats and support Republican Dwight D. Eisenhower for president in 1952. His concern over taxes was not based purely in self-interest. In Reagan's view, the Democrats' proclivity for high tax rates was harmful to the wider economy, hitting the pockets of ordinary Americans and deterring them from putting in more hours at work.[58] While anti-communism was the first step on Reagan's journey to conservatism, it was his antipathy towards high federal taxes that pushed him further away from Democratic liberalism and towards an ideological commitment to small government.

This anti-statism deepened during his time as a spokesman for General Electric in the 1950s, during which his thinking was heavily influenced by the unambiguously capitalist culture of GE's management. Reagan's role entailed grueling cross-country trips to visit plants and speak to company workers, part of a program to generate wider support for GE's political priorities: deregulation, lower corporate taxes, and limits on the power of unions. The program's architect, senior executive Lemuel Boulware, acted as a mentor to Reagan, encouraging him to read conservative political science and economics, and to gradually align his views—and particularly the content of his speeches—with GE's agenda.[59] A fear of flying forced Reagan to undertake countless long journeys by train, during which he immersed himself in books such as Friedrich Hayek's *The Road to Serfdom* (1944) or Henry Hazlitt's *Economics in One Lesson* (1948), absorbing arguments that added intellectual substance to his already conservative instincts. An aide assigned to travel with Reagan, Earl Dunckel, later claimed, "Everything that went into that mind stayed there. He could quote it out like a computer any time you wanted."[60] Such texts unquestionably influenced Reagan's political philosophy, strengthening his belief that the expansion of government portended the rise of socialism—potentially even a communist takeover of the United States—and bolstering his growing faith in the benefits of free market economics.

The transformation in Reagan's thinking echoed developments on the right of the Republican Party. By the late 1950s, the so-called Old Guard on the Taftite wing were being replaced by a less traditionalist, more ideologically driven generation of conservatives, with Barry Goldwater foremost among them.[61] At the same time, a theoretical underpinning for this new wave of conservatism was emerging. Writers such as Russell Kirk, William Rusher, and William Buckley railed against the national Democratic Party—as well as the moderate establishment in the Republican Party—and provided a counterbalance to the liberal intellectualism that prevailed in academia.[62] Each man was, like Reagan, a keen reader of Hayek and other mid-twentieth-century advocates of free market economics and limited government, and each played a significant role in establishing conservatism as an intellectual phenomenon. William Buckley was particularly effective in giving it philosophical weight. As editor of the *National Review*, which he had founded in 1955, Buckley created a vital forum for conservative debate. Published by William Rusher and employing Russell Kirk as a writer, the magazine was, as David Farber observes, "an institutional beachhead on which conservative political activists could sort out their worldviews and organize their campaigns to take on what they perceived as an establishmentarian liberal consensus."[63]

This new generation of conservatives, both inside and outside Congress, had strong links to the old Taftites. After entering the Senate in 1953, Barry Goldwater had regarded Robert Taft as a mentor during the brief time they served together.[64] Numerous writers at the *National Re-*

view, including William Buckley and Brent Bozell, had been supporters of Taft against the moderate Republicanism of Dewey and Eisenhower. In many ways, the leading figures of the new Republican right were the heirs to Taftite conservatism, particularly in their emphasis on small government and low taxes, and their resolve that the power of labor unions should be heavily restricted.

In several crucial areas, however, the new conservatives marked themselves out as a different breed of Republican. Interested in more than merely fighting internal party battles against the eastern GOP establishment, their faith in a radical anti-statist ideology produced a brasher, more dynamic style of politics than that of their predecessors. Unlike Taft, their ideological belief in conservative principles was buttressed by their vehement anti-communism. Taft's own opposition to communism had often been mitigated by his suspicion of foreign entanglements. He had, for example, opposed both the Marshall Plan and American involvement in Korea.[65] But for Taft's successors on the right of the GOP, their dedication to anti-communism both strengthened and reframed their already anti-statist instincts, enabling them to formulate a new discourse of patriotic American conservatism that emphasized individual freedom above all else. Anti-communism became a framework through which conservatives could define their own ideals as traditionally American values, while at the same time suggesting that liberalism was un-American. Because communism mandated state control, Americans must defend personal liberties, and because communist regimes sought to manage their nations' economies, Americans should always seek to preserve the free market and free enterprise. During the 1950s, anti-communism became the foundation stone for the new Republican conservative movement.

Turning away from the traditional, midwestern conservatism of the Taftites, the locus of this new Republican right was in the West and Southwest, in expanding, newly affluent, Sunbelt metropolises such as Los Angeles, San Diego, and Phoenix. The early Sunbelt boom occurred just as anti-communism was beginning to influence and—through the actions of Senator Joseph McCarthy and the House Un-American Activities Committee—overshadow national political debate. Anti-communist sentiments became especially ingrained in Sunbelt suburbs which owed much of their growth to the burgeoning military-industrial complex. Hundreds of thousands of Americans had been attracted to Sunbelt cities by the promise of jobs in defense and aerospace manufacturing. Consequently, a pro-military, anti-communist culture developed—one which encompassed an anti-statist, at times libertarian, approach to domestic politics. For many new residents of the Sunbelt, the struggle against communism overseas necessitated defending the free market at home, which in turn was contingent on preventing the federal government from encroaching on the economic freedom of American citizens.[66] During the 1950s, these sentiments gave rise to discontent among Sunbelt suburbanites over rising property and income taxes and increasing federal regulation. As Lisa McGirr has asserted, before long these white, middle-class "kitchen-table activists" had begun to form "the nucleus of a broader conservative matrix evolving in the Sunbelt and West."[67]

Added to this matrix was a hard-edged capitalist business culture. "Sunbelt capitalists [were] decidedly unsupportive of compromises made by the old rich over unions and welfare," sociologist James Salt noted in 1989. Instead, they tended to "favor laissez faire economic policies that allow them free reign [sic] to defend their profits and reject state attempts to ameliorate the impact of capitalism."[68] In her study of Phoenix, Elizabeth Tandy Shermer argues that the creation of this pro-business climate in the Southwest was crucial to the development of the Republican right. Local boosters—primarily business and political elites—worked hard to attract external investment, reinforcing an ethos that prioritized low corporate taxes, deregulation, and opposition to unionization.[69] This aggressively capitalist mindset inevitably merged with the Sunbelt's anti-statist character. Pro-business policies blended seamlessly with typically American notions of personal liberty and self-determination. Efforts to undermine union activity, for example, were framed as supporting the freedom of the American worker. Promoting deregulation and corporate tax breaks was portrayed as liberating American entrepreneurialism from government constraints.

Many priorities of this new conservatism—low taxes, decentralization, and opposition to labor unions—had been at the heart of Robert Taft's congressional agenda. However, it also encompassed positions that Taft himself would have thought imprudent. The anti-communism of the new Republican right led it away from the protectionism and isolationism of the Taftites and towards a passionate defense of global free trade and a determination that the United States should drive back communist advances around the world. Furthermore, in certain domestic areas Taft had displayed a level of pragmatism, accepting that federal support in education and housing was sometimes necessary. Now, conservatives more ideologically committed to cutting bureaucracy and promoting free enterprise were calling for the termination of programs Taft had once favored.[70]

In image terms, too, the new conservatism was very different. As an emerging figure on the Republican Right in the late 1950s, Barry Goldwater's energetic campaigning was far removed from the straight-laced and dour Taft. A former fighter pilot in the Air Force Reserve, he often appeared on the campaign trail wearing cowboy boots and a Stetson. He retained the Sunbelt capitalist's antipathy towards unionization and employment regulations from his days as manager of his family's successful department store. Moreover, his political philosophy, combining vehement anti-communism, a resolute belief in individual liberty and entrepreneurialism, and an assertive emphasis on American military power, fused the mid-twentieth-century Sunbelt with the nineteenth-century frontier.[71] Goldwater's self-consciously "western" persona played a vital role in recasting the image of Republican conservatism. Though the conservative movement owed far more to the concerns of the Sunbelt's business class and suburbanites than to the old West, it came to be wrapped in frontier symbolism and later acquired the label "cowboy conservatism."[72] It was, Sean Cunningham notes, "anchored by pre-existing notions of entrepreneurialism; rugged individualism; self-help or 'bootstrap politics' [and] limited and local government."[73] No politician exemplified cowboy conservatism more than Barry Goldwater.

While Goldwater established himself as the congressional leader of the Republican right, William Buckley, Russell Kirk, and others were expertly using the media to thrust the new conservative movement from the political fringes towards the mainstream. They explained it to a generation of American voters that was largely unacquainted with such an aggressively anti-statist ideology, frequently doing so by framing it in the context of anti-communism. In addition to editing the *National Review*, by the early 1960s Buckley was writing a twice-weekly nationally syndicated newspaper column and was a regular guest on televised political debates, eventually being given his own talk show, *Firing Line*, in 1966.[74] He employed his natural wit and growing celebrity to publicize the kind of anti-statist views that were increasingly common in Sunbelt suburbs, but which were not yet widely appreciated by an American populace accustomed to New Deal liberalism and an expanding federal government. By far the most influential literary work on the new conservatism—Barry Goldwater's 1960 book *The Conscience of a Conservative*—was ghost-written by Buckley's brother-in-law and fellow *National Review* writer, Brent Bozell, a former Taftite and speechwriter for Goldwater. The book became a huge bestseller, propelling Barry Goldwater to national prominence and demonstrating the effectiveness of Buckley and his cadre of conservative writers.[75]

During the late 1950s, Ronald Reagan gravitated ever closer to this emergent Republican conservatism. His education in conservative theory mirrored national developments—indeed, Reagan was an early subscriber to the *National Review* and read it throughout his political career.[76] The political priorities of his GE bosses echoed those of Sunbelt capitalism, particularly in their antagonism towards unionization and government regulations. Significantly, although GE was a long-established corporation based in the Northeast, in Lemuel Boulware it had a conduit to the newer, more aggressive entrepreneurs of the Sunbelt. Boulware forged strong links to political and business figures in the Southwest—particularly in Phoenix where he sought to expand General Electric's operations—and allied with them to restrict the power of labor unions. As well as being Reagan's philosophical mentor, Boulware was steeped in the capitalist culture of the Sunbelt, was one of the founding backers of the *National Review*, and later struck up a close friendship with Barry Goldwater. Thanks to his influence, Reagan's philosophy did not develop in isolation from the rise of the new conservative movement.[77]

Reagan had begun his journey towards anti-statist conservatism prior to his time with General Electric, and his political transformation was driven primarily by personal experiences. Indeed, he regularly related stories from his life (real or imagined) to explain his views. But the forces that molded his anti-statism unquestionably reflected broader trends that were transforming the Republican right nationally. By the early 1960s, Reagan had arrived at the same point on the political spectrum as Barry Goldwater, William Buckley, and countless residents of affluent, middle-class Sunbelt suburbs. The stories of Reagan's political evolution and the rise of the new Republican conservatism truly merged when Reagan delivered a speech on national television in support of Barry Goldwater's 1964 presidential campaign. Though Goldwater's campaign markedly failed to persuade Americans of the merits of anti-statist conservatism and was defeated in a landslide by the Democratic liberalism of President Lyndon Johnson, it established Ronald Reagan as an emerging political figure. In the eyes of many in the GOP, he was a potentially transformative leader who could spearhead the new conservative movement. Little more than a decade later, Reagan was the unquestioned leader of the Republican right. By the start of the 1980s, he was so inextricably linked to this ascendant conservatism that it had come to bear his name.

At a time when Democratic liberalism was at its zenith in the early 1960s, a new, ideologically anti-statist conservatism was emergent in the Republican Party. Within two decades, it would control both the GOP and the White House. In the South, meanwhile, the region's peculiar brand of conservatism was in the latter stages of a reconfiguration—adapting to the inevitable end of segregation and formulating in its place new social, political, and economic priorities. In Part One, this book tracks these two strands of conservatism through Ronald Reagan's pre-presidential career, examining how his personal popularity in the South—which dated back to the 1950s—led white conservative southerners to place their trust in him and subsequently drive his campaigns for the presidency. Chapter One considers how Reagan established his popularity among white southerners during his nascent political career, at a time when white southerners disillusioned with the Democratic Party were looking for a leader to represent them on the national political stage. The deep bond of affection and trust that white southerners forged with Reagan later proved vital in holding together an uneasy conservative coalition during his time in the White House. As we will see, it also led to Reagan repeatedly being absolved of personal blame for administration policies which southern conservatives vehemently opposed.

Chapter Two focuses on Reagan's presidential campaigns. It highlights the importance of his southern popularity in rescuing and sustaining his presidential candidacy, and effectively his career in politics, in 1976, and how conservative southerners—especially the ascendant Christian Right—played a key role in Reagan's 1980 election victory over a southern-born incumbent president, Jimmy Carter. But it also highlights early differences between culturally conservative southerners and Reaganites who preferred to focus on economic issues. Southern influence on the 1976 Republican platform, the first to explicitly oppose abortion and gun control, was only grudgingly supported by Reagan and his advisors. Likewise, Reagan's rhetorical embrace of Christian Right leaders in 1980 was accompanied by a reluctance to appear aligned too closely with their agenda on social issues. Together, these early chapters illustrate the importance of Reagan's personal appeal in drawing millions of conservative white southerners towards the Republican Party and presage the tensions and conflicts that ensued during his eight years in the White House.

The divergence in priorities and political culture between Reaganism and southern conservatism is the central focus of this book. Parts Two and Three explore the difficulties faced by the Reagan administration in handling these conflicting agendas, what they meant for his achievements and presidential legacy, and how they illustrated the white South's increasing power in the Republican Party. In the decades since Reagan left office, the dominant foreign policy concerns he confronted have fallen down the political agenda. Instead, it has been on the domestic front that Americans have become increasingly divided over how they perceive themselves and their country's direction. The threat of communism—which helped to unite Reaganism and southern conservatism during the 1970s and 1980s—abated after the end of the Cold War and, except for the War on Terror, the major battlegrounds in US politics have been over economic, social, and cultural issues. As debates over domestic issues became more acrimonious, the divide within conservatism became sharper and gained greater significance. For these reasons, this book will concentrate predominantly on domestic and economic policy.

Part Two considers economic issues, particularly the ways in which Reagan's anti-statist agenda of tax cuts and reductions in government spending aligned with, or more often came into conflict with, southern regional interests. Chapter Three examines the crucial role played by conservative southern Democrats in enacting Reagan's tax and spending cuts. But in doing so it highlights significant disagreements, as these so-called Boll Weevils exhibited both the longstanding southern penchant for big government and a populist skepticism towards Reagan's signature tax cuts on the grounds that they disproportionately benefited the wealthy. As Chapter Four illustrates, southern conservatives also opposed the Reagan administration on issues of trade and agriculture. Throughout Reagan's presidency, they fought to preserve and increase federal subsidies for their region's farmers and demanded limits on US textile imports to protect the southern economy. As these chapters show, the Reaganite commitment to a deregulated, free market economy, combined with low taxes and local control, repeatedly met resistance from conservative southerners—Republican and Democrat—who had become accustomed to copious sums of federal money flowing into their home states, and who were driven far more by regional interest and custom than by ideological principle.

In Part Three, the focus moves on to the social and cultural issues that have long been priorities for conservative southerners. Chapter Five examines how the economic focus of Reaganism led to discontent among fundamentalist southern evangelicals, as the Reagan administration prioritized cutting taxes and reducing spending over acting on abortion or school prayer. It also assesses how, despite their grievances, Reagan was able to retain the support of groups like the Moral Majority by preserving a rhetorical alignment with their agenda. Lastly, Chapter Six addresses the racial issues that constituted a political minefield for the Reagan administration. In dealing with disputes surrounding Bob Jones University, Martin Luther King Day, and the extension of the Voting Rights Act, the administration's efforts to retain the support of racially conservative white southerners provoked intense criticism from civil rights organizations who argued that its positions were racially insensitive.

As this book demonstrates, Ronald Reagan's career was propelled not just by those who shared his radical anti-statism, but also by voters, politicians, and religious leaders who typified the racial insecurity, cultural traditionalism, and economic populism of the white conservative South. While Reagan played a crucial role in turning the South into a Republican stronghold, first at the presidential level and subsequently at the congressional and state levels, his relationship with southern conservatives was often fractious, and they determinedly pursued their own political priorities even when it meant going against Reagan's agenda. Through their support for Reagan's campaigns or by exercising influence in Congress during his presidency, southern conservatives were able to achieve considerable power in the Republican Party. Subsequently, the GOP itself came to bear many characteristics of the conservative South.

The consequences were drastic for both the Republican Party and American politics. "As the new Southern-state Republicans lurched their party organizations to the right, they unbalanced the GOP nationally," former Republican operative Chris Ladd lamented in *Forbes* in August 2017.[78] After their awkward coalition with Reaganites began to fracture during the 1990s and 2000s, southern conservatives were at the heart of a grassroots insurgency that erupted in the 2010s, sparking an intraparty power struggle that resulted in prominent Republican leaders losing primary elections or being forced to resign. The Republican Party came under the sway of a populist, racially- and culturally-conservative base that paid little heed to the Reaganite agenda. White conservative southerners were at the forefront of a revolt which "energized extremists all over the country, fueling the rise of a strange, previously unimaginable white nationalist fringe in the Party of Lincoln."[79] It was an insurgency that transformed the modern GOP, led to the election of President Donald Trump, and pitched American politics into turmoil.

This book examines the roots of that transformation—Ronald Reagan's role in drawing white southerners to the Republican Party and the subsequent divide between Reaganism and southern conservatism. In doing so, it explores a telling paradox at the heart of modern American political history: Ronald Reagan's career brought forces into the Republican Party which eventually overwhelmed the Reaganite agenda and changed the GOP in ways that Reagan himself would barely recognize. The legacy of Ronald Reagan's complex relationship with the white South continues to have a profound influence on the course of US politics.

I. Courting the South

1. "He Brought Them the Gospel"
Ronald Reagan, the White South, and the GOP, 1953–1975

By the time Ronald Reagan emerged onto the political stage in his new role as a conservative Republican in the early 1960s, he had been appearing and speaking before enthusiastic southern audiences for over a decade. His speeches, focusing on anticommunism, hostility to big government, and disaffection from the national Democratic Party— all delivered with unaffected charisma—resonated powerfully in the white South. Yet, at the time of his first appearance in the region in 1952, he was still in the early stages of his unlikely transformation from liberal Hollywood actor to conservative political icon. He remained a registered Democrat, and his only connection to the ferment of southern politics had been on a Hollywood film set. In 1951, he had starred in the movie *Storm Warning*, playing a county prosecutor attempting to bring the hooded killers of a newspaper reporter to justice in a fictional southern town. The story was inspired by reports of real-life lynchings in the South, and its portrayal of the Ku Klux Klan—including a particularly menacing depiction of a KKK meeting—was so disturbing that studio executives were nervous the Klan might take legal action.[1] As reviews of the "hard-hitting" movie suggested, *Storm Warning*'s viewers were left in no doubt as to its liberal political leanings.[2]

The following year, in his role as head of the Screen Actors Guild, Reagan traveled to Dallas, Texas, in June 1952 to preside over a film industry conference. While there, his charisma and eloquence caught the attention of the *Dallas Morning News*, which described him as a "dynamic speaker."[3] A return trip to Dallas in 1953 was even more auspicious. On this occasion Reagan fell into conversation with Billy Graham and W. A. Criswell at a charity fundraising event. After a skeptical Criswell told Reagan he believed the film industry was "of the devil," Billy Graham watched in admiration as Reagan proceeded to win Criswell over. "Ron had not only changed a man's mind," Graham

3

later recalled, "but he had done it with charm, conviction, and humor."[4] Reagan and Graham would become lifelong friends, while Criswell's subsequent rise to the leadership of the Southern Baptist Convention helped to forge a movement that would prove politically beneficial to both Reagan and the Republican Party, as millions of fundamentalist evangelicals coalesced into a formidable conservative voting bloc. As early as 1953, Ronald Reagan was making valuable acquaintances in the South.

The following year, with his film career stalling, Reagan accepted an offer to become host of a new television show, *General Electric Theater*. As well as bringing him into the living rooms of millions of Americans, the role entailed touring company plants around the country to meet General Electric's workers and give speeches. In eight years with GE, he crisscrossed most of the southern states. In Toby Glenn Bates's phrase, he laid "trails to be followed in future political campaigns: Texas, Louisiana, Arkansas, Kentucky, Tennessee, Georgia, North Carolina, and Virginia."[5] According to Reagan, the GE plant in Louisville, Kentucky, had "forty-six miles of assembly line" which he claimed to have walked twice. "I had to meet the night shift too. . . . *But I enjoyed every whizzing minute of it.*"[6]

His appearances involved more than simply meeting GE workers and often made quite an impression on their wider communities. In the small town of Anniston, Alabama, for example, anticipation began to build weeks prior to Reagan's arrival. The *Anniston Star* excitedly announced, "Handsome star Ronald Reagan of the screen, television, and radio, will visit Anniston this month."[7] Each visit was enthusiastically followed by reporters and included dinners, autograph signings, and photo opportunities away from GE's facilities. On a three-day trip to Kentucky in March 1955, inspections of two GE plants were scheduled alongside a country club luncheon and a service at the Central Christian Church in Lexington, where Reagan was even invited to give a "layman's witness" from the pulpit.[8] Many of the facilities Reagan toured in the South were recently constructed, products of the region's crusade to attract outside investment. A visit to South Carolina to see "General Electric's impressive and busy new Irmo capacitor plant" was combined with a meet-and-greet with locals at Irmo High School and a lunch in Columbia with civic and business leaders, before Reagan and his party moved on to appearances at other newly built company plants in Florida.[9]

Reagan's period with GE gave him invaluable experience in political networking and demonstrated his seemingly innate ability to connect with ordinary Americans. As time went on, it also served to propel his political shift from liberalism to conservatism. Reagan's philosophy was shaped not only by the works of political science his company bosses encouraged him to read, but also by what he perceived as the instinctive small-government conservatism of the average American worker. His speeches evolved during the mid-1950s from promoting General Electric, boosting the morale of workers, and recounting Hollywood stories, to more overtly political topics. Increasingly, audiences wanted him to both hear and echo their own grievances regarding taxes or federal bureaucracy, and so he adapted his words, forging a new identity for himself as a champion of individual freedom. "At many Southern locations," Bates has observed, "Reagan took his first baby steps with words and phrases that would become familiar in later decades."[10]

For white southern audiences seeking certainty and reassurance in turbulent times, Reagan's straightforward rhetoric on personal liberty, the threat of communism, and the dangers of big government was exactly what they wanted to hear. Reagan was, moreover, not merely a bombastic local politician or preacher but a charismatic national celebrity—one of the most recognizable men in the nation thanks to his television work. In the view of his audiences, by appearing regularly in the South at a time when southern whites felt their region was being persecuted, Reagan was lending them his support and recognizing their fears and anxieties. This perception was crucial to his burgeoning southern appeal, but in reality, Reagan's message was largely the same no matter where he was speaking. As Kurt Ritter notes, Reagan "did not fashion a southern rhetoric. . . . Instead, Reagan's standard political rhetoric resonated so well with conservative white southern Democrats that they embraced him and would not let him go."[11] His words were reflective of his own anti-statism far more than they were tailored to audience demands. Though he regarded his speeches as "nonpartisan as far as the two major political parties were concerned," as time went on his evolving conservative ideology became more apparent. Transcripts of these speeches are scarce, but Reagan later wrote that he made a determined effort to highlight to his audiences "the problems of centralizing power in Washington, with subsequent loss of freedom at the local level."[12] Eventually "it became basically a warning to people about the threat of government," Reagan recalled. "I'd emphasize that we as Americans should get together and take back the liberties we were losing."[13] To southerners facing dramatic changes to their way of life, such themes acted to reinforce their own convictions.

Personal affection for Reagan among white southern conservatives deepened with his every appearance in the region. His warnings about communism, in particular, were music to the ears of those listening. However, given the key role that anti-communism played in "massive resistance," those warnings were likely interpreted in a far more racialized way than Reagan intended. When filtered through the cultural fixations of conservative southerners, his strident anti-communism would have instead become an endorsement of the racial and social customs of the white South. It is open to question whether he fully understood how his words were being construed. Remarkably, given the climate of the period, Reagan makes no reference to segregation or civil rights in his subsequent recollections of his time with GE, so the extent to which he was conscious of the South's racial tumult as he traveled around the region is difficult to discern. Nonetheless, even before he entered politics, the particular way in which white southerners interpreted Reagan's anti-statist and anti-communist rhetoric was at the core of his appeal in the region. It remained so throughout his political career.

Occasionally, Reagan's repeated warnings about the dangers of big government collided with the South's political and economic interests. In 1959, Reagan started to include strong criticism of federal funding for the Tennessee Valley Authority (TVA) in his standard speech, suggesting that "the annual interest on the TVA deal is five times as great as the flood damage it prevents."[14] TVA representatives informed bosses at General Electric that the company's $50 million worth of business was in jeopardy if the criticism continued, and the offending passage was removed from Reagan's speech—something he later claimed to have done voluntarily.[15] The episode foreshadowed differences that would resurface years later between Reagan's deeply held commitment to free markets and small government on the one hand and the entrenched economic interests of the South on the other.

As his speeches became more overtly political, Reagan's audiences came to resemble those of a candidate on the campaign trail. He recalled that his trips began to feature "more important annual events: state Chamber of Commerce banquets, national conventions, and groups recognized as important political sounding boards."[16] One such event was the 1957 Rose Festival in Tyler, Texas, which Reagan attended as part of a trip to visit the town's GE plant. During the festival, Reagan introduced the state's most prominent senator, Democrat Lyndon Johnson, and spoke to an audience including local leaders from the oil and gas industry, agriculture, aerospace, and defense contracting, as well as federal and state politicians. "In short," observes Ritter, "it was an audience that two future US presidents thought was worth addressing."[17]

At the time of Reagan's travels with GE, the political establishment in the South—along with most business and industry leaders—remained overwhelmingly Democratic. While the Dixiecrat revolt in 1948 had been a significant crack in the edifice of the Solid South and demonstrated that southern conservatives were increasingly mistrustful of the national Democratic leadership, this had not translated into Republican electoral success. At the start of the 1950s, as Earl and Merle Black have written, "the Southern Republican party had almost no followers, no leaders, and no candidates for public office."[18] In terms of state and congressional politics, the party's prospects remained bleak for the rest of the decade. At the presidential level, however, the nomination of Dwight D. Eisenhower as GOP candidate in 1952 gave the "experienced defeatists" in the southern Republican Party some cause for hope.[19]

Running against a tired Democratic Party and with a backdrop of rising antipathy in the white South for the welfare and racial policies of the Truman administration, Eisenhower's status as a war hero was immensely appealing to conservative southerners.[20] His opponent, Adlai Stevenson, was an establishment Democrat from Illinois who chose Alabama senator John Sparkman as his running mate in an effort to sway southern voters. But four years on from the Dixiecrat campaign, the resentment that prominent southern Democrats felt towards their party's national leadership had only intensified. Many of them, including 1948 Dixiecrat presidential candidate Strom Thurmond, Louisiana governor Robert Kennon, and Texas governor Alan Shivers, now formed a "Democrats for Eisenhower'" movement.[21] With their support, Eisenhower won Texas, Virginia, Florida, and Tennessee as part of a convincing nationwide victory, and almost made a breakthrough in the Deep South, losing narrowly in South Carolina. First as Dixiecrats in 1948 and then by supporting Eisenhower in 1952, segregationist leaders had "effectively loosened the moorings of southern political allegiance at the national level, weakening the custom of automatically supporting Democratic Party nominees."[22] Though Democratic loyalties remained entrenched at the local and state levels—in many southern elections during the 1950s Democrats faced no opposition whatsoever—the party's presidential candidates could no longer count on the white South.

Still, it was also true that Eisenhower's personal appeal in the region was moderate at best. His support was largely concentrated in urban and metropolitan areas, his candidacy had little impact further down the ballot, and his vote share never exceeded 60 percent in any southern state.[23] But largely through careful political calculation, Eisenhower retained this southern electoral beachhead during his first term in office. Following the *Brown v. Board of Education* decision in 1954, his administration refused to publicly endorse the Supreme Court's ruling. Instead, recognizing the electoral dangers, Eisenhower chose to avoid appearing too sympathetic towards civil rights. In 1956, for example, the carefully worded Republican platform merely accepted and concurred with the Supreme Court's rulings on *Brown* and school desegregation.[24] With the Democratic leadership continuing to head in a liberal direction—endorsing federal interventions in support of civil rights while making unsubtle attempts to appease white southerners come election time—Eisenhower's calculated reticence over *Brown* proved effective. He won six southern states in another comfortable victory over Adlai Stevenson in 1956, even breaking into the Deep South by adding Louisiana to the Republican column for the first time in eighty years.

Eisenhower's actions early in his second term, especially his response to events in Arkansas, turned many of his southern supporters against him. When, in September 1957, the school board in Little Rock began the gradual integration of the city's Central High School, Governor Orval Faubus sent Arkansas National Guardsmen to prevent nine black students from attending classes. Tensions escalated when a crowd of white segregationists, led by the local Citizens' Council, gathered outside the building. Having ignored a similar incident in Mansfield, Texas, a year earlier—prior to his re-election as president —Eisenhower now had little option but federalize the Arkansas National Guard and send soldiers from the 101st Airborne Division to Little Rock to escort the black students into the school and bring order to a situation that threatened to spiral out of control.[25] For their part, segregationists were incensed to witness the federal government sending troops to the South to protect the rights of African Americans for the first time since the end of Reconstruction.[26] Eisenhower further enraged southern conservatives when, in the wake of events in Little Rock, he supported a civil rights bill that had been introduced to Congress months earlier. The Civil Rights Act of 1957 was passed after being heavily watered down to avoid a southern filibuster, but as the first such act since Reconstruction it was nevertheless highly symbolic.[27] Its passage paved the way for further legislation in the mid-1960s and, ultimately, marked the point at which southern resistance to racial integration became doomed to fail.

Though he had never publicly supported the civil rights movement, by the end of his presidency Dwight Eisenhower was viewed with mistrust by many southern conservatives and seen as a tyrannical hate figure by the more fervent segregationists. In the 1960 election, the same air of mistrust lingered over Eisenhower's vice president, Richard Nixon. Facing off against a Catholic Democrat, John F. Kennedy—whose faith was a cause of suspicion among conservative Southern Baptists and who was running on a platform that contained a significant pro-civil rights plank—Nixon won only four southern states. Despite the inroads Eisenhower had made into the white South in 1952 and 1956, when presented with an election between two candidates they regarded with deep skepticism, most white southerners still, grudgingly, leaned towards the Democrat.

Throughout the late 1950s and into the early 1960s, Ronald Reagan had continued his appearances for General Electric. As the years passed, he gravitated ever closer to the right of the Republican Party, and his increasingly apocalyptic warnings about communism—regularly depicting an America under siege—began to garner occasionally negative media coverage. After a speech in North Carolina in October 1961, two of the state's more liberal newspapers, the *Carolina Israelite* and the *Charlotte News*, criticized Reagan for his inordinate fearmongering.[28] Indeed, his doom-laden rhetoric appears to have played a significant role in the decision by a new generation of GE executives to try a different promotional strategy. When Reagan parted company with GE in 1962, by his own recollection his conversion to conservatism was complete and he was increasingly focused on his role as a conservative speaker, writer, and campaigner. His active involvement in partisan politics was growing and he finally registered as a Republican in 1962 after years of feeling alienated from the "tax and spend" liberals at the top of the Democratic Party.[29] His popularity in the white South, though, was essentially undiminished. On a tour of Texas in February 1962, he hinted at a socialist conspiracy in Washington. "Under the high flown phrases of 'freedom from want,' 'human rights' and so on, we have seen the federal government lay its hand on almost every facet of our existence," he told a five thousand-strong audience in the Dallas Memorial Auditorium.[30] The speech received fulsome praise. Reagan "exploded a score of liberal myths, built a foolproof case against centralized government and outlined one of the best platforms for conservatism ever heard in Dallas," according to the *Dallas Morning News*. "His statements came from deep conviction and this conviction was transferred to most of those who heard him."[31]

Reagan's connections to southern politics deepened in early 1964 when he campaigned in support of Charlton Lyons, the Republican candidate for the Louisiana governorship and a friend since the 1950s. Lyons was a recent Democratic convert to the GOP, but remained a southern conservative and a committed segregationist. His rhetoric on race, both in 1964 and in a previous 1960 congressional campaign, was almost indistinguishable from that of his Democratic opponents in Louisiana. His claims that the 1960 Democratic platform was "a veritable blueprint for a complete Socialist State" and that the GOP now offered the "greatest hope of perpetuating Constitutional Government in America" spoke to white anxiety at the racial and social change that was hitting Louisiana and the rest of the South.[32] At the core of Lyons' campaign was a theme that was becoming ever more potent: the national Democratic leadership's abandonment of its once loyal southern supporters.

Reagan echoed these sentiments when he addressed an audience of both Democrats and Republicans in Baton Rouge. Describing himself and Lyons as "ex life-long Democrats," he said, "We changed parties. . . . States' rights, limited government, adherence to the Constitution—no longer are these the principles of that national party."[33] His words reflected his own loss of faith in the Democratic Party. In correspondence with his "old friend" Lyons, Reagan argued Democrats had abandoned Woodrow Wilson's philosophy that "Liberty cannot exist where govt. takes care of the people, it can only thrive where the people take care of the govt."[34] Reagan clearly "believed in states' rights," as his biographer Lou Cannon has argued, and his antipathy towards the growth in size and power of the federal government was undeniable.[35] Nonetheless, Reagan's use of "state's rights" in the South, where the phrase had become a widespread euphemism for resistance to integration, highlighted the often-ambiguous nature of much of his rhetoric. To an audience of white southerners, Reagan was condemning a party that had betrayed generations of steadfast support by advocating black equality and was now threatening to overturn their region's entire social structure. It is difficult to know the extent to which Reagan—a man entirely convinced of his own lack of prejudice—was aware of this, but his genuine feelings of anger and sadness at the Democratic Party meant he was perfectly placed to speak to similar emotions among white southerners. Certainly, his anti-statist rhetoric increasingly chimed with southern resentment at federal efforts to impose civil rights on the region.

Despite Reagan's efforts on his behalf, Charlton Lyons failed to win the Louisiana governorship. Despite being repeatedly derided by Lyons' opponent as a "carpetbagger," Reagan's campaigning helped Lyons achieve 38 percent of the vote.[36] Given that the previous Republican candidate had received 17 percent and no Republican had won more than 20 percent since 1888—most won less than 5 percent—this was a remarkably high tally. Significantly, in the next gubernatorial election four years later the GOP did not even field a candidate.[37] The spike in Republican support that Lyons received in March 1964 was seemingly the first electoral evidence of Reagan's popularity in the white South.

Certainly, his appearances on the stump in Louisiana had been well received. During a stop in Lafayette, Reagan had trialed a new speech that contained elements familiar from his previous addresses in the South, but which would go on to become one of the most famous of his career. "You and I have a rendezvous with destiny," Reagan told his audience. "We can preserve for our children this, the last best hope of man on earth, or we can sentence them to take the first step into a thousand years of darkness." It was perhaps the starkest elucidation yet of Reagan's good-versus-evil interpretation of the Cold War. But his language also spoke obliquely to conservative southerners of their own struggles against the encroaching enemies of liberalism, civil rights, and the federal government. Reprinted in its entirety in newspapers, as well as later being broadcast to audiences in cities across Louisiana, Reagan's address unquestionably captured the attention of the state's voters. The *Shreveport Times* thought it "a speech that perhaps could not be excelled by any North Louisianian in its sound and solid conservatism."[38] The speech garnered much wider attention six months later when Reagan delivered it on national television in support of Arizona Senator Barry Goldwater's presidential campaign. Amended, refined, and given the title "A Time for Choosing," it signaled Reagan's emergence as an influential presence on the national political scene.

Nationally, the 1964 presidential election was a clash between the prevailing philosophy of Democratic liberalism and the insurgent ideology of "cowboy conservatism." In his first year as president, Lyndon Johnson had ridden a wave of sympathy following the assassination of John F. Kennedy and had already cajoled Congress into passing some of the most liberal legislation since the New Deal. In the summer of 1964 Johnson signed both the Economic Opportunity Act—the first salvo in his "War on Poverty"—and the landmark Civil Rights Act. Formally at least, the latter brought an end to Jim Crow by outlawing segregation in public schools, government buildings, transportation, hotels, theatres, and restaurants. The Civil Rights Act also prohibited discrimination in employment and voter registration, though Johnson was aware that, as Martin Luther King and other civil rights leaders argued, the act offered only limited protection for African American voting rights.[39] Nonetheless, as the November election approached, Johnson's command of the American political landscape appeared absolute.

On the Republican side, 1964 saw an acrimonious nomination battle between conservative champion Barry Goldwater and the epitome of moderate northeastern Republicanism, New York governor Nelson Rockefeller. To the fury of GOP moderates and liberals, and thanks to an army of conservative activists who had worked for more than two years to take control of party committees at both national and state level, Goldwater triumphed at the Republican National Convention in San Francisco in mid-July. His campaigning to that point had been energetic but ill-disciplined and gaffe-prone, including suggesting he would make Social Security voluntary and that NATO commanders should be allowed to use nuclear weapons at their own discretion.[40] His acceptance speech at the convention, in which he declared that "extremism in the defense of liberty is no vice" and "moderation in the pursuit of justice is no virtue," did little to shake off the increasingly common perception of him as impulsive and overzealous.[41] Still, Goldwater's nomination for the upcoming presidential election meant that, for the first time, the party was under the control of the Republican right and its anti-statist ideology. The antipathy of Goldwater supporters towards Johnson and his federal activism at times bordered on hostile, and they were similarly disdainful of their defeated Republican counterparts. As Lewis Gould has written, "they intended to win or lose the presidency on their own terms."[42]

The national contest may have been an ideological struggle, but in the South the 1964 election was about one issue: race. Having backed Kennedy, white southerners had watched with displeasure as Democratic Party leaders became ever more supportive of black civil rights during the early 1960s. In the 1962 midterm elections, the Republican National Committee had exploited white southern discontent by pursuing its own "Operation Dixie" strategy and winning 1.4 million more votes across the region than the GOP had ever previously won in congressional elections.[43] With the passage of the Civil Rights Act in 1964, the white South's backlash against racial integration reached a boiling point. On national television, the region was defined by news footage of water cannons and police dogs being turned on black civil rights protesters, while bigoted local officials and KKK leaders spouted racist invective. One of the most prominent figures in the southern resistance was Alabama governor George Wallace, who had announced himself to a national audience with his 1963 inaugural address from the Alabama State Capitol Building in Montgomery. "I draw the line in the dust and toss the gauntlet before the feet of tyranny," Wallace proclaimed, "and I say segregation now, segregation tomorrow, segregation forever." The following year, he mounted a primary challenge to Lyndon Johnson, one that was futile but nevertheless embarrassing for the Democratic Party as it attracted enough support in Indiana, Maryland, and Wisconsin to suggest that antipathy towards liberalism and civil rights was not confined to white southerners.[44] On a trip around the South during the national campaign, the president's wife, Lady Bird Johnson, was publicly snubbed by leading southern Democrats and encountered hostility from white crowds. Speeches she made in Georgia and South Carolina were drowned out by booing and heckling, while audience members at an event in Charleston carried signs saying, "Johnson's a Nigger Lover" and "Black Bird Go Home." In Florida, the First Lady was met with bomb scares and death threats.[45]

The mood of many in the white South towards Lyndon Johnson and his supporters was poisonous. However, the fact that so many in the hostile crowds were holding pro-Goldwater placards only served to tarnish the Republican nominee, further branding him as an extremist in the eyes of the national electorate. Like Ronald Reagan, Barry Goldwater had for years been making apocalyptic speeches warning of the dangers of communism and big government. Since the beginning of the 1960s, he had been doing so with the specific aim of winning southern conservative votes, "shaking his finger in the face of Kennedy liberalism" to appreciative southern audiences.[46] In 1961, he told an audience of Republicans in Atlanta, "We're not going to get the Negro vote as a bloc in 1964 and 1968, so we ought to go hunting where the ducks are."[47] Goldwater, for all his ideological zeal and occasionally clumsy rhetoric on the campaign trail, was a shrewd political operator. By the late summer of 1964, the tactic of deliberately chasing white southern votes, combined with his fiery anti-statist language, had made Goldwater the preferred presidential candidate among southern whites by margins as big as four to one in some states.[48] Though lacking the emotional bond Reagan had built up over a decade of visits to the region, Goldwater's status in the white South in 1964 rivalled that of the former Hollywood actor.

The Arizona senator's southern appeal was founded entirely on the race issue. Goldwater never advocated racial segregation—he had made his name by opposing segregation as a city councilor in Phoenix and later vetoed a proposed 1964 campaign film because he felt it was racist—but he was philosophically wedded to the idea that the issue should be one of state jurisdiction. Despite having voted in favor of civil rights legislation in 1957 and 1960, he opposed the 1964 Civil Rights Act on the grounds that the sections prohibiting discrimination in employment and segregation were unconstitutional.[49] Goldwater's rationale notwithstanding, in the eyes of millions of white southerners his campaign was the ideal vehicle for them to rage at national Democrats over civil rights and desegregation. His popularity rested on the interpretation that white southerners placed on his anti-statist, anti-communist language. As Ronald Keith Gaddie observed, this constituted "a meeting of his deeply felt libertarian convictions about limited government and the appeal of limited government as a codeword for segregation and rolling back federal intervention."[50] Like Ronald Reagan, Goldwater was perceived as an ally in the fight to repel the threat of social change in the South.

Yet his campaign also symbolized something rather less tangible— the last gasp of the dying Jim Crow era. Reporting for the *New Yorker* on the Goldwater campaign, Richard Rovere described Goldwater's southern rallies as opportunities for "great numbers of unapologetic white supremacists to hold great carnivals of white supremacy." With little concern for the national Republican campaign, white southerners attended Goldwater rallies to celebrate a way of life that, thanks to the liberal interventionism of the Johnson administration, was now fated to end. The atmosphere was "essentially non-political," Rovere observed. Rather than typical campaign events, "they were revels, they were pageants, they were celebrations. The aim of the revelers was not so much to advance a candidacy or a cause as to dramatize a mood, and the mood was a kind of joyful defiance, or defiant joy."[51]

Goldwater's popularity among segregationists in the South made it easy for the Johnson campaign to characterize him as being well outside the political mainstream. Polling prior to the election showed Johnson with a huge lead, and indeed Goldwater subsequently went down to a landslide national defeat.[52] Though he won only the five Deep South states plus his home state of Arizona, Goldwater's campaign marked a significant fracture in the Democratic Party's once impregnable hold on Dixie. As well as bringing the Deep South into the Republican fold for the first time since Reconstruction (including winning 87 percent of the vote in Mississippi), Goldwater came within fifty thousand votes of carrying Florida.[53] Demonstrating the importance of race and the recently passed Civil Rights Act to the election in the South, Goldwater also won a majority of whites in North Carolina, Tennessee, Arkansas, and Virginia, states where Johnson only prevailed thanks to a sharp increase in the number of black voters.[54] Postelection analysis in the *Los Angeles Times* noted that Goldwater's southern backing was strongest among "voters in rural areas who were more interested in white supremacy and less interested in economic issues."[55]

In the immediate aftermath of the election, many observers were focused more on the abysmal outlook for the GOP at the national level than on the forces Goldwater's campaign may have unleashed in the South. But writing a year later in *The Making of the President*, Theodore White's assessment was remarkably perceptive. "The Republican Party is now, finally, deeply rooted in the South," he noted, "but these roots may nourish bitter fruit."[56] In the longer term, Goldwater's campaign provided the trigger for the more ardent segregationists in the South to begin their migration to the GOP. The support he received from South Carolina senator Strom Thurmond bears this out. One of the leading segregationist Democrats in Congress, and the man who had led the Dixiecrat revolt against Truman's civil rights policies in 1948, Thurmond had switched allegiance to the Republican Party in September 1964 and campaigned in the South on Goldwater's behalf.[57] Men like Thurmond, and Ronald Reagan's old friend Charlton Lyons in Louisiana, were prominent harbingers of what would become, over the next decade, an "influx of Democratic segregationists" into southern Republican parties, creating by the early 1970s a "new kind of grassroots Dixie GOP."[58]

Ronald Reagan was one of the few Republicans to emerge from Goldwater's landslide defeat with his reputation enhanced. Alongside his televised "A Time for Choosing" address, which had prompted a flood of donations in the last week before the election, Reagan had chaired Goldwater's California campaign and appeared regularly on the stump, demonstrating his natural charisma, political skill, and speechmaking ability. Awaiting Goldwater's inevitable defeat, conservative Republicans had begun to talk of Reagan as the new standard-bearer for the GOP right even prior to election day.[59] Many regarded him as the perfect messenger for conservative ideals in the mid-1960s: a smoother, less erratic campaigner than Goldwater, as well being as more convivial and unifying on a personal level. Within weeks of Goldwater's defeat, Republican donors were urging Reagan to challenge incumbent Democrat Edmund "Pat" Brown for the governorship of California. By late December 1964, Reagan was telling Charlton Lyons that he was "doing some real soul searching" about his future in politics. He would decide "based on what I believe is the best way I can continue to serve in this fight we must win."[60]

Within months, he was preparing his challenge for the California governorship and was already being viewed by pollsters as a potential Republican presidential candidate for 1968, albeit as an outside bet.[61] Reagan's progress in California would also be watched with keen interest in the white South, where he had been making regular appearances for over a decade and where many viewed him with trust and affection. Indeed, his gubernatorial campaign would be boosted by the fact that around 1.6 million white residents of California were southern-born, and millions more descended from earlier generations of white southerners who had migrated during the first half of the twentieth century.[62] Most had settled in California's southern counties, in the rapidly

expanding suburbs of Los Angeles and San Diego that Barry Goldwater had won in 1964 and where Reagan enjoyed his highest popularity
in the state.[63] As political scientist James Q. Wilson observed in 1967,
28 percent of Southern California residents had migrated from dust-
bowl states: from those neighboring the South including Oklahoma
and Kansas, from peripheral southern states such as Texas and Arkansas, and notably from one state of the Deep South, Louisiana.[64] Reagan's popularity in the white South seemingly translated, at least in
part, into popularity among these white Californian "southerners." A
prominent Reagan backer claimed the "one-half million Texans living
in Los Angeles County" would be a huge source of support for his 1966
gubernatorial campaign.[65]

This diaspora had imbued Southern California with some of the
white South's social and cultural conservatism. Consequently, by
the 1960s, Californian politics bore a passing resemblance to that of
the southern states. In November 1961, Strom Thurmond had visited
Southern California on an anti-communist tour.[66] He returned in February 1964 to campaign in support of a constitutional amendment to
mandate prayer in public schools.[67] Both times he was met by appreciative audiences and his trips served to strengthen conservative links
between Southern California and the South. Likewise, the 1964 debate
surrounding California's Proposition 14 referendum revealed southern overtones in the Golden State's politics. The proposition sought to
overturn the 1963 Rumford Fair Housing Act prohibiting discrimination in the sale of property based on race or religion. Leading the opposition to the initiative was California's liberal Democratic governor
Pat Brown, who decried it as "a provision for discrimination of which
not even Mississippi or Alabama can boast."[68] Among those supporting the campaign in favor of Proposition 14 were prominent southern
conservatives, including Thurmond, and fundamentalist evangelicals
in the Southern Baptist Church.[69] Between 1940 and 1970 the Southern Baptist General Convention of California expanded from around
twelve congregations to over 250,000 members, many of whom had
migrated from the South and brought with them their racially infused
and culturally conservative religious beliefs.[70] Proposition 14 won landslide approval from 65 percent of voters in November 1964, but was

struck down eighteen months later by the state's Supreme Court as a violation of federal rights of equal protection.[71]

In California's southern-infused political environment, Reagan's decision to campaign in 1966 on a pledge to repeal the original Rumford Fair Housing Act was strategically wise, and an early example of his ability to finesse issues of race.[72] Though Reagan always rejected any accusation of racism, and his stance on housing owed more to his belief in personal liberty than a desire to see communities racially segregated, he nevertheless possessed an instinct for subtly aligning his political agenda and campaign rhetoric with the racial concerns of middle-class whites. As British journalist Alistair Cooke, a perceptive observer of American politics, commented in November 1966, "Many of the things [Reagan] has talked about—crime in the streets, the high cost in taxes of welfare schemes, the constitutional right of people to rent houses to whom they choose—these all strike an association in the voter's mind."[73]

Also helpful to Reagan's gubernatorial campaign were his stances on the 1964 Civil Rights Act and the Voting Rights Act of 1965. Like Barry Goldwater, Reagan had opposed both as unconstitutional expansions of federal authority over the rights of states and private citizens. Such views enhanced his appeal among California's southern immigrants— as did his use of harsh, racially-tinged language that would have resonated equally with white audiences in the South. Following riots in the heavily black Watts area of Los Angeles in August 1965, for example, Reagan warned when he announced his candidacy that the streets of Californian cities had become "jungle paths after dark."[74] Moreover, what incumbent Governor Pat Brown described as "white backlash" was, according to Reagan, "nothing more than the concern people have for . . . extremists in the civil rights movement taking to the streets, the use of violence, of demonstrations, instead of an orderly process of appealing wrongs through legitimate channels." To call it white backlash, he argued, "isn't fair."[75] Such provocative statements may not have been commonplace in Reagan's campaign rhetoric, but they undoubtedly resonated with the racial conservatism of transplanted southerners in California and with white anxiety across the state about increasing unrest in black neighborhoods. They also revealed the candidate's talent for deploying dog whistle rhetoric when he believed it politically necessary. As Alistair Cooke noted, in the gubernatorial race, with around 20 percent of voters seemingly undecided as the election approached, Reagan "must have looked at the polls" and chosen to "come out firing with both barrels."[76]

Prior to those final weeks, Reagan's campaign had been a positive one. Its theme was the "Creative Society," a slogan and manifesto that combined the anti-statist conservatism of the Republican right, with its emphasis on individualism and entrepreneurialism, and the confidence, personal charisma, and innate positivity that were central to Reagan's political persona. By framing longstanding conservative critiques of big government in more upbeat terms, the notion of the "Creative Society" represented a huge step towards creating the brand of conservatism with which Reagan would be inextricably linked for the rest of his life.[77] Donors and commentators on the right of the Republican Party were by now convinced they had found their new leader. In the *Los Angeles Times*, William F. Buckley described Reagan as "developing a political know-how which astounds the professionals" and as having "the mind of a true conservative."[78] The parallel stories of Reagan's personal journey to conservatism and the ascendance of the postwar Republican right had fully merged. As it became ever more closely identified with Ronald Reagan's political persona, what had once been the cowboy conservatism of Barry Goldwater was on the way to becoming Reaganite conservatism.

If the California gubernatorial race represented the first electoral test for Reaganism, it passed with flying colors. In November 1966, Reagan defeated Governor Pat Brown in a landslide. His message of optimism won the support of moderate and conservative suburbanites across the state. Notably, his victory was marked by crushing vote margins in heavily populated counties that had seen significant white southern immigration, including Orange County, Los Angeles, San Diego, Riverside, and San Bernardino.[79] California's politics incorporated strong liberal and libertarian elements, but the migration of southern whites to the state had helped to create an ideal electorate for Reagan's first political candidacy, particularly considering his first-rate education in dealing with conservative southerners over the previous decade.

His anti-statist rhetoric resonated with southern conservatives' racial insecurity and hostility to government intrusion whether they lived in Shreveport or San Diego. Reagan's success in building a powerful base in the southern-tinged counties of California acted as a foretaste of his national campaigns.

As California governor, Reagan continued to make appearances in the South. When he attended a fundraising dinner with Strom Thurmond in Columbia, South Carolina, in September 1967, his visit made front page news. He was welcomed at the airport by a thousand-strong crowd, the adulation that greeted him demonstrating that his popularity in the region had only increased since his victory in California.[80] According to local media reports, at the packed fundraising event later that evening Reagan's "charisma . . . warmed the hearts" of the audience, which "literally mobbed him as he moved about the room, shaking hands, signing autographs and kissing pretty girls."[81] A fundraiser designed to help pay off $30,000 of the state Republican Party's campaign debt ultimately raised $170,000.[82] The *Atlanta Constitution* observed that, to the overwhelmingly white audience of around 3,500—as well as hundreds in the overflow outside and many watching on television across the state—Reagan had "brought them the gospel." His "opposition to present economic policies, big government, social welfare, indecision in Vietnam, and U.S. trade agreements to help Russia's economy" was so well received, reported the *Constitution*, that "the only way to describe the reaction is that it was fanatic." Reagan once again returned to his personal narrative as a former Democrat, saying "I know the feeling of betrayal. . . . I say to you, you did not leave that party, but the leadership of that party left you." The event in Columbia was widely viewed as Reagan testing the waters for a presidential run the following year. When that possibility was raised, his response was hardly opaque: "How many more chances do you think we'll get if we don't do it this time?"[83]

By the summer of 1968, Reagan was indeed contemplating a presidential bid. By some distance, he was white southerners' preferred candidate in either major party. He did, however, have a rival for the affections of the white South: the former Democratic governor of Alabama George Wallace, now running on a third-party ticket. As Lou

Cannon has pointed out, "Wallace posed a special problem for Reagan. Without Wallace, Reagan was the strongest potential nominee of any party in the South. With Wallace, he was a question mark, for their appeal to white conservatives overlapped."[84] Before embarking on a tour of southern states in July 1968, Reagan was asked about his and Wallace's similar appeals to southern conservatives. In response, he clumsily attempted to walk a tightrope of maintaining his appeal to white southerners without explicitly agreeing with Wallace's advocacy of racial separation. When questioned, he was forced to acknowledge that differences between the two men "would be kind of hard to pin down." Reagan eventually fell back on Wallace's economic populism, stating he disagreed with Wallace because "as a governor he showed no opposition particularly to great programs of federal aid and spending programs etc." Asked directly what he would say to those whose support for Wallace was based on segregation, Reagan responded curtly, "Why should they ask for my opinion?" Pressed further, he replied, "If they seek my advice and someone asks me on an outright segregation or racist basis, I'd have to tell them that I think racism is wrong." The *Los Angeles Times* pointedly observed that "the governor appeared reluctant to discuss Wallace's segregationist views" and reported that Reagan "had no plans to initiate a discussion of racial problems in the South" on his upcoming trip.[85] As an emergent national political figure, Reagan appears to have become increasingly conscious that courting white support in the South could pose acute dangers for someone with presidential ambitions. Aware of how Barry Goldwater's campaign had become closely associated with the white South's defense of segregation four years earlier, Reagan's strategy was simply to avoid the issue.

A few days later he left California for what an aide described as "a Southern solicitation."[86] Nominally, this was a fundraising trip for southern Republican parties en route to the Republican National Convention in Miami Beach, Florida. In reality, it was a test of southern support for a potential, but very belated, challenge to frontrunner Richard Nixon for the 1968 GOP presidential nomination. Reagan and his advisors were aware that if he was to build a groundswell of support among GOP members and convention delegates, that surge would have to begin in the region where his popularity was highest: the South.

If Nixon did not win on the first ballot, they believed, the nomination would go to Reagan. For his part, Richard Nixon had spent the previous years building allegiances with party leaders around the country with a view to winning the nomination, but even he was nervous about the threat posed by Reagan's southern popularity.[87] After travelling to Texas, Arkansas, Virginia, and Kentucky, Reagan stopped in Alabama on 24 July.[88] Addressing a crowd of 3,800 in Birmingham, he denounced "bearded beatniks and so-called intellectuals" and sounded, as the *Los Angeles Times* noted, rather like George Wallace.[89] While in Alabama, he met that state's Republican delegates as well as some from South Carolina, Georgia, Mississippi and Louisiana. In its main aim of convincing Nixon-supporting delegates to switch sides, Reagan's southern trip met with some success. "Reagan's Southern raids unquestionably are slicing away a delegate here and a delegate there from Nixon's massive strength," reported the *Boston Globe*. "A Mississippi defection, coupled with Reagan infiltrations in South Carolina and Louisiana, would hurt Nixon badly on the first ballot."[90]

Despite making his candidacy official when he reached the Miami Beach convention, and spending hours in his trailer attempting to win over southern delegates, Reagan's strategy failed. Though Nixon later wrote of his concern that "Southern delegates could be lured at the last minute by [Reagan's] ideological siren song," it was, ironically, Strom Thurmond who played an instrumental role in keeping southern delegations on Nixon's side.[91] Thurmond's backing for Reagan remained strong—he repeatedly told fellow Republicans, "I love that man. He's the best we've got." But, like many senior GOP figures, he viewed Nixon as the candidate best placed to win the presidency in 1968.[92] Thurmond's thinking reflected wider concerns among southern delegates that, for all his popularity and charisma, Reagan was still a political neophyte. His ideological position on the right of the GOP also likely worked against him in a party still scarred by the Goldwater debacle.

While Richard Nixon narrowly won the nomination on the first ballot, this was not a sign that Reagan's popularity in the South was waning. Rather, as Theodore White argues in his study of the 1968 election, it was the Reagan campaign's late entry into the contest which cost him the support of the South and potentially the GOP nomination.

"At any moment in 1967, had he chosen, Reagan might have captured this bloc of Southern delegates and deadlocked the nomination," White contends. Instead, Reagan was trying to win delegates in states "where Richard Nixon's lieutenants had long preceded him." By the time the Reagan campaign was attempting to persuade individual southern delegates, many were unwilling to renege on their commitment to Nixon, despite their personal affection for Reagan. One Louisiana delegate, Reagan's old friend Charlton Lyons, was on the verge of tears after telling him he could not offer his support. Reagan's campaign manager said of Lyons, "He agrees with everything we say—but he can't get off his commitment to Nixon."[93] In response, Reagan wrote to Lyons a few weeks later to reassure him, "[I] would not want you to think for a moment that I was hurt or disappointed or that this in any way affects our friendship."[94] The Miami Beach convention was ultimately a failure for Reagan, but it signified that his southern support would be a crucial springboard in future presidential campaigns. As an editorial in South Carolina's *State* newspaper observed in the wake of the convention, Ronald Reagan remained "the sentimental and ideological choice of most Southerners."[95]

As the 1968 election demonstrated, postwar social and economic change had produced a white southern electorate that was increasingly fragmented. The region had seen two decades of uneven economic growth, with southern metropolises continuing to prosper and expand while around them the rural economy stagnated. This in turn had forged two broad trends among southern conservatives, closely linked to the geographic and economic divide. In 1968, the South's more affluent urban and suburban areas proved fertile ground for Richard Nixon, as middle-class whites employed in skilled jobs in defense or high-tech industries displayed typically middle-class electoral priorities: low taxation, law and order, housing, and education.[96] Chiefly, these voters were more conventional Republicans of the kind that Dwight Eisenhower had attracted when establishing a GOP beachhead in the South during the 1950s. But, in the decade since Eisenhower's last election, the economic boom had also drawn Republican-inclined voters from outside the South. As Bruce Schulman has written, "The region imported Republicanism much as it had imported new industry and a new technical workforce."[97]

Away from these "Sunbelt" oases, however, much of the South remained a heavily agricultural and economically beleaguered place. Overall, the South remained the nation's lowest paid, most poorly skilled region, with higher unemployment and lower life expectancy than the rest of the United States. While the southern political establishment had continued to embrace federal largesse for business, welfare for southerners in rural areas was scarce. The ongoing southern crusade to bring in outside investment and federal money had "ignited growth at the top, but neglected the poverty smoldering at the bottom."[98] Whites in rural areas had predominantly supported Barry Goldwater in 1964, and four years later were still intensely hostile to civil rights. In many parts of the rural South, the Civil Rights Act had little immediate effect, with segregation remaining largely unchallenged and whites able to live much as they had always done. Yet the old narrative of white southerners being persecuted by outside forces, including the federal government, Supreme Court justices, civil rights campaigners, and communists, retained its power. Segregationist Democrats like Georgia Governor Lester Maddox won office by fulminating against the Civil Rights Act even three years after it was passed.[99] In the election of 1968, the man who spoke to this anti-civil rights sentiment was a former Democrat, now the presidential nominee for the newly formed American Independence Party, George Wallace.

Each of these two broad conservative trends featured race as a core motivating factor. Even away from the racial tensions of the rural South, affluent middle-class voters existed in a world where both their workplaces and their comfortable suburbs were overwhelmingly white. Despite new federal anti-discrimination laws, African Americans continued to be discouraged, or in some instances barred, from moving into suburban communities and acquiring well paid jobs by housing and employment practices that were designed for exactly that purpose. In the late 1960s, as Kevin Kruse has argued, Atlanta's suburbs were marked by a "secessionist attitude" towards housing and education—rooted in the desire of whites to keep public housing away from suburban areas and to prevent the racial integration of local schools.[100] The situation was comparable in the workplace. In 1966, aerospace was one of the South's fastest growing industries, yet black workers accounted for less than 2 percent of white-collar jobs and less than 7 percent of blue-collar jobs at aerospace companies.[101] By supporting Richard Nixon's presidential campaign—with its call to the "silent majority" and its rhetorical focus on law and order—it was this world that southern middle-class whites were seeking to maintain.

Race was, unsurprisingly, a far more obvious element of George Wallace's 1968 campaign. Yet it was notable that when appealing to rural, working-class whites still enraged by civil rights and federally mandated integration, Wallace made only limited references to segregation—arguing again that it should be an issue of state jurisdiction—and sought to expand his platform into one that combined economic populism with backlash politics. The American Independence Party's nominee called for greater federal investment in education, health care, Social Security, and transportation, while at the same time condemning liberals, hippies, protesters, and federal judges. In many ways, Wallace was reflecting the traditional Southern conservative mindset, demanding federal government action as long as it was directed solely in ways that benefitted white southerners. But while he had certainly moderated the nakedly racist language he had used in previous campaigns, it was also true that Wallace's appeal was still rooted in the southern attitude to race. As one of his senior aides later admitted, "He was really trying to reach the common, ordinary white person out there who did not like black people."[102]

In different ways, the Wallace and Nixon campaigns of 1968 indicated a shift in southern discourse. Segregation and white supremacy were no longer the alpha and omega of the South's politics, as they had been as recently as 1964. Race now had a more complex and nuanced rhetorical context, though it simmered just beneath the surface of most political arguments. Across the region, heightened concerns about "white rights" came to the fore, taking the place of overt opposition to desegregation.[103] The white South's vernacular of states' rights, anti-communism, and hostility to welfare remained the same, but it now spoke to fears of increased black political and economic power and anxiety about the threat this posed to white southern identity.

The late 1960s saw something of an existential crisis for conservative white southerners, rooted in their entrenched insecurity and aversion to change. It was not simply a racial backlash. There were also many southern whites who had been ambivalent about segregation and abhorred the idea of violent resistance to black rights, yet who now, as Jason Sokol observes, "deplored riots, feared a civil rights struggle shorn of its nonviolent heart, and chafed under court-ordered school integration, busing, and the tax burden imposed by an active federal government."[104]

What both Nixon and Wallace campaigns also demonstrated very clearly was the depth of white southern aversion towards the national Democratic Party. Though the 1968 presidential election was one of the closest in US history, Democrat Hubert Humphrey won just one southern state: Texas. A prominent liberal, Humphrey had been a hate figure to segregationists in the South for twenty years, firstly when he spoke passionately in favor of civil rights at the 1948 Democratic Convention and sparked a walkout of southern delegates, and subsequently as Lyndon Johnson's vice president during the height of the civil rights revolution. Among white southerners in 1968, fully 80 percent of votes went to either Nixon or Wallace, with the latter winning Alabama, Georgia, Louisiana, Mississippi, and Arkansas—a strong showing for a third-party candidate.[105] Though Democratic loyalties remained strong at the state and congressional levels, the party's presidential reliance on the white South was now shattered.

On a national level, the assassinations of Martin Luther King Jr. and Robert F. Kennedy and widespread unrest over American involvement in Vietnam meant the 1968 election took place in a uniquely febrile climate, against the backdrop of a society that appeared to be coming apart at the seams. Moreover, Nixon's win was the culmination of years of growing tension, as across the nation white support for civil rights began to wane. As Lewis Gould points out, support for racial integration among whites outside the South had been high in the early 1960s, largely because segregation was seen as a primarily southern problem. When new federal civil rights legislation began to impact other areas of the United States, many white Americans "saw it as a threat to property values, neighborhood integrity, and ethnic cohesion."[106] On top of this,

the rise of the Black Power movement epitomized increasingly assertive African American demands for equality, while each summer race
riots erupted in black ghettos across the nation, a despairing response
to police brutality and poor living standards. Consequently, by 1968,
anxiety over racial tensions and social disorder had severely damaged
the image of the Democratic Party among white voters across the nation and prepared the ground for Richard Nixon's success. That year's
presidential election therefore highlighted how political themes that
many had once thought characteristically southern—such as racial
division and white resentment—were spreading ever further beyond
Dixie's borders.

In California, meanwhile, Ronald Reagan was building his reputation on a combination of ideological anti-statism and political pragmatism. After it became clear that liberals in the state legislature, both
Democrat and Republican, would fight hard to preserve the Rumford
Fair Housing Act, for example, Reagan quietly backed away from his
pledge to repeal it and instead accepted revision of the legislation.[107]
In doing so, he could avoid a potentially damaging political battle and
at the same time blame the legislature for preventing him fulfilling his
campaign promise. The issue arose again some months later, but after
meeting with leaders of minority groups Reagan stated that the Act
had become a "symbol" for California's minority communities, and
he would veto any attempt at outright repeal.[108] Ultimately, the debate
over the Rumford Act was superseded by fair housing provisions in
the 1968 Civil Rights Act. This was just one area in which Reagan's
California governorship highlighted the pragmatism that would be a
recurring theme throughout his subsequent career. Yet his supporters
on the Republican right, along with the many white southerners who
regarded Reagan with admiration and affection, maintained their support for him. "Conservatives were not blind to Reagan's pragmatism,"
Lou Cannon has written. "They liked what he said, even when it required ignoring what he did."[109]

Reagan was utterly convinced of the rightness of the conservative
cause, and expertly conveyed that conviction to his audiences, but he
did not see himself as a die-hard right-wing ideologue. Instead, his
self-image was that of a "citizen-politician" who reflected the concerns

of average Americans.[110] In Reagan's interpretation, those concerns were chiefly economic. His eight years as governor provided ample evidence that he placed greater emphasis on personal and economic freedom than on enforcing moral or social values, including his support for a program led by Californian industrialist H. C. McClellan which provided African Americans in Watts with employment and his reluctant decision to sign a bill liberalizing the state's abortion laws.[111] In 1967, he tightened gun controls by signing the Mulford Act, though this was motivated in part by fears of guns being used in race riots after a heavily armed protest by Black Panthers outside the state Capitol building.[112] Although Reagan was often personally dubious about the effects of such legislation, he was nevertheless willing to adopt relatively liberal stances on social issues if he thought it politically necessary.

Conversely, during his time as governor, Reagan's embrace of the Southern Baptist church helped to strengthen his ties to the conservatism of the white South, as well as giving him a valuable education in how to maintain evangelicals' support while keeping their religious zeal in check. Reagan was astute enough to understand that he needed to keep personal relations with evangelical leaders cordial and to incorporate religious rhetoric into his speeches. "To hold their confidence and continue tapping their considerable resources, the governor enshrouded the ceremonial side of his politics in an aura of heartfelt, homespun Protestantism," Darren Dochuk writes. Still, Reagan and his advisors regarded evangelicals with caution, "always courting the patricians and power brokers among them but controlling the populist preachers and activists."[113]

In 1969, Reagan introduced his friend Billy Graham at a Southern California Crusade that Graham had organized in Orange County, which was attended by some 384,000 worshippers in Anaheim Stadium over a ten-day period. Reagan's speech was a prime example of the way he made sure to remain publicly in tune with evangelicals, despite giving them scant reward for their support in policy terms.[114] Reagan told his audience, "People have become so concerned with church-state separation, that we have interpreted freedom of religion into freedom from religion." He went on to call for a rediscovery of "our spiritual heritage."[115] Alongside his widely publicized meetings with prominent Southern Baptist leaders, Reagan's appearance at the event was designed to provide evangelical voters and activists with reassurance. Ultimately, his handling of transplanted southern evangelicals in California was indicative of how he would handle the Christian Right on the national stage two decades later. By embracing them rhetorically but doing little to advance their political agenda, Reagan offered conservative evangelicals little more than the illusion of influence when it came to policymaking.

As he approached the end of his governorship, Reagan's displays of pragmatism in California had done little to dent his popularity among southern conservatives. He was again talked of as a Republican presidential candidate and many leading southern Republicans now regarded him as the best vehicle for furthering their cause within the GOP. In a letter to Reagan, Strom Thurmond wrote that he could not think of "a more articulate and knowledgeable spokesman for the conservative position."[116] Reagan was conspicuous in supporting Republican candidates for office in many southern states, including writing fundraising letters, such as one for Thurmond in 1970, and recording television campaign advertisements.[117] One campaign endorsement helped Jesse Helms win a Senate seat in North Carolina in 1972, a favor Helms would repay during Reagan's campaign for the 1976 Republican presidential nomination.[118] Reagan also continued to receive rapturous welcomes on his regular appearances in the South. At a GOP fundraiser in Jackson, Mississippi, in November 1973, he was feted as the man white southerners wanted to see as the next president. One Mississippi Republican told him, "Nowhere else in this country are you better understood and respected," and in return Reagan described his audience of southern Republicans as "the wave of the future."[119] Similarly, after a visit to Alabama in October 1974, an editorial in the *Mobile Register* declared Reagan had seemed "right at home" before claiming that "he talked the language of Alabamians . . . and has the ability to follow up his talk with action. That's strong medicine. Come back to see us again, Governor Reagan. We could form a mutual admiration society!"[120]

During the early 1970s, while Reagan was serving his second term as governor of California, the South appeared to be on a positive trajectory, at least to outsiders. Though regional power still rested largely with conservative whites, black political participation was increasing across the region. Several heavily African American districts emerged, enabling the election of black local officials and sending liberal Democrats to Congress. By 1972, even George Wallace was making pro-integration statements and appealing to black voters.[121] The fever of the 1960s had subsided. Reporters visited symbolic cities like Birmingham, Alabama, and Little Rock, Arkansas, in search of positive stories of integration, and optimistic talk of a "New South" began to appear in national newspapers.[122] But even among those white southerners who had grudgingly adjusted to racial integration, relatively few fully accepted it. For many, the emergence of black voters as a political force served to deepen anxieties around white identity. Added to this was concern over the steady decline of white southern power in Washington. By 1975, several long serving southern Democrats had either died or left office, including Georgia senator Richard Russell, Louisiana senator Allen Ellender, Alabama senator Lister Hill, and Arkansas senator William Fulbright. As chairs of powerful senate committees, these men had used their influence and seniority to protect the interests of the white South for much of the postwar era. Their passing, combined with rising black electoral strength, left the white conservative South politically diminished.[123]

In that context, it is unsurprising that Reagan's anti-statist rhetoric continued to attract white southerners who were fearful of losing their identity and who felt the federal government's approach to civil rights was authoritarian. Reagan was now more than a celebrity whose speeches provided succor to anxious or angry southern audiences. By the mid-1970s, he was a significant political figure who appeared to offer white southerners a chance to reassert themselves and make their voices heard at the national level. Alienated from the leadership of the Democratic Party, white southerners had been in search of a national political standard-bearer for years, as southern support for Reagan's short-lived candidacy in 1968 had indicated. This had been a significant factor behind the partisan fluctuations in the white South in the wake of the civil rights movement. For many southerners, George Wallace had been the solution. However, as a third-party candidate in 1968 he was highly unlikely ever to reach the White House. When he was paralyzed in an assassination attempt while campaigning for the Democratic nomination in 1972, Wallace largely ceased to be an influence on national politics, despite continuing to feature in presidential primary races.[124]

The other alternative was Richard Nixon. Though he had seen off Reagan's primary challenge in 1968, for many conservatives support for Nixon did not translate into personal affection. As Robert Mason observes, Nixon was "no better than the second choice of many activists representing the party's new conservatism."[125] Among those selecting the GOP presidential candidate that year he had simply been the pragmatic option. This was particularly true for those southerners who regarded Ronald Reagan as "a soul brother" (in the phrase of one Georgia Republican) but still too politically inexperienced.[126] Consequently, though Nixon had won the presidency that year with the help of millions of white southern voters, their faith in him was far from wholehearted. Indeed, he had barely won a plurality of southern votes: 34.7 percent to Wallace's 34.3 percent.[127] During Nixon's first term his popularity in the South had been bolstered by his vice president Spiro Agnew—whose belligerent political style struck such a chord with southern whites that "Spiro Is My Hero" bumper stickers began to appear around the region—until Agnew was forced to resign over corruption allegations.[128] Nixon's re-election campaign in 1972 saw him fully deploy what had come to be termed the "southern strategy," aiming to combine his urban and suburban support from 1968 with those working-class white southerners who previously backed Wallace. Though he won every southern state, Nixon's landslide victory owed much to the identity of his opponent. By choosing one of the most liberal senators in Washington, George McGovern of South Dakota, as their nominee, Democrats effectively sealed their fate. In many parts of the South, support for Nixon was almost entirely down to a rejection of McGovern's liberalism. As Sean Cunningham has written of the 1972 election in Texas, "Nixon was considered a moderate, still distrusted by most Texas conservatives."[129]

Throughout the early 1970s, therefore, many white southerners had continued to look to Ronald Reagan, not only as a trustworthy ally but now as a potential president. This perception only grew stronger after the Watergate scandal led to Nixon's downfall in 1974. His successor,

Gerald Ford, was regarded with even greater skepticism by conservatives in the white South. Their perception of him as part of the liberal establishment was cemented by his choice of vice president: former New York governor Nelson Rockefeller, the leading GOP moderate who had lost to Barry Goldwater in the 1964 Republican primaries. At the same time as Ronald Reagan was addressing large, rapturous southern audiences, a tour of the region by President Ford in October 1974 drew crowds that were, according to the *Atlanta Constitution*, "warm and friendly but small."[130]

By the mid-1970s, after watching him win two terms as California governor and rise to national prominence, white southern audiences were once again giving Reagan overwhelming encouragement to seek the presidency. Reagan himself remained coy about another presidential run, telling Barry Goldwater in May 1975 that he was "waiting in the wings."[131] Though he and his advisors had long been looking to 1976 as a potential opportunity, he would now have to challenge an incumbent Republican president, something they were deeply reluctant to do. Moreover, after his abortive last-minute candidacy at the 1968 Republican National Convention in Miami Beach, he was wary of another failure. To the frustration of many supporters, Reagan hung back, keen to maintain his political influence but wary of committing to a campaign that would divide his party and had only a slim chance of success—no incumbent president had been unseated by their own party since 1884.[132] Nevertheless, confidence remained high among Reagan's devotees in the South that their region could propel him to the nomination. "We could take just about every Southern delegate vote for him," one supporter optimistically declared to the *Atlanta Constitution.* "He'd win two-to-one in every state primary in Dixie."[133]

As conservative anger towards the Ford administration deepened, and his own supporters grew restive, Reagan drew closer to entering the race. In speeches, he began to justify a potential challenge to a sitting Republican president by suggesting that the "mandate" of 1972 was being "obscured." The country did not need a conservative third party, he argued, but "a new second party—the Republican Party—raising a banner of bold colors, with no pale pastels."[134] Though he was careful not to attack President Ford personally, the inference to Reagan's supporters was clear: under Ford's moderate leadership, conservative values were being betrayed. On 24 July 1975, Reagan attended a GOP fundraising event with Jesse Helms in Raleigh, North Carolina which helped set the scene for a likely Republican primary battle the following year. As well as rallying support for a future campaign, Reagan's appearance before a two thousand-strong audience was, according to William Link, "designed to consummate the Helms-Reagan alliance."[135] Returning to familiar southern themes, Reagan likened Helms to Confederate General Thomas "Stonewall" Jackson for his unwavering conservatism, avowed that Americans had "repudiated the welfare state," and attacked an extension of the Voting Rights Act as "pure cheap demagoguery." His speech finished to a standing ovation as some in the audience held aloft "Reagan for President" posters.[136]

Four months later Ronald Reagan was back in North Carolina, addressing hundreds of cheering supporters in Charlotte to promote his candidacy for President of the United States. Having declared his intention to run at a Washington press conference the previous day, Reagan had embarked on an intensive two-day, five thousand-mile tour of early primary states including New Hampshire, Florida, Illinois, and North Carolina.[137] As in 1968, the South would act as a catalyst for his campaign. Over the coming year, southern conservative support would prove pivotal in driving his challenge to a sitting Republican president. In Charlotte, a delighted Jesse Helms once again introduced Reagan, describing him as "our party's most articulate and exciting conservative spokesman. He has the personal magnetism and leadership ability to capture the imagination of the American people."[138] Though some polls showed Reagan and Ford neck and neck, in reality Ford's incumbency gave him a significant campaigning advantage over Reagan.[139] But when Jesse Helms introduced the newly announced candidate, he spoke for many white southerners who saw Reagan as the man to restore their region to a position of influence and power in Washington and as someone who, above all else, had been a loyal ally for two decades. Reagan was, in essence, one of them. Helms declared, "Isn't it great that, as of yesterday, *we* have a presidential candidate!"[140]

2. "This Is Reagan Country"
The South in Reagan's Presidential Campaigns, 1976–1980

In the mid-1970s, state Republican parties across the South were divided. Following the Goldwater campaign in 1964, large numbers of racially conservative white southerners, increasingly disgusted by the liberalism of the national Democratic leadership, had gravitated towards the GOP in search of a political home. Many had done so via support for George Wallace's campaign in 1968 and carried with them lingering segregationist sentiments and feelings of anger and disillusionment. They demonstrated a willingness to confront any internal opposition that might prevent them from gaining a foothold in the GOP. "Politically conservative, fervent to the point of amateurism, their aim is to overthrow the establishment," observed David Nordan of the *Atlanta Constitution*.[1] Power struggles between these tenacious, socially conservative insurgents and comparatively moderate Republican establishments were being played out across the South, most prominently in North Carolina, Texas, and Tennessee.[2]

The 1976 primary battle between Ronald Reagan and President Gerald Ford would bring these struggles into national focus. Conservative insurgents viewed Reagan as their ideal candidate, while the southern GOP establishment remained loyal to the president. "The foot soldiers of the GOP in the South are swinging towards Reagan," claimed one Virginia Republican following heated exchanges between the two sides at the 1975 Southern Republican Conference in Houston. A Reagan backer from Mississippi told journalists, "The South is Reagan country. . . . Some leaders have aligned themselves with the Ford effort, but they're just out of touch with the grass roots."[3] In October 1975, the *Atlanta Constitution* correctly predicted that southern primaries would be pivotal in deciding the upcoming nomination contest. The South was "vital to both of these leading Republicans, but it is more vital to Reagan, who knows he is basically stronger here than any other region."[4]

By early March 1976, the Ford campaign had eked out victory by little more than 1,300 votes in the first primary in New Hampshire and followed this with a comfortable win in Massachusetts.[5] The next primary in Florida was now crucial to Reagan's challenge. The first contest in the South, it was "a major key to our entire effort" in the view of Reagan's southern campaign coordinator David Keene.[6] Far ahead in the polls at one stage, Reagan saw Ford eventually sweep home by a 53–47 percent vote margin. Afterwards, Reagan declared himself "delighted" to have won 47 percent of the vote and argued he had lost because Florida was "not a typical Southern state."[7] When it came to Republican primary voters, his claim had some validity. The *Los Angeles Times* explained that "only 13% of Florida's 1 million Republicans were born here and only 14% more were born elsewhere in the South. The rest migrated from other regions, bringing with them views that are not as strongly conservative as those of most southern Republicans." Reagan ran strongly in Florida's more socially and racially conservative northern counties, which were "close to the rest of the South not only in geography but in ideological outlook," but this was not enough to offset his losses in the rest of the Sunshine State.[8]

Following Reagan's defeat, his campaign manager John Sears told journalists he was now looking to "Texas, Alabama, Georgia, Kentucky, and Tennessee, which are more natural grounds for us."[9] In the short term, Florida was followed by defeats in Illinois and Vermont. By the time the contest returned to the South in mid-March, Reagan's campaign was around $2 million in debt, senior staff were working without pay, and donations were drying up. Ford's team used surrogates such as Texas senator John Tower to publicly and privately pressure Reagan to concede defeat for the sake of the party. Even Nancy Reagan repeatedly encouraged her husband to leave the race.[10] Despite their entreaties, Reagan was undeterred. The next primary was in North Carolina, where he had enjoyed enormous popularity since the 1950s. It was also home to Senator Jesse Helms—his most ardent southern supporter and a conservative scourge of the Republican establishment.

The two had first met in Raleigh in the early 1960s when Reagan visited WRAL, the television station where Helms was executive vice president. According to Helms, they hit it off immediately, bonding over shared interests in "Hollywood and the media" before inevitably getting around to talking politics.[11] Over the years they developed a mutual admiration and friendship. Both men were from modest, small-town backgrounds and both had forged careers in television and the media before launching themselves into the political fray. Reagan did so via his work for GE, while Helms wrote and presented editorials on WRAL that became a forum for his conservative views and a springboard for his political career.[12]

Like Reagan, Helms had been a lifelong Democrat prior to switching parties in 1970. Unlike Reagan, however, Helms was not a former liberal. He had been a traditional southern Democrat, and his popularity among conservative Democratic voters was such that so-called "Jessecrats" comprised a substantial portion of North Carolina's electorate. By the mid-1970s, Rob Christensen has observed, "Helms was a conservative Democrat in Republican clothing. He carried to Washington the southern conservative and segregationist tradition of [former North Carolina senator] Sam Ervin, coupled with the angry belligerence of a George Wallace."[13] In 1950, the young Helms had been an unofficial strategist for the Senate candidacy of Democrat Willis Smith when he defeated a liberal, anti-racist opponent, Frank Porter Graham. In a closely fought election, Helms engaged in some of the most explicit race-baiting in US campaign history, including the circulation of doctored photographs of Graham's wife dancing with an African American man.[14] During his later years in print and broadcast journalism Helms was an outspoken opponent of federal desegregation efforts, which he "liked to convert into another Yankee war on [his] beloved South."[15] In editorials he railed against enemies including communists, liberals, intellectuals, and civil rights protesters, deploying these labels interchangeably against anyone he believed was conspiring to undermine the foundations of the white South. In the turbulence of the 1960s, Helms became, in Ernest Furgurson's description, a "conspicuous hero to the Carolinians who were angry but seemingly helpless to resist the crumbling of the world they held dear."[16]

Helms carried this reactionary populism into politics and after Ronald Reagan recorded a television advert for Helms's successful 1972 senatorial campaign, their personal friendship evolved into a political alliance. Over lunch at Reagan's California home in October 1973, Helms promised Reagan, "If you ever decide to run for President, and if you feel that I can be helpful, count me in. I'll be honored to do anything I can."[17] In 1976, he was true to his word. On the stump in Florida Helms attacked the Ford administration with glee, describing Henry Kissinger as a "proven failure" and claiming President Ford was being "led around by the nose by his advisors." Criticizing Ford's policy of détente with the Soviet Union, he said, "Jerry Ford is getting rid of the word détente, but he is keeping Henry Kissinger. That's like throwing away the safety pin and keeping the soiled diaper."[18] In short, Helms was the perfect ally for Reagan's faltering campaign.

Helms could also call upon one of the most effective conservative political machines in the United States, the North Carolina Congressional Club. The NCCC was chaired by Tom Ellis, whom Helms had known since they both worked on Willis Smith's 1950 campaign. A "shrewd, pipe-smoking Raleigh attorney," Ellis had been a well-connected and influential figure in North Carolina conservatism for over a decade. Both he and Helms switched to the GOP in 1970, and it was Ellis who persuaded Helms to run for the Senate in 1972. The two became politically inseparable. Ellis managed Helms' senatorial campaign and remained his closest ally and strategist for the rest of his career.[19] With Tom Ellis in charge, the NCCC began life as a political action committee formed to retire Helms' 1972 campaign debt. It subsequently became a vehicle to provide strategic guidance and money—raised through a technologically advanced direct mailing operation—to conservative candidates across the South and nationwide. The NCCC epitomized the conservative insurgency that was rapidly gaining ascendance in the southern GOP, acting as a channel through which embittered conservative Democrats in search of a new home could be drawn towards the Republican Party.[20]

The NCCC typified the aggression of southern conservative political campaigning. Former state party chairman, Frank Rouse, recalled of the committee's leadership, "They go out there and they don't take any damn prisoners—from day one they're in it to win."[21] Though nominally a Republican organization, the NCCC prioritized electing conservatives and even refused to allow moderate Republicans to appear at their rallies and events. Like other southern Democrats who were newly converted to the GOP, NCCC leaders' commitment to the social and cultural conservatism of the white South often bordered on zealotry. Rouse's recollection was that Helms, Ellis, and their associates were "a closed society" who felt they were "on a mission from God."[22] As was the case in state Republican parties across the South, this conservative faction was regularly in conflict with the North Carolina GOP establishment. In 1976, the traditional party elite lined up behind President Ford, with Governor James Holshauser serving as the Ford campaign's southern coordinator, while Reagan's campaign gave Helms and Ellis the chance to gain control over a state Republican Party they had joined just six years earlier. As the *Greensboro Daily News* put it, the Reagan-Ford primary was "a test of political strength."[23]

Infuriated by Reagan's failures in New Hampshire and Florida, Helms and Ellis demanded control over the campaign in North Carolina. Though Jesse Helms chaired the campaign, its day-to-day management was in the hands of Tom Ellis and his staff at the North Carolina Congressional Club.[24] The NCCC was viewed with circumspection by Reagan's circle but understood instinctively how to appeal to conservative southern voters. Reagan advisor Lyn Nofziger later described Tom Ellis as "a right-wing zealot," but also lauded him for "almost single-handedly turning the campaign around."[25]

Ellis's plan was to focus on exploiting North Carolinians' existing affection for Reagan and to use his celebrity to generate media exposure, while at the same time taking an aggressive approach to issues that spoke emotionally to white southern discontent. To attract publicity, and to recreate the feeling of glamour that Reagan had brought to small southern towns in the 1950s, the NCCC sought to involve some of his old Hollywood friends. Jimmy Stewart was enlisted to introduce Reagan at several campaign stops. "I can't believe it!" one woman who attended a Reagan event in Greensboro exclaimed to a *New York Times* reporter. "I've seen Ronald Reagan, but there's Jimmy Stewart!"[26] Ellis also arranged for a thirty-minute television broadcast to be shown on fifteen stations across the state in prime-time. Reagan spoke directly into the camera and expressed his sadness that Americans had to "celebrate our bicentennial beset by troubles that have us in a time of discontent." He also restated a claim that had long been at the center of his appeal: that he was simply a concerned citizen with a desire to change how things were being done. Of his time as California governor, Reagan said, "I didn't think of myself as part of government. I was a citizen, temporarily serving and representing my fellow citizens, and my loyalty was to them."[27] It was a performance akin to that which thrust him onto the national stage in 1964. "It was Reagan talking from the heart and nobody talks from the heart better than Reagan," observed Lyn Nofziger.[28]

Under continued pressure from Ford surrogates to pull out of the race, Reagan also started to employ more trenchant language on issues that spoke to feelings of anger, insecurity, and betrayal among conservative North Carolinians. In particular, the NCCC alighted on an issue that provoked a visceral reaction among southern voters: the proposed return of the Panama Canal to the Panamanian government. Both Reagan and Helms had raised the subject in Florida, but too late to change the outcome of the primary. Now, it became central to the campaign's theme of the betrayal of ordinary Americans by the Washington establishment. On the stump, Reagan asked rhetorically, "What kind of foreign policy is it when a little tinhorn dictator in Panama says he is going to start guerrilla warfare against us unless we give him the Panama Canal?"[29] For his part, Jesse Helms demanded to know what George Washington would have made of those "who cringe, in fear and terror, at the threats of two-bit communist puppet dictators who demand, among other things, that we give away the Panama Canal which was bought and built with the blood and resources of the American people?"[30]

Of course, ownership of the canal itself was not the issue for most North Carolina voters. More important was what it represented. On an emotional level, it resonated with the sense of grievance and betrayal southern conservatives felt towards the Democratic Party. It was also symbolic of a nation in decline both at home and abroad, a decline that was not merely political but moral and social. To white southerners resentful at the changes their region had undergone over the previous decade, the issue spoke to a conviction that the Washington establishment was deceitful, weak, and increasingly liberal. For many,

President Ford was as much a part of this untrustworthy elite as leading Democrats. In Florida, the issue had failed to generate the powerful response it did in North Carolina. As the *Baltimore Sun* observed,
this reflected differences in the Republican electorate, and particularly
the growing preponderance of conservative former Democrats in the
southern GOP. "[In] New Hampshire, Illinois—and, yes—Florida, the
majority of the registered Republicans are the same breed of voter.
They are traditional Republicans, supporters of the party of Lincoln
and even Hoover," the *Sun* reported. "But in the real South, traditional
Republicans are a rarity." The GOP's southern primary electorate was
increasingly dominated by voters who "did not become Republicans
because they believed in just not rocking the boat, as traditional Republicans elsewhere did."[31] Instead, they sought ways to demonstrate
their anger, overthrow the liberal order in Washington, and reassert the
white South's political power.

Though a decade had passed since the civil rights revolution of the
1960s, race remained a central factor in North Carolinian politics, as it
did in much of the South. "It's race in North Carolina. That is not sup-
position. That is a fact," Frank Rouse later recalled. "The Democrats
by and large were pro-busing, pro-integration, pro-welfare, pro-some-
thing for nothing. The Republicans resent the fact that blacks bloc vote
for Democrats and white Democrats resent the fact that blacks have
such a stranglehold on their party. . . . Folks who live in suburbia or
folks who moved to North Carolina don't understand it, but it is an
absolute fact of life."[32] In North Carolina, the men who knew best how
to exploit these racial tensions were the strategists at the NCCC. Tom
Ellis and his colleagues printed leaflets suggesting that Gerald Ford was
considering black Massachusetts senator Edward Brooke for the vice
presidency—without noting that he was only one of several possibilities under consideration—and distributed them to the predominantly
white crowds at Reagan rallies. The racial overtones were clear.[33]

When Reagan found out about the flyers, he ordered Ellis to stop
the distribution and informed the media that he had done so. Given
Helms' past involvement in racist campaigning and Ellis's love of
"Southern slash-and-burn politics," it is unlikely that Reagan could
have been genuinely surprised by the NCCC's tactics.[34] The episode

was evidence that an unwavering certainty about his own righteousness when it came to issues of race—along with an unshakeable faith
in the conservative cause—meant Reagan was often willing to blind
himself to the South's racialized political climate. When questioned
about his opposition to civil rights legislation by an audience of black
Republicans back in 1966, the usually sanguine Reagan had reacted
with genuine outrage, shouting "I resent the implication that there is
any bigotry in my nature." Yet when the Reagan campaign responded
to the furor over the Brooke leaflets by insisting their candidate had
"never campaigned on race or used it as an issue, never will," their
claim was clearly disingenuous.[35] In his denunciations of the Rumford
Act during the latter weeks of his first California governor's race, Reagan had shown an inclination to follow in Barry Goldwater's tracks
and go "hunting where the ducks are" when electoral circumstances
required it. In the North Carolina primary, the fact that the Brooke
leaflets originated with the NCCC enabled Reagan's campaign to send
out a loud dog whistle to white voters while the candidate himself publicly asserted his opposition to racist campaigning. In the same way
that he could remain convinced of his own racial innocence even as he
was speaking to white southerners of states' rights, so Reagan was also
willing overlook the race-baiting instincts of his southern allies, at least
until they caused a stir in the media. Though he personally never made
overtly racist appeals, Reagan was undoubtedly skilled at having it both
ways when it came to the politics of race.

Ultimately, his campaign was unscathed by the brief storm that surrounded the leaflets. But the NCCC had clearly identified their target
electorate: racially conservative white voters disenchanted with the
political establishment, in particular disaffected Democrats and those
who had fallen off electoral lists. Newspaper advertisements declared,
"You can vote your beliefs by re-registering Republican in order to cast
a ballot for Ronald Reagan. . . . Regardless of party registration, all citizens of North Carolina are invited to work and contribute to the Reagan for President effort."[36] These were just one element of an efficient
and innovative direct mail and get-out-the-vote operation in which the
NCCC repeatedly contacted voters by mail and telephone. Ellis and his
staff amassed a computerized database of 80,000 voters in North Car-

olina and a further 350,000 conservative supporters nationwide who would make up a fundraising base for Reagan's campaign in the Tar Heel state and beyond.[37]

The NCCC's expertise and commitment made Reagan's operation in North Carolina a formidable one. To some, it was more than merely a nomination challenge. According to Jules Witcover, for many "Helmsites" the campaign was nothing less than "a holy war."[38] Theirs was not a cause tethered by partisan affiliation. Little thought was given to shaping a nuanced message to please the varied interest groups within the GOP. Instead, it was a campaign aimed at harnessing the southern conservative insurgency that had been gaining traction in the party since the late 1960s. Feeling betrayed by the Democrats, these southerners had found a new political home in the GOP and through Reagan's candidacy they sought to exert as much influence over it as possible at both state and national levels.

When the results came through, Reagan was victorious by 52 percent to 46 percent. "Just when President Ford thought he had Ronald Reagan staggering on the ropes," editorialized the *Los Angeles Times*, "the former California governor came slugging back."[39] The differing approaches of the two campaigns had been critical. While Helms and Ellis were turning Reagan's candidacy into a holy war, Ford spent just two days in North Carolina and fully expected an easy win to wrap up the nomination. Reagan's support in the eastern part of the state, Jesse Helms's electoral stronghold, enabled him to offset Ford's strength in mountainous western counties, home to more traditional, long-standing Republican voters.[40] The factional battle within the state GOP further encouraged a strong showing by the Helms-led insurgents. As Reagan advisor Peter Hannaford observed, "control of the state party was at stake."[41]

Though Jesse Helms received widespread credit, it was Tom Ellis and the NCCC who masterminded Reagan's win. Ellis's campaign strategy—combining a state-wide media blitz with discreet but intensive voter registration and direct mailing—had proved remarkably effective. It was the first time a sitting president had been defeated after actively campaigning in a primary contest, and the result elevated Helms and his allies to a position of dominance in the state Republican

Party. Tom Ellis would chair the North Carolina delegation to the Republican convention that summer, with Governor James Holshauser not even allowed to be a member.[42] Reagan's fightback proved that his candidacy was a viable vehicle for southern conservatives to assert greater influence within the national Republican Party. North Carolina had rescued Reagan's campaign, possibly even his political career. Fifteen years later, he wrote to Jesse Helms: "I'll never forget what you did for me in 1976. I shudder to think how things would have turned out had North Carolina not gambled on this guy."[43]

In the weeks after his victory, Reagan's momentum stalled as the campaign moved away from the South. Financially motivated concessions in Wisconsin, Pennsylvania, and New York meant Reagan's advisors again looked to the South to revitalize his campaign, this time in the Texas primary. As Jimmy Carter began to wrap up the Democratic nomination and deflate George Wallace's final presidential campaign, culturally-conservative Wallace supporters became potential Reagan voters. In Texas, radio advertisements were aired featuring a Wallace supporter from Fort Worth, Rollie Millirons. "George Wallace can't be nominated. Ronald Reagan can," Millirons told listeners. "He's right on the issues. So for the first time in my life I'm gonna vote in the Republican primary. I'm gonna vote for Ronald Reagan."[44] After Reagan aide Jeff Bell advised that "appeals to like-minded Democrats to cross over should be renewed whenever possible," Reagan's personal narrative, as a former Democrat who believed the party had abandoned its principles, was resurrected in his stump speeches. It proved especially resonant in the Wallace stronghold of East Texas.[45] A rally in Fort Worth featured former Wallace campaign workers on the platform alongside Reagan, and an audience of three thousand that "seemed much more like a typical Wallace rally—women in housedresses, sport-shirted men, lots of small American flags."[46]

Crowds like these—former southern Democrats and Wallace supporters—responded with fervent applause when Reagan touched on social issues, decrying school busing as an experiment which treated children as "guinea pigs" and criticizing a White House proposal requiring the manufacture and sale of handguns to be approved by the

Secretary of the Treasury.[47] On a variety of subjects, President Ford proved an easy target. Reagan condemned the decline of Christianity in public schools, Ford's signing of an unpopular energy bill that placed price controls on oil companies, and an expansion of the Voting Rights Act which brought Texas under that law for the first time. "Into each topic, Reagan infused anti-government animus and dire warnings of impending national insecurity," writes Sean Cunningham. "The public's awareness of this appeal acted as a self-fulfilling prophecy, drawing even larger numbers of undecided conservative Democrats into the Reagan tent."[48]

As had happened in North Carolina, the Texas primary exacerbated the divide between conservative insurgents and the GOP establishment. The main victim of the intraparty struggle was John Tower, a leading Texas Republican since winning election to the Senate in 1961. Though Tower had endorsed Reagan's bid for California governor in 1966, after taking on the role of Ford's state campaign chairman he now found himself at odds with the Texas GOP's grassroots membership, most of whom adored Reagan as a conservative hero and reviled Gerald Ford as a liberal. Reagan criticized Tower, with some justification, for backtracking on social issues to align himself with the Ford campaign.[49] Reprising a popular theme from North Carolina, Reagan's Texas campaign chairmen also declared it "shocking" that John Tower "could travel around this state saying that Mr. Ford has no intention of giving up U.S. sovereignty and control over the Panama Canal. . . . If the President and his Texas campaign chairman cannot be believed on issues as important as these, where *can* we believe them."[50] Unsurprisingly, Tower's reputation among conservative Texans took a severe hit from the Reagan team's personal attacks.

A remarkably high turnout on 1 May gave Reagan victory by 66 percent to Ford's 33 percent, the heaviest defeat ever suffered by a sitting president. The *New York Times* reported that a "massive Democratic crossover vote" had helped Reagan win many East Texas districts by more than three to one.[51] After the primary, alarm spread among Ford's campaign staff about the energy and enthusiasm of Reagan's conservative supporters, chiefly those recently converted Democrats who had propelled his success in the South. Many voters, an internal report noted, "have not been involved in the Republican political system before; they vote overwhelmingly for Reagan." Reagan was benefiting from "skillful organization by extreme right-wing political groups in the Reagan camp operating almost invisibly through direct mail and voter turnout efforts," including gun ownership advocates, George Wallace supporters, and right to life organizations. These were "not loyal Republicans or Democrats," the report observed, and the Ford campaign was "in real danger of being out-organized by a small number of highly motivated *right-wing nuts*."[52]

Southern conservatives were certainly providing Reagan with vital strategic and fundraising assistance. Tom Ellis had travelled to Texas to offer tactical advice, and the NCCC's direct mail operation had raised around $778,000 for the Reagan campaign since the North Carolina primary.[53] It was also true that Jesse Helms and the NCCC operatives leading these efforts were not especially loyal to the GOP, having been Republicans for less than a decade. Journalist Ferrel Guillory noted that "from a long range perspective, the continued existence of the Republican Party as it is now known is not central to Helms' political concerns."[54] Likewise, the American Conservative Union—which provided Reagan with fundraising help—was chaired by M. Stanton Evans, a pugnacious southern conservative born in Texas and raised in Tennessee. In Evans' view, the Republican presidencies of Ford and Nixon were merely "an extension of the Kennedy-Johnson administrations." In 1975, both Helms and Evans had publicly toyed with the idea of forming a conservative third party.[55] The influence of these southerners effectively turned Reagan's 1976 candidacy into a nationwide version of the conservative insurgency that had been splitting the southern GOP in recent years. As such, it appealed powerfully to a white southern electorate that felt abandoned by the Democratic Party but was still a long way from trusting the Republican establishment.

For the remainder of the primaries, Reagan and Ford traded victories, with Ford winning in the Northeast and Midwest and Reagan winning in the South and West. Reagan's wins included dominant victories in Georgia, Alabama, and Arkansas—each propelled by crossover voting by George Wallace supporters.[56] Reagan's popularity in southern states provided his campaign with crucial momentum, with two notable exceptions. In Kentucky and Tennessee on 25 May, he suffered defeats in southern primaries his advisors had been confident of winning. Both were indicative of a tension that would recur throughout Reagan's political career, whenever the anti-statist ideology of Reaganite conservatism clashed with the economic priorities of his southern supporters.

As Reagan and his former bosses at General Electric had learned in the late 1950s, criticizing the Tennessee Valley Authority was akin to wandering into a southern political minefield. Since then, the TVA had expanded even further, branching out into nuclear power and remaining economically vital to huge swathes of Tennessee and Kentucky. By the mid-1970s, it was politically and economically embedded in the South. Reagan had largely avoided criticizing the TVA after entering politics, but he could not avoid the subject when campaigning for the Kentucky and Tennessee primaries. Questioned by reporters in Knoxville shortly before election day, Reagan claimed the TVA's expansion meant it was now "competing with private enterprise . . . able as an agency without the consent of the people to amass a debt against the people, to put the people into debt for hundreds of millions of dollars." Asked directly if he would privatize the TVA, Reagan replied "I don't think I can give you an answer. . . . It would be something to look at."[57] Ford surrogates jumped on Reagan's comments. Kentucky Representative Tim Lee Carter described TVA privatization as "a disaster to Southcentral and Western Kentucky, as well as to Tennessee," while Tennessee Senator Howard Baker said it was "simply out of the question to seriously talk about selling it."[58] Reagan tried to backpedal, but the damage was done. He went on to lose the Tennessee and Kentucky primaries by such narrow margins—around two thousand votes and five thousand votes respectively—that the TVA backlash is almost certain to have made the difference. Both results showed just how the white South's economic self-interest could trump its anti-government sentiment once a federal project or subsidy had, like the TVA, become "a cherished part of the status quo" in the region.[59] It was a mindset that Reagan's southern supporters would demonstrate repeatedly throughout the 1980s.

Following the final primary contest, Reagan told senior advisors that he wanted to choose a presidential running mate prior to the Republican convention rather than waiting until he had won the nomination, as was customary. With Ford holding a slim lead in the delegate count, Reagan's national campaign manager John Sears agreed. If Reagan named a running mate, Sears concluded, Gerald Ford would be forced into the uncomfortable position of doing the same.[60] Incumbent vice president Nelson Rockefeller had effectively been forced into withdrawing from the ticket by conservatives the previous November —nominating a replacement during a divisive primary campaign meant Ford would run the risk of alienating crucial delegates. In the end it was Reagan's choice of nominee that proved deeply problematic, causing the first major rift with his southern conservative allies. Pennsylvania senator Richard Schweiker was a practicing Catholic who took relatively conservative stances on abortion and school prayer but was otherwise one of the most liberal Republicans in the Senate. He had opposed the Vietnam War, was an ally of national labor unions, and advocated the break-up of large oil companies. Not only did Schweiker receive a 100 percent rating from the AFL-CIO in 1975, but he had also received an 89 percent rating from Americans for Democratic Action, the same as Democrat George McGovern.[61] Importantly for Reagan and Sears, choosing Schweiker seemingly increased the prospects of winning over a large bloc of uncommitted Pennsylvania delegates and getting Reagan back in the nomination fight. With an eye on the longer term, the choice of a northeastern liberal also chimed with Reagan's personal inclination to reunite a riven party.

Reagan's political pragmatism, however, sparked fury among his southern supporters. "Instead of relying upon Southerners, Mr. Reagan has written them off—and in a manner that can only be described as callous," claimed an editorial in the *Charleston News and Courier*. "He is one who wants the presidency badly enough to resort to graceless betrayal of an early and enthusiastic constituency which deserves better of him."[62] Correspondence echoing the *Courier's* fury arrived at Reagan headquarters from conservatives across the South. A Texan rancher who had donated "several hundreds of dollars" to Reagan's campaign described the choice of Schweiker as "the worst rape of the South since the Civil War" and demanded that Reagan withdraw his candidacy: "I believe this is the only choice left to a turncoat!" A Charlotte resident asked that his earlier donation to the "deceptive" Reagan be used to buy flowers for the candidate's "political grave." Other letters were less overwrought but equally embittered. A correspondent from Woodville, Mississippi, wrote, "I now feel that you have lost a major portion of your Southern support. This is very disappointing because you were really our man." With a similarly mournful air, a long-time Reagan supporter from Louisiana stated simply, "I feel that you have stabbed your friends in the back."[63]

Likewise, Reagan's most prominent southern backers reacted with bewilderment and fury. Though he said little to the media, Strom Thurmond was privately stunned and "badly shaken," repeatedly telling aides "I can't believe it."[64] Jesse Helms found out when Reagan phoned him at 9:05 p.m. the evening before the Schweiker announcement, later remarking that he "wanted to record for posterity the exact time I received the shock of my life."[65] He wrote in his memoirs that Reagan had reassured him "Jess, you know where my heart is. . . . It's all right."[66] But at a subsequent gathering of North Carolina Republicans, Helms declared, "I will not go along with political expediency, whether intended to be that or not," and described the previous days as "a week that I wish had never been."[67] While he continued to believe in Reagan's commitment to conservatism and urged his state's delegates to remain loyal, Helms did so with the intention of forcing the campaign to replace Schweiker once the nomination had been won.

The *Atlanta Constitution* reported that the fallout was widespread: "All across the south Reagan supporters appeared to be slipping away."[68] Some Louisiana delegates who had pledged to vote for Reagan claimed his actions had "negated" their support. One told the *Advocate*, "I recognize a responsibility to the people who elected me to vote for Reagan, but whether I honor that commitment is totally another matter."[69] A prominent Texas Republican admitted "I'd be less than candid if I didn't express substantial disappointment. . . . [I] had operated under the faith that when Governor Reagan selected a vice president, it would be someone compatible with himself and the South."[70] Ultimately, however, the position of South Carolina governor James Edwards reflected the views of many conservative southerners who backed Reagan: Schweiker should be removed from the ticket after the convention, but

Reagan's campaign was too important for southerners to simply abandon it. "I can see an opportunity for the South like we haven't had since 1968," Edwards told journalists. "There's no advantage for us in the South to dump our candidate."[71]

Publicly, Reagan cited GOP unity as the main reason behind his choice, saying he wanted to "bring two groups of the party together, that have been more or less estranged."[72] Choosing Schweiker was bound to enrage those southerners who had left the Democratic Party because they believed it had betrayed them, but even years later Reagan remained convinced the choice was not a mistake. "I had not abandoned my belief, nor will I, that the man suggested for the second spot on the ticket should be one who would carry on the programs enunciated by the presidential nominee," he wrote in 1979.[73] Reagan's southern supporters required a similar rationalization process to remain loyal. Many, like Helms and Edwards, decided it was more important to focus on helping Reagan win the nomination before ousting Schweiker from the ticket. Others absolved Reagan of personal blame by directing their anger towards his advisors, particularly John Sears. In their eyes, Reagan would not have resorted to such expediency had Sears not talked him into it. Within weeks, the "long knives" would be out for Sears, "wielded by some of Reagan's most conservative, and most chagrined, supporters."[74] It was not the only reason Sears would become a hate figure among southern conservatives in the wake of the 1976 convention.

Choosing Schweiker certainly damaged Reagan in the eyes of southern delegates, but it was not the reason for the eventual defeat of his nomination challenge at the 1976 Republican Convention. Events at the Kansas City Convention were complex and arcane. In short, the nomination was decided when an attempt by John Sears to change convention rules was voted down. In a last roll of the dice, Sears proposed a change to Rule 16-C that would require all candidates to name their vice-presidential running mate before voting began for the party's nominee—an unsubtle attempt to back Gerald Ford into a difficult corner. But the rule change became, in effect, a proxy nomination vote. With some irony, it was an internal vote by a southern delegation, Mississippi, which signaled the end of Reagan's nomination chances. By just three votes, Mississippi delegates elected to oppose Rule 16-C. The state's 30 delegates on the convention floor would go in Ford's favor. The few remaining uncommitted delegates started to publicly side with Ford, not only on 16-C but also in the nomination battle, and Reagan finally had to acknowledge defeat.[75] The white South had revitalized and propelled Reagan's nomination challenge but, in the end, it was a handful of southern votes that kept victory out of his reach.

By the time of the final convention votes, most of the southern delegates angered by Reagan's choice of Schweiker had moved warily back to his camp. Still, despite the momentum he had received from his victories in the South, Reagan had never managed to overhaul Ford in the delegate count at any point in the primary campaign. In the nomination vote, President Gerald Ford defeated Ronald Reagan to win the nomination by 1,187 votes to 1,070.[76] Reagan's southern supporters reacted to his defeat with grief, anger, and disgust. For many, the prime target for blame was John Sears. The Texas delegation, for example, had remained loyal and voted unanimously for Reagan, but one angry delegate singled out Sears for vitriol: "If Reagan is dead, it's because of Sears."[77] Jesse Helms contemptuously referred to the Rule 16-C tactic as "that Mickey Mouse thing of John Sears."[78] Though Sears' missteps did not cost Reagan many southern delegates, they had certainly undermined southern faith in the Reagan campaign. As the *Atlanta Constitution* put it, the choice of Schweiker had "demoralized some of the Reagan faithful without adding any substantial number of new recruits to the cause."[79]

Nonetheless, as the GOP platform demonstrated, Reagan's campaign had created an exceptional opportunity for southern conservatives to increase their influence over the direction of the Republican Party. At a meeting in Atlanta in July—a gathering that Reagan's national advisors initially tried to prevent—Jesse Helms, Tom Ellis, and others had devised a plan to replace policy positions they regarded as too liberal with a series of hardline conservative principles drafted predominantly by John East, a Helms protégé and political science professor from North Carolina. Predictably, many of these principles ran "directly counter to Ford administration policies." Demands for constitutional amendments to ban abortion and forced busing sat alongside unambiguous opposition to gun control. Conversely, pro–Equal Rights

Amendment language would be removed entirely.[80] At the convention, Reagan's senior advisors wanted to avoid fights over platform issues, fearing they would alienate moderate delegates, but Reagan's southern allies were now so powerful they could not be ignored. The conservative platform challenge went ahead with the reluctant approval of Reagan's team. In response, also wanting to avoid divisive policy disputes, Ford capitulated. Platform committees approved most of the conservative policy planks. Language on busing, abortion, and welfare was hardened substantially. A commitment to deal with the "root causes" of segregation was removed, while a pledge to prevent the sale of cheap handguns was replaced with an unequivocal pro-gun statement: "We support the right of citizens to keep and bear arms. We oppose federal registration of firearms."[81]

On foreign policy, the changes were milder than Helms and Ellis wanted, but still represented a thinly veiled critique of Ford's record. Declarations such as "Ours will be a foreign policy which recognizes that in international negotiations we must make no undue concessions" and "We are firmly committed to a foreign policy in which secret agreements, hidden from our people, will have no part" were clearly designed to undercut Ford and Henry Kissinger's actions over the Panama Canal and détente.[82] Despite being "furious" when he first read it, Ford nevertheless accepted the plank, fearing that a possible fight over the issue could cost him the nomination.[83] Though they were more evident in domestic policy than foreign policy, the entire GOP platform bore conspicuous hallmarks of southern conservatism.

Southerners like Jesse Helms and his allies were undoubtedly more interested in advancing their conservatism than healing a divided party. As one columnist observed just prior to the GOP convention, "Helms believes the same thing about political parties that he believes about wishbones: It doesn't matter if you tear them apart, just as long as you get the biggest piece."[84] While Reagan had benefitted greatly from the support of southern conservatives, the reverse was also true. It is inconceivable that Helms, Ellis, and others could have forced such significant changes to the GOP platform had it not been for their role in Reagan's campaign. "It was because of the Reagan victories that began in North Carolina," Helms wrote to Stanton Evans a few weeks later, "that we were able to project the conservative message to millions of Americans and to have considerable influence on the drafting of the Republican platform, the most conservative in recent memory."[85] Their influence in 1976 was an early manifestation of a profound transformation in the GOP's character. From that point on, it became unthinkable that a Republican platform could, for example, be pro-choice on the issue of abortion. Southern social and cultural conservatism was on the way to becoming a central feature of the Republican Party's political identity.

After accepting the Republican nomination in Kansas City, Ford invited Reagan to speak from the convention podium in a gesture seemingly aimed at restoring party unity. Instead, Reagan's speech— condemning "the erosion of freedom that has taken place under Democratic rule in this country, the invasion of private rights, the controls and restrictions on the vitality of the great free economy that we enjoy"—made many conservatives even more certain the wrong man had won.[86] Carl Rowan, writing for the *Atlanta Constitution*, came away from the GOP convention with some perceptive "nagging thoughts" about the direction of the party. "I left Kansas City wondering if that throng of delegates, clamoring and weeping for Ronald Reagan long after the battle was lost, screaming that [Ford's running mate] Bob Dole wasn't conservative enough, begging for North Carolina's Sen. Jesse Helms, could be the wave of the future."[87]

Though Reagan appeared on Ford's behalf in twenty states during the subsequent presidential campaign, he often made little mention of the president. Stops in Louisiana and Mississippi, for example, were designed chiefly to promote Republican candidates for Congress.[88] Likewise, he received an enthusiastic welcome during a rally at the Houston Music Hall before delivering a speech "centered on the Republican platform" rather than the presidential race.[89] Unsurprisingly, Jesse Helms and Tom Ellis pursued the southern conservative agenda in their own way, adopting the label of the "Platforms Education Committee" and creating five-minute long television advertisements promoting the cultural conservatism of the Republican platform while completely ignoring the top of the ticket.[90]

In November, Reagan's southern support split between Ford and Jimmy Carter, though both were viewed with profound circumspection by conservative southerners. Most Wallace Democrats, for example, ultimately preferred Carter over Ford. Still, Carter's moderate stance on civil rights and his popularity among black southerners meant support from Wallaceites was guarded at best.[91] As a *Dallas Morning News* editorial colorfully phrased it, many of Carter's white southern voters were "conservative sheep . . . who went trotting off at the sound of a gentle Southern voice but who no longer care for some of the things that voice is saying."[92] While Gerald Ford narrowly lost the presidential election to Jimmy Carter by fifty-seven Electoral College votes and a popular vote margin of 2 percent, results in the South were more clear-cut. Aside from a Ford victory in Virginia, Carter's appeal among his fellow southerners enabled him to win the entire region. An unnamed Ford advisor argued the results showed that "blood was thicker than philosophy" in the South and described southern support for Carter as an "emotional binge."[93]

Following the election Ronald Reagan sought to keep himself in the public eye, including arguing in an interview that he "could have broken into the Solid South" and beaten Carter to the presidency.[94] For all Reagan's undoubted political skills and the deep well of affection for him among white southerners, this was a dubious claim. Reagan would have provided a stiffer challenge in the South, but it is unlikely he had the required electoral strength in the rest of the country. In 1976, with Watergate still a painful recent memory, polling on party identification showed the trend was not in the GOP's favor. As a Democrat and an outsider to Washington, Carter's appeal was formidable. Most Americans wanted a new face in the White House, but they were probably not yet inclined to move their country further to the right. Nevertheless, when it came to both his own political future and the prospects for Republican conservatism, Reagan remained upbeat as ever. In Lou Cannon's phrase, he continued "selling the conservative elixir" throughout the late 1970s, embarking on what amounted to a four-year campaign for the 1980 Republican nomination. By making hundreds of appearances at GOP events nationwide, penning newspaper columns, and writing and presenting daily radio talks on a range of political topics, Reagan maintained his position as the unofficial leader of the Republican right.[95] At the same time, a movement was emerging which would serve as a vehicle for southern conservatism and alter the political landscape of both the South and the United States: the Christian Right.

Since the start of the 1960s, fundamentalist evangelical leaders had been increasingly determined to exercise political power and to defend the social and religious values of the white conservative South. W. A. Criswell, Bob Jones Jr., and Billy James Hargis, among others, fulminated against the Supreme Court over decisions in 1962 and 1963 to prohibit officially sponsored prayer and Bible readings in public schools. They also condemned the civil rights movement and fervently supported southern segregation, which Hargis described as "one of Nature's universal laws."[96] As the threat of federal government action on civil rights grew, fundamentalists turned their fire on the Kennedy and Johnson administrations and looked to George Wallace for political leadership. Wallace was even awarded an honorary doctorate at Bob Jones University in May 1964.[97] However, with the white South's inevitable defeat in the battle to preserve racial segregation came a shift in focus for fundamentalist leaders in the late 1960s. Horrified by the apparent collapse of American morality symbolized by the "Summer of Love" in 1967, they embarked on a campaign to hold back the tide of cultural liberalism on multiple fronts, denouncing drug use, sexual freedoms, women's rights, pornography, homosexuality, and vocally supporting the Vietnam War in the face of nationwide anti-war protests. In 1968, Billy James Hargis moved the focus of his Christian Crusade from the fight against communism to resisting sex education in public schools. Other fundamentalists opted out of the public education system altogether. Following the example of Bob Jones University in South Carolina, from the mid-1960s private Christian schools and colleges began to appear across the United States, predominantly in the South. As well as escaping the secularization of public education, from a southern conservative perspective such institutions also had the benefit of enabling selective admissions, leading to student bodies that were—almost without exception—entirely white.[98]

Throughout this period, some fundamentalist leaders made a deliberate effort to move beyond the overt racism of their earlier years, with the intention of exerting influence on the national political stage. The transformation of the Southern Baptist Convention exemplified this strategy. Though he had publicly renounced his segregationist views, the election of W. A. Criswell as SBC president in 1968 still represented a significant rightward shift in an organization that had been led by mainstream evangelicals for much of its recent history. From that point on, conservatives in the SBC maneuvered ruthlessly to increase their control, including spying on moderate opponents and secretly recording their conversations. As Paul Harvey has observed, "Fundamentalists, who proclaimed themselves defenders of the spirituality of the church, in fact were savvy political operators who successfully organized for a political victory in taking over the nation's largest Protestant denomination."[99] Within a decade, the coup was complete. Once in control of its leadership positions, fundamentalists pushed the SBC into increasingly hardline stances on social issues and towards a deeper involvement in partisan politics as part of the emergent Christian Right. By the start of the 1980s, the agenda of the SBC leadership embodied the social values of white southern conservatives: opposition to abortion, demands for the restoration of prayer in public schools, resistance to women's rights, and a deeply traditionalist, patriarchal stance on family values. "The fundamentalists were the successful dissenters," writes Harvey, "and now they reigned as the power elite."[100]

Other conservative evangelical pastors created their own organizations with a view to increasing their political power. Jerry Falwell had founded a private school in Virginia, the Lynchburg Christian Academy, in 1967—the year in which Virginia's public education system was ordered to desegregate by the state's commissioner of education. Initially entirely white, Falwell's school admitted its first few black students in 1969. Like W. A. Criswell, Falwell had remained a committed opponent of racial integration until the early 1960s but had begun to support civil rights sooner than many of his fellow fundamentalists.[101] By the mid-1970s, he was directing a multimillion-dollar evangelical empire. Alongside the Christian Academy, Falwell preached to over ten thousand members at his Thomas Road Baptist Church, and had created summer camps, kindergartens, drug rehabilitation programs, and Liberty University, a private college founded in 1971. In addition, Falwell's radio and television program, "The Old-Time Gospel Hour," attracted around one and a half million viewers nationwide.[102] During the 1970s, he steadily gained prominence as a leading figure in the burgeoning Christian Right, participating in widely publicized campaigns against the Equal Rights Amendment, abortion, gay rights, and other "national cancers" identified by fundamentalist evangelicals as typifying the disintegration of American morality. These multifarious crusades merged in September 1979, when Falwell stood on the steps of the Capitol Building and announced the formation of the Moral Majority campaign—which quickly became the Moral Majority Inc.—to bring back "the America our founding fathers established."[103]

Fundamentalist evangelicals had long decried Supreme Court decisions and federal government intrusion into the southern way of life, particularly when it came to segregation. But their determination to wield national political influence by forming groups like the Moral Majority—or by aggressively taking control of existing organizations such as the Southern Baptist Convention—was a new trend. The Christian Right's campaigns functioned as an outlet for the political and cultural revanchism of the conservative South in the post–civil rights era. It epitomized many of the white South's age-old preoccupations. The founding of organizations such as the Moral Majority occurred not in the immediate aftermath of *Roe v. Wade* (1973) but following the Carter administration's 1978 revocation of tax exemptions from racially discriminatory Christian schools in the South, suggesting that the movement's rallying point in its early years was not abortion, but race.[104] Not coincidentally, the movement's coalescence in the mid-1970s also occurred in the aftermath of the decline of southern congressional power, which had for so long acted to protect the region's customs and traditions. As a result, new ways to project southern influence in Washington were needed. When Christian Right groups "fleshed out their platforms to include issues not ordinarily dealt with in Sunday School" these too epitomized southern conservatism: fervent anti-communism (including denouncing US-Soviet treaties limiting nuclear arms), support for white African regimes, opposition to relinquishing control of the Panama Canal, and demands for increased military spending.[105]

In essence, the Christian Right was a new variation on an old theme: the white South waging a rear-guard action in the face of threats to regional traditions from a changing America.

By the late 1970s, evangelical Protestants—including moderates and liberals as well as conservatives—were the largest religious denomination in the United States. Around a third of adult Americans, almost fifty million people, declared themselves to be "born again." But it was the number of conservative evangelicals that was truly surging. The Southern Baptist Convention reached more than thirteen million members by the end of the decade, at the same time as its leadership was moving ever further to the right. Private Christian colleges continued to expand, evangelical congregations grew to become so-called megachurches, books aimed at conservative evangelical audiences outsold even some secular bestsellers, and Christian Right organizations produced an array of religious television programming.[106]

Ronald Reagan understood that tapping into the Christian Right voting bloc was crucial if he was to challenge Jimmy Carter for the presidency. Though he was politically moderate, Carter's past as a former Southern Baptist layman had proved persuasive to white southerners in 1976. In contrast, while Reagan had developed connections to Southern Baptists as California governor, in the late 1970s he was still comparatively inexperienced in dealing with evangelical voters. Former Nixon aide Charles Colson—who became an evangelical Christian after being imprisoned because of Watergate—recalled a reporter asking Reagan if he was "born again." Colson said, "Reagan shrugged, like the fellow had landed from Mars. He didn't know what it meant."[107] In 1976, Reagan's speeches had begun to include more discussion of traditional morality once Jesse Helms and the NCCC had stamped their mark on his campaign. But following the Christian Right's emergence as a political force, such language became even more important. Reagan honed his moralistic rhetoric and learned how to, in the words of journalist Kenneth Briggs, "[play] the themes—the personal morality themes, his opposition to abortion, his emphasis on the family . . . through direct address, and perhaps through some code words, he conveyed to them that he was one of them."[108]

Yet Reagan remained instinctively libertarian when it came to social issues, as made clear by his intervention in the debate over California's Proposition 6 in 1978. Republican state senator John Briggs placed on the ballot a proposition calling for the removal of gay teachers from public schools. The so-called Briggs Initiative was strongly supported by anti–gay rights campaigners across the nation, including the Christian Right.[109] When the measure was defeated, Briggs himself attributed the result to a late intervention by Reagan, after the former governor argued that Proposition 6 "has the potential of infringing on basic rights of privacy and perhaps even constitutional rights. . . . Innocent lives could be ruined."[110] In response, Jerry Falwell condemned Reagan for taking "the political rather than the moral route." Reagan, he said, would "have to face the music from Christian voters two years from now."[111] Perhaps aware of a need to repair the damage, as the 1970s came to an end Reagan's rhetoric on social issues hardened. On abortion, for example, he told a supporter in October 1979, "My position is that interrupting a pregnancy means the taking of a human life. In our Judeo-Christian tradition, that can only be done in self-defense. . . . I will agree to an abortion only to protect the life of the prospective mother."[112] But the fundamentalist tone to his language did not change the fact that Reagan was more focused on economics and shrinking the size of the federal government than on religious morality. His priorities were evident in a letter to another supporter in July 1980, when he wrote that "threats to our economy and prosperity" were the "major issues facing this country today."[113]

Still, Reagan courted Christian Right leaders persistently. His criticisms of welfare and food stamp programs and the deliberate framing of his anti-communism in religious terms—such as describing American efforts in Vietnam to combat the "godless tyranny of communism" as an "act of moral courage"—helped to redeem him for his stance on the Briggs Initiative.[114] By 1980, Jerry Falwell had forgiven Reagan enough to declare support for his presidential candidacy. Falwell echoed Reagan's language on communism and welfare, denouncing "godless, not-to-be trusted Russian Communists" and describing welfare as "needless giveaways for people who wouldn't work in a pie shop eating holes in a doughnut."[115] By the time Reagan attended the National Affairs Briefing in Dallas on 22 August 1980, he was the Christian Right's preferred candidate for the White House. ·

Even at that event, however, differences between Reaganite

anti-statism and the fervent religious and social traditionalism of the white South were very apparent. Prominent attendees included Jerry Falwell, Jesse Helms, and president of the SBC Bailey Smith, who stirred controversy by claiming that God did not hear the prayers of non-Christians. The event was organized by Texan pastor James Robison. Speaking prior to Reagan, Robison warned his audience, "We are to fight a war. Our weapon is faith. . . . We'll either have a Hitler-type takeover, or Soviet domination, or God is going to take over this country." According to another attendee, Reagan's aides were "cringing and saying 'Where the heck did that guy come from?'"[116] Though Reagan and his circle courted the Christian Right, they understood the dangers of appearing too closely associated. At a press conference before his speech, Reagan had refused to answer when asked if someone who supported the Equal Rights Amendment, abortion, and gay rights could still be described as Christian.[117] A few months earlier, Reagan advisor Martin Anderson had been keen to emphasize that, while Reagan would not ignore conservative evangelicals, "they're certainly not going to dictate to him."[118]

Reagan's speech to the National Affairs Briefing was strongly critical of federal attempts to revoke tax exemptions for segregationist Christian schools, a policy designed, in his view, "to force all tax exempt schools—including church schools—to abide by affirmative action orders drawn up by—who else?—IRS bureaucrats."[119] In response, some in the audience shouted "Amen" and "Preach on!"[120] Significantly, his speech failed to directly address the issue of abortion. While the anti-abortion campaign was of the utmost importance to southern evangelicals, Reagan's advisors were seemingly aware that it lacked the urgency of the tax exemption issue. For many fundamentalist evangelicals and conservative southern whites, the revocation of tax exemptions was a federal assault on their institutions and traditions of the kind they had faced in the 1950s and 1960s. Reagan's decision not to discuss abortion, even before an audience of Christian Right leaders, also suggested a sense of caution within his immediate political circle when it came to contentious social issues—a caution that only became more apparent during his presidency. Nonetheless, Reagan's appearance at the National Affairs Briefing was widely regarded as the consummation of his political alliance with the Christian Right. In a line given to him by Robison, Reagan told his audience, "I know this is a nonpartisan gathering, and so I know that you can't endorse me, but . . . I want you to know that I endorse you and what you're doing."[121]

In the 1980 Republican primaries, Ronald Reagan's popularity in the white South helped him fend off challenges from an adopted southerner, the Massachusetts-born former Texas congressman George H. W. Bush, and a native southerner, former governor of Texas John Connally. Following a defeat to Bush in Iowa, Reagan staged a comeback in New Hampshire, before landslide wins in four southern states—South Carolina, Alabama, Georgia, and Florida—gave him an unbreakable grip on the GOP nomination in early March.[122] At the start of Reagan's national campaign, the South's racial politics took center stage when he became the first presidential candidate to address the Neshoba County Fair in Mississippi, historically a forum for segregationist politicians.[123] Speaking just a few miles from where three civil rights activists had been brutally murdered by Klansmen and local police in 1964, he asserted "I believe in states' rights. . . . I believe that we've distorted the balance of our government today by giving powers that were never intended in the constitution to that federal establishment."[124] Just as when Reagan and Goldwater had spoken of states' rights in the 1960s, the connotations would have been easy for white southerners to decipher. The atmosphere, too, was reminiscent of Reagan's visits to the South in his GE days, with local newspapers describing "a cult attitude on the part of the Mississippi crowd towards him. An attitude that makes issues almost unimportant."[125]

Even accounting for Reagan's popularity in the region, rural Mississippi was not an obvious place to make an early campaign stop. In late 1979, a leading Mississippi Republican had suggested a visit to the Neshoba County Fair would help to win over "George Wallace inclined voters."[126] Reagan's appearance and speech in Neshoba were unquestionably designed to reinforce his appeal among conservative southerners, indicating that senior campaign figures viewed wresting southern states back from President Carter as a key campaign target. To that end, Reagan also held a rally in Columbus, Mississippi, with the state's former Democratic governor John Bell Williams, a vocal opponent of racial integration in the 1960s.[127] Likewise, Mississippi representative (and Reagan's state campaign chairman) Trent Lott extolled Strom Thurmond's segregationist presidential campaign of 1948 at an event in Jackson, saying, "If we had elected this man 30 years ago, we wouldn't be in the mess we are today." For his part, Thurmond told the audience, "We want that federal government to keep their filthy hands off the rights of the states."[128] From the very start of the 1980 campaign, Reagan's national advisors were evidently more primed to target the racial preoccupations of white southerners than they had been four years earlier.

On 4 November 1980, Ronald Reagan won 61 percent of southern whites on his way to an overwhelming election win.[129] Except for Jimmy Carter's home state of Georgia, Reagan swept the South. The region provided him with over 10.5 million votes, around a quarter of his overall total, and 127 Electoral College votes in a national landslide victory by 489 votes to 49.[130] Several southern Republicans were also elected to the Senate, House, and state governorships on his coattails. John East, the Jesse Helms protégé who had drafted a significant portion of the 1976 Republican platform, became North Carolina's second Republican senator alongside Helms. Mack Mattingly and Paula Hawkins won Senate seats in Georgia and Florida respectively, while Frank White beat Democratic incumbent Bill Clinton to win the Arkansas governorship. In Alabama, Donald Stewart lost the Democratic primary and his Senate seat was won by Republican Jeremiah Denton.[131] But below the presidential level the white South's partisan shift was still tentative, and certainly did not reflect a change in southern political culture. As a report in the *Christian Science Monitor* observed, "Most Southern Democrats are, on most issues, already fairly conservative. What this election saw, in many cases, was the defeat of conservative Southerners by even more conservative Southerners."[132]

The 1980 election proved Ronald Reagan's personal popularity in the white South was undimmed and demonstrated just how far President Carter had fallen in the estimation of his fellow southerners. Carter's reputation declined particularly steeply among conservative evangelicals, with Reagan winning 61 percent of Americans who identified as born again.[133] Each time Carter had adopted moderate positions on the

ERA or gay rights he was met with furious disapproval, condemnatory SBC resolutions, and questions about the authenticity of his Baptist faith.[134] Southern evangelicals seemingly voted against Carter at least as much as they voted in favor of Reagan, though Reagan's intensive courting of the Christian Right had positioned him as an appealing alternative. Still, senior figures around the newly elected president maintained their caution about appearing too close to Christian Right leaders. When Jerry Falwell claimed that the Moral Majority had registered four million voters and encouraged a further ten million to go to the polls—almost certainly an exaggeration—the incoming vice president, George Bush, was quick to dismiss the notion that the new administration would owe conservative evangelicals a political debt.[135] It was certainly the case that Reagan's victory in 1980 represented the emergence of the Christian Right as a formidable voting bloc for the Republican Party. It was now, unquestionably, a partisan movement.

For many conservatives in the South, seeing Reagan win the presidency fulfilled a wish they had harbored for over a decade. They had rescued Reagan's political hopes in 1976 and forgiven him for transgressions such as choosing Richard Schweiker and opposing the Briggs Initiative. Now, the man they believed would help restore southern political influence in Washington had finally reached the White House. His language on social issues and tax exemptions for segregationist Christian schools—alongside the anti-statist and anti-communist rhetoric that had been central to his appeal for over two decades— meant white southerners expected his administration to be aligned with their agenda. But, as the early years of his presidency proved, the priorities of Reaganite conservatism and southern conservatism would often diverge.

II. Southern Interests

3. "We Really Seem to Be Putting a Coalition Together"
Boll Weevil Democrats and the Reagan Revolution

"I had come to Washington with my mind set on a program and I was anxious to get started on it," Ronald Reagan recalled of his first days in office.[1] His administration's legislative blitzkrieg during the first half of 1981 has become fundamental to Reagan's image as a transformational president. But as they entered the White House, Reagan and his aides knew that winning the votes of around fifty conservative southern Democrats would be crucial if his agenda was to stand any chance of being enacted. Despite his landslide victory, the situation on Capitol Hill was not entirely in Reagan's favor. Republicans had won control of the Senate, but in the House of Representatives—where the Democrats held a majority of fifty-three—it was essential to forge a bipartisan conservative coalition. For a president who had placed the restoration of American economic vitality at the heart of his election campaign, the early success or failure of Reagan's administration rested on the passage of his economic program. That, in turn, required exploiting his popularity in the white South to win the votes of southern Democrats.

The administration's legislative agenda aimed to turn the philosophy of Reaganism into reality. A program of massive tax reductions and unprecedented cuts to domestic programs was designed to tackle what Reagan viewed as the "greatest economic emergency since the Great Depression. The most immediate priority was dealing with double-digit inflation, high unemployment, and a prime interest rate of 21.5 percent."[2] In a televised address, Reagan warned the American people, "We cannot delay in implementing an economic program aimed at both reducing tax rates to stimulate productivity and reducing the growth in government spending to reduce unemployment and inflation."[3] He laid out the details in his first appearance before a joint session of Congress on 18 February. At the heart of his economic package was a proposed 30 percent reduction in personal income taxes over

67

three years—a reduction of 10 percent in each fiscal year beginning in 1982. "This proposal for an equal reduction in everyone's tax rates," Reagan declared, "will expand our national prosperity, enlarge national incomes, and increase opportunities for all Americans." Then came the second major pillar of his economic program: "I'm asking that you join me in reducing direct federal spending by $41.4 billion in fiscal year 1982." These reductions would come from eliminating some government agencies, such as the Economic Development Administration, tightening eligibility for various welfare programs, including the Food Stamp program and school lunches, and reducing subsidies to business and industry as well as to governmental bodies such as the Postal Service and the Department of Energy.[4] Reagan's proposals amounted to the most significant reduction of federal expenditure in half a century.[5] Though he made only brief reference to it, his proposed budget would also include huge increases in funding for the US military, in line with his belief that "my duty as President requires that I recommend increases in defense spending over the coming years."[6]

Reagan's agenda met with broad approval among conservative southern Democrats in the House. Texan Marvin Leath later recalled, "We agreed with a lot of the things Ronald Reagan said he wanted to do. We agreed that the tax system needed to be reformed, that our defense effort needed to be strengthened, and that the Great Society programs should be cut back and eliminated."[7] Aware that their influence was likely to increase with Reagan in the White House, southern Democrats had formed the Conservative Democratic Forum (CDF) in November 1980. The chair of the group was Texas representative and former cotton farmer, Charles Stenholm, who admitted that brief consideration had been given to a mass defection to the GOP, but told reporters, "The first decision the members of our group made was to stay in the Democratic Party."[8]

In response to derision from congressional liberals—who branded the CDF as the "redneck caucus"—the group embraced the term "Boll Weevils," a label previously applied to southern Democrats in the postwar era and derived from a notoriously resilient beetle which periodically infested southern cotton farms. In the weeks after Reagan's inauguration, the Boll Weevils went from being a largely unheeded group of backbenchers to becoming "the fulcrum of political power."[9]

Though Stenholm nominally chaired the CDF, the Boll Weevils had no designated leader. The office of Mississippi representative Gillespie "Sonny" Montgomery, decked out with flags and swords, was used as the group's "war room" to debate strategy, as these conservative southern Democrats sought to follow the tradition of their predecessors and act as a unified bloc to increase their power.[10]

Compared to previous generations of southern Democrats, few Boll Weevils were known nationally. But in early 1981, several members of the group, including Stenholm and Montgomery as well as Texans Phil Gramm and Kent Hance, John Breaux of Louisiana, and Georgian Billy Lee Evans, gained prominence thanks to their newfound influence. Their districts reflected the South's huge economic disparities. Some, like those represented by Gramm and Hance, exemplified the Sunbelt economic boom. In Hance's district, the city of Midland was an affluent hub of the Texan oil and gas industry—"a little bit of Beverly Hills or West Houston in the desert."[11] In places like Midland, the popularity of Reagan's economic plan, particularly the tax cuts, was understandable. "Reagan won 72 percent of the vote in my district," Hance told the *New York Times*. "It's mighty tough to go against a popular President in a district like mine, especially when he's pushing for the same kind of economic policies I've been talking about all along."[12]

Other Boll Weevils, in contrast, represented rural districts in states like Alabama, Georgia, and South Carolina. Such areas were economically reliant on agriculture or textile production, industries that had been struggling for years. These parts of the white South were characterized by "rural poverty and low skills and the lingering belief that the Democratic Party is, on bread and butter issues, the party of the people."[13] When it came to federal spending, particularly on agriculture, Boll Weevils from rural districts did not regard big government as the enemy. Instead, they retained a traditionally southern desire to protect regional interests and to represent the populist nature of their electorates. Several of these Boll Weevils would, for instance, reject Reagan's proposed tax cuts as a giveaway to the rich. Many members of the CDF relished the pivotal role they now played in Congress and were eager to make it clear exactly where their priorities lay. "A congressman's final vote," warned Sonny Montgomery, "is in the interest of his district."[14]

Indeed, the congressional voting records of the Boll Weevils reflected the conservatism of their districts. On issues such as welfare and abortion, they were often well to the right of their Democratic colleagues. Some, notably Sonny Montgomery and Georgia representative Lawrence McDonald, had voting records to the right of all but a handful of Republicans.[15] By 1981, these southern conservatives had grown increasingly frustrated at the liberal course their party's leadership was taking under Speaker Tip O'Neill. Charles Stenholm summed up the resentments that had been building since the mid-1970s: "We're people with a conservative philosophy who've been on the losing end of the majority of votes in the last couple of years."[16] Stenholm's claim was based more on perception than reality—conservative Democrats had experienced some notable victories during the Carter years, including supporting a $16 billion tax cut against the administration's wishes and obstructing the passage of liberal welfare and healthcare legislation.[17] Nonetheless, Stenholm was reflecting the disillusionment of many southern Democrats. The chance to push a conservative economic agenda through Congress was payback for the disrespect they believed senior House Democrats had shown them. "Suddenly, the good ol' boys who sit together on 'redneck row' on the House floor are pressuring the Democratic leadership to satisfy their wishes or face a reborn Dixie-GOP coalition."[18]

The Boll Weevils were also acutely aware that the Democrats' grip on the South had been loosening for more than a decade. Louisianan Jerry Huckaby estimated that his district was "97 percent registered Democrat." Yet, he continued, "on a national level philosophically, most of the people in my district think more in tune with Republicans. It's just that they've been Democrats since the War between the States."[19] This residual Democratic loyalty enabled many Boll Weevils to win elections throughout the 1970s with little Republican opposition, just as previous generations of southern Democratic congressmen had done. Charles Stenholm was among those who ran unopposed in 1980. The few serious electoral tests they faced tended to come in wealthier, suburban districts. When Kent Hance was first elected in 1978, he narrowly defeated a challenge from future Republican president George W. Bush.[20] But in early 1981, most Boll Weevils found themselves representing districts Reagan had won the previous November and were mindful that their political careers could be at stake. Maintaining loyalty to the liberal Democratic House leadership was already difficult and Reagan's electoral strength in the South gave them further reason to rebel. As Stenholm acknowledged, "The similarities between my personal platform and the President's program are such that if I did not support the President, I could not explain it to my constituents in any manner except that he is a Republican, and that doesn't bother them."[21] Several Boll Weevils, including Phil Gramm, Kent Hance, John Breaux, Sonny Montgomery, and Billy Lee Evans, were candid in their approval of Reagan's agenda. They needed little encouragement to support the new president's economic plan, at least in principle.

Georgia Republican Newt Gingrich even believed his party should create a formal grouping with the Boll Weevils and attempt to oust Tip O'Neill. The speakership could then be occupied by a conservative southern Democrat, with committee chairmanships being divided between Republicans and southern Democrats, effectively implementing a conservative-led takeover of the House. His vision foreshadowed the future of the House GOP from the mid-1990s onwards, as southern districts turned Republican and southern conservatives rose to positions of influence. In early 1981, however, senior Republicans rejected Gingrich's strategy. "If people think we're already in charge, they won't see any need to vote in more Republicans," reasoned Max Friedersdorf, Reagan's chief congressional liaison. The Reagan White House and the House GOP leadership instead sought a less formal coalition, one similar, the *Baltimore Sun* explained, "to the GOP-Southern Democratic alliance that thwarted liberal legislation in the 1950s and 1960s."[22]

Unlike southern Democrats in the mid-twentieth century, almost all of whom had been committed segregationists, the Boll Weevils whom Reagan was seeking to win over had first been elected in the wake of the civil rights era—many in the wake of Watergate. Yet their economic priorities, and those of the conservative electorates who had sent them to Congress, retained a racial dimension. Their determination to scale back Great Society welfare programs, for example, disproportionately affected ethnic minorities, and racially coded anti-welfare rhetoric had become commonplace in the political vocabulary of white southern conservatives in the post–civil rights era. Mississippi Republican Trent

Lott declared that the basis for this refashioned conservative coalition was to be "economics, strictly economics. . . . We're not talking about abortion or busing, we're talking about budget controls, spending cuts, and tax rate cuts."[23] As would soon become evident, the Boll Weevils viewed economic policy from a distinctly southern perspective. But in the early weeks of Reagan's presidency their conservative orthodoxy was at its peak. When he hosted a breakfast meeting with them on 5 March, they urged extra spending cuts above what the administration had proposed. The Boll Weevils were, Reagan noted in his diary, "Gung ho for our [economic package] but went further & gave us their recommendation for 10 [billion dollars] in additional budget cuts."[24]

The first test of Boll Weevil support was a vote on the budget resolution bill in May, which set out the broad framework for spending reductions. A Budget Reconciliation Bill—enacting the specific reductions decided by congressional committees—and Reagan's tax cut legislation would both follow later in the summer. Boll Weevils were finding themselves alternately wooed and pressured by leaders of both parties. Democrats on the House Budget Committee presented their own plan which proposed more modest reductions in federal spending and was designed to keep the Boll Weevils from straying over to Reagan's side. It was a sign of Reagan's political potency in the early weeks of his presidency that the Democratic resolution followed the same overall direction on spending cuts.[25] Indicating the importance of Boll Weevil votes, one senior Reagan advisor acknowledged, "In a very real sense, this economic campaign will be won or lost in the South." In mid-April, as Reagan recuperated from an attempt on his life less than three weeks earlier, his aides announced what they called a "blitz" of fifty-three districts across the region.[26] Masterminded by South Carolinian White House strategist Lee Atwater, this was a large-scale effort aimed at reinforcing support for Reagan's budget proposals among southern voters, thereby placing pressure on their Boll Weevil representatives to vote in favor. With internal administration polling suggesting popular approval for Reagan's budget plan stood at 68 percent in the South, Atwater outlined the operation's purpose in a memo: "Overwhelming positive public opinion will encourage their support and therein mitigate toeing the Democrat Party line."[27]

Financed by groups such as the Moral Majority as well as the Republican National Committee, the blitz initially comprised three days of campaign-style events featuring appearances from, among others, Strom Thurmond, Jesse Helms, Trent Lott, the Republican governors of Louisiana and Tennessee—David Treen and Lamar Alexander—and Vice President George Bush.[28] These were followed in subsequent weeks by direct mailing and television and radio advertisements. "We're not going in there [the South] to intimidate or blackmail," claimed a White House aide. "We're going in positively to help these congressmen."[29] Still, Reagan and his advisors understood the political pressure their campaign would exert. "Behind the carrot of friendly persuasion," the *Washington Post* noted, "lies the potential club of political opposition in the 1982 elections. . . . White House political strategists are aware of Reagan's enormous popularity in the South."[30] Given Reagan's strong electoral showing in the South the previous November, the possibility that he might actively campaign against them in the midterms was a threat many Boll Weevils took seriously. Some even sought to help Reagan in his efforts to persuade wavering southern Democrats. Stenholm, Montgomery, Breaux, and Hance were among eight CDF members to sign a letter declaring that "in every respect" Reagan's budget was "superior to the budget reported by the House Budget Committee. . . . [We] urge you to join us in this effort to put the interest of the American people ahead of partisanship."[31]

When Reagan began a campaign of personal coaxing during late April and early May, he had more success with conservative southern Democrats than with recalcitrant members of his own party. During an address to Congress on his economic plan on 28 April, around forty Boll Weevils joined Republicans in giving him a standing ovation.[32] The following week Reagan hosted a meeting with several of them in the Oval Office, where Arkansas representative Beryl Anthony told the president of his "concern that many South Arkansans may feel these budget cuts very deeply." His constituents, he said, were willing to make sacrifices but "not unfairly." However, Anthony was reassured when Reagan told him that his "door will be open in the coming months as the effects of the budget cuts are felt."[33] Their exchange was an early indication that many southern conservatives, though keenly supportive of Reagan's agenda in principle, had concerns about the impact of spending cuts in their region. The populist, regionally focused priorities of southern congressmen would soon begin to cause headaches for the administration.

Still, after meeting the Boll Weevils, Reagan was confident. He noted in his diary, "These [Democrats] are with us on the budget. . . . We really seem to be putting a coalition together."[34] His confidence was borne out on 7 May, when the House approved his budget plan by 253 votes to 176, with 45 Boll Weevils among the ayes.[35] The name of the legislation, Gramm-Latta, highlighted the crucial part played by one Boll Weevil in particular. Texan Phil Gramm stood out among southern Democrats as the strongest supporter of Reagan's agenda. Gramm cosponsored the budget bill and pursued even greater spending reductions than Reagan's original proposal had demanded. He was also an old friend of Office of Management and Budget director David Stockman—the man largely responsible for formulating the details of Reagan's economic legislation—and liaised with him throughout the congressional debates. Gramm helped to thwart the rival budget resolution proposed by Budget Committee chair, James Jones of Oklahoma.[36] His prominence gave Reagan's plan a bipartisan gloss that made it easier for other Boll Weevils to break ranks with the Democratic leadership. For his efforts in support of Reagan, Gramm was labelled a "collaborator" by Democratic House majority leader (and fellow Texan) Jim Wright.[37] Equally important in winning Boll Weevil support, however, was the pressure applied by Lee Atwater's southern blitz. Prior to the vote, it was not just Republicans exerting pressure on the Boll Weevils. Alabama's Democratic governor Forrest "Fob" James called Ronnie Flippo, a Boll Weevil and fellow Alabaman, to urge his support for Reagan. The governor's office drily informed the White House that "James has 'persuaded' Flippo to vote for the president." Similarly, Dan Mica of Florida received calls from a local Democratic mayor urging him to vote for the administration's budget.[38]

This victory was merely the first hurdle in enacting Reagan's economic agenda. Next came the Budget Reconciliation Bill laying out precisely which spending programs Reagan planned to cut. During the upcoming debate, one editorial predicted in mid-May, "The Southern conservative bloc can look forward to being courted even more heavily." This was a marked change for representatives who had previously been side-lined by both parties: "A Democrat from south of Mason and Dixon's line can enjoy being treated no longer as the proverbial illegitimate at the family picnic."[39] As their influence grew, the Boll Weevils became more organized and demanding. "We never dreamed we would become the swing vote in the House," admitted Georgian Bo Ginn, "and we're pleased to have an open line to Reagan." But he was quick to add, "The White House needs to understand that we can't be taken for granted."[40] Realizing they had a rare—and potentially brief— opportunity, the Boll Weevils set about exploiting their newfound power to extract concessions for their districts.

Max Friedersdorf would later recall that while Phil Gramm was the administration's "most open channel" when it came to budget negotiations, CDF chair Charles Stenholm acted as the Boll Weevils' political link to the White House. "Stenholm was the one who corralled these guys. Stenholm was the one we would talk to about who we should go after. Give us a list of who you think is vulnerable—that's where Charlie was good."[41] After the first budget vote had demonstrated the Boll Weevils' importance and willingness to back Reagan's agenda, efforts to retain their votes for the Budget Reconciliation Bill frequently descended into open horse-trading. Some southern Democrats demanded changes to an agriculture bill then under debate by Congress. Georgia representatives wanted increased protection for peanut farmers, while Louisiana congressmen John Breaux and Wilbert "Billy" Tauzin won Reagan's agreement to introduce price supports for sugar.[42] As well as contradicting Reagan's ideological opposition to agricultural subsidies, such arrangements carried fiscal costs that hurt the administration's drive to cut federal spending. Publicly, the administration denied it had struck any deals. In reality, as Friedersdorf admitted, the White House was quick to comply with Boll Weevil demands. "I mean, are you going to let the peanut subsidies rule your life? Or are you going to let the budget rule your life? So we'd call Stockman and we'd say, 'Houston we've got a problem. We need a little sugar in Louisiana, some peanuts in Georgia,' whatever it was. . . . That's the way it worked."[43]

Further concessions included a victory for Georgia congressmen in getting cotton warehouses exempted from costly user fees, and changes to the Fuel Use Act demanded by several Texan Democrats in aid of the oil and gas industries in their districts. A restoration of $400 million for veterans' programs won the support of Sonny Montgomery.[44] Similarly, Reagan called Texan representative Ralph Hall on the evening before the budget reconciliation vote and asked, "What do we need to do to get your vote?" As the *Miami Herald* reported, "Hall wasn't stumped for an answer." He immediately requested changes to energy laws which would benefit the natural gas industry critical to his district's economy. That same evening, David Stockman and Chief of Staff James Baker telephoned Hall to say the changes would be made.[45] According to the *Washington Post*, funding for the construction of a nuclear reactor in Tennessee also found its way into the bill. "The controversial Clinch River fast breeder reactor project, which is strenuously opposed by Stockman as a waste of federal funds, nonetheless receives $230 million more in the Republican budget plan." Deals of this nature were ultimately crucial to the passage of the Budget Reconciliation Bill. "I went with the best deal," John Breaux admitted, pointedly joking that while his vote could not be bought, "it can be rented."[46] For all their public agreement with Reagan's desire for dramatic spending reductions, the preservation of federal assistance to the South remained uppermost in Boll Weevil minds.

The extent of the bartering subsequently led David Stockman to claim, in his book *The Triumph of Politics*, that many Boll Weevils "weren't even remotely genuine fiscal conservatives."[47] A few, notably Phil Gramm, were clearly ideologically committed to enacting the Reaganite agenda, but most took stances more typical of traditional southern conservatives. The populist anti-government sentiment that remained deeply ingrained in the white South meant Reagan's proposed spending reductions were popular, at least in theory. But the overriding instincts of conservative southerners were to be fiercely protective of regional interests and strongly supportive of federal aid to important southern industries, as Reagan had found to his cost on the campaign trail after criticizing the Tennessee Valley Authority. While liberal Republicans were also bartering with the White House for concessions in return for their support—requesting increased funding for the National Endowment for the Arts, provision of student loans to more families, and a higher Medicaid cap for example—Boll Weevil demands were focused to a far greater degree on predominantly southern industries, be it sugar, cotton, peanuts, or oil.[48] Such was their focus on regional interests, many Boll Weevils remained unclear as to the details of the enormous and complex budget bill even as they were about to vote on it. On the day of the vote, House Majority Leader Jim Wright of Texas wrote to warn them of "unpleasant surprises in this clandestine deck of cards" and pleaded with them to pause and reflect before supporting the president. "Have you read the Gramm-Latta substitute, and can you honestly say that you know what's in it?" Wright wrote to Marvin Leath. "Please think it over carefully. . . . Do what you do in good conscience. If you can honestly face yourself in the morning, you'll have no quarrel from me. But be honest with yourself."[49] Despite his entreaties, 38 southern Democrats supported the Budget Reconciliation Bill as it passed the House by 232 votes to 193.[50]

The budget debate demonstrated the impulse to protect regional interests that lay at the heart of southern conservatism. The Boll Weevils had shown they were committed to preserving, even increasing, federal assistance to the South while at the same time demanding government spending be reduced. Their approach stood in sharp contrast to the anti-statist ideology of Reaganism. "They talked a good budget-cutting game," wrote a frustrated David Stockman, "but they loved even more their own regional pork."[51] Still, the importance of Boll Weevil support for Reagan's budget cuts cannot be overstated. If the administration's efforts to cut federal spending had been thwarted, Reagan's proposed tax cuts would almost certainly have failed too. The Reagan Revolution would have been over before it began. Instead, thanks to Reagan's coalition with conservative southern Democrats, the 1981 budget was the first major legislative victory for Reaganite conservatism. It made sweeping cuts to domestic funding—largely by tightening eligibility for various welfare programs and reducing funding to government agencies—while at the same time dramatically increasing defense spending. Southern conservatism was once again a decisive influence on the direction of US politics. One Boll Weevil, Georgia representative Charles Hatcher, was certainly proud of what the coalition had achieved, telling a constituent that his "working relationship" with Reagan was "excellent." "He and I have agreed that we share the same goals and have expressed our mutual hope that we will be able to work closely to implement them."[52] After years of being side-lined in Washington, the passage of the budget bill illustrated to millions of white southerners that by allying with Ronald Reagan and the Republican Party, their region's economic interests could return to the top of the agenda on Capitol Hill.

Southern votes remained critically important when the White House sought to drive its tax cut bill through Congress later that summer. Reagan's tax plan broadly favored the wealthy over lower- and middle-class Americans, reflecting his belief that growth could be promoted by reducing the tax burden on the rich and thereby increasing the incentive to invest and create jobs. Along with 30 percent across-the-board income tax cuts, it included an immediate reduction in the top marginal tax rate from 70 percent to 50 percent and an 8 percent cut in capital gains tax.[53] Many Boll Weevils were far more circumspect about the president's tax bill than they had been about his spending reductions. As one *New York Times* reporter commented, cutting federal programs, particularly welfare, "had been gospel in their region for years." However, for the Boll Weevils, "the situation is quite different on the tax issue." Some, like Kent Hance, represented districts where cutting taxes for rich Americans was popular. Midland's oil wealth meant it was "the kind of place that welcomes President Reagan's proposal to give the wealthy the same tax breaks as the poor and middle-class." Hance would act as cosponsor of the tax cut in the House, the role Phil Gramm had played for the budget.[54]

But Hance's colleagues who represented agricultural areas and mill towns in the rural South—places far removed from the affluent Sunbelt—felt rather differently. In those districts, both representatives and constituents were deeply skeptical of cutting taxes for the rich. "We're all for spending reductions," observed Ed Jenkins, a founding member of the Conservative Democratic Forum. "The administration tapped that feeling in the budget fight. But there is a populist approach when it comes to taxes."[55] Jenkins, a man raised in a small Georgia town of two thousand people and whose largely rural district had suffered textile mill closures and job losses, was cautious about the administration's economic radicalism: "I'm a product of my area. . . . We're not quick to change." Likewise, Ken Holland argued that his poor South Carolina district would benefit little from Reagan's tax cuts: "The per capita income in my district is $7,125. . . . Most of my constituents will only pick up enough to pay for a few gallons of gas." As Holland told reporters, for many Boll Weevils this new legislative battle had "a little less passion than the first one."[56]

The administration understood that support among Boll Weevils was not the same as it had been for the budget bills. As early as mid-March, Max Friedersdorf had warned Reagan's senior advisors: "While the budget reduction portion of the President's program seems to be going well, our staff continues to pick up disturbing intelligence with regard to the tax reduction side."[57] Reagan received a memo stating that even Kent Hance was "more skittish about the process than Phil Gramm was about the spending cuts" and that a phone call was required to "buck him up." After calling Hance, Reagan jotted a note on the memo saying, "He's solid."[58] Aware that other southern Democrats were rather less solid, Reagan held a meeting with several Boll Weevils in late May at which, according to Charles Stenholm, he offered them "a shopping list" of potential compromises on the tax cut bill.[59] He sought to ease their nervousness still further at another meeting on 4 June. When asked if he would campaign against them in the 1982 midterm elections even if they supported his tax cuts, Reagan reportedly replied, "I couldn't look myself in the mirror in the morning if I campaigned against someone that helped me on my program." Presidential aides later attempted to backtrack on Reagan's pledge, but the concession served to assuage concerns among the Boll Weevils about his potentially powerful electoral influence.[60]

Democratic leaders again proposed alternative legislation designed to lure wavering Boll Weevils back into the fold. Their tax plan featured an individual tax cut over two years, smaller cuts for the wealthy and larger cuts for people on low incomes. In response, Reagan mounted a campaign of personal lobbying. This involved both friendly persuasion—including hosting a barbeque at Camp David for a group of Boll

Weevils—and strategically directed pressure, such as calling into a radio talk show in the district of Texan Democrat Ralph Hall to promote his tax plan.[61] He also telephoned Boll Weevils personally, but this time found them decidedly more tentative in their commitment. According to Reagan's notes, Buddy Roemer of Louisiana was undecided but nevertheless reassured Reagan that he was "enthusiastic about our plans generally." Doug Barnard of Georgia was also broadly supportive but concerned about "how to explain to his low-income constituents the [Democratic] bill offering a bigger break." When Tennessee's Bill Boner warily pledged his support, Reagan "assured him I'll remember come election time."[62] All three men ultimately voted with the administration. Democratic leaders found the president's ability to cajole these conservative southerners both depressing and remarkable. "I was supposed to be a good communicator," Jim Wright later recalled. "In Ronald Reagan I'd met my master."[63]

The administration also reprised its southern blitz, this time incorporating a series of television advertisements promoting Reagan's tax cuts. These covered thirty-two media markets across the South but focused particularly on states which were home to the most reluctant Boll Weevils.[64] One target was North Carolina representative L. H. Fountain. The *Greensboro Daily News* reported that Fountain was "angered" by an advertisement which "praised [him] for supporting Reagan's budget cuts, but warned that he was under pressure from House Speaker Thomas P. 'Tip' O'Neill . . . to vote against the president's tax plan." Though Fountain decried the advert as "unprecedented and unwarranted," it was effective.[65] According to Reagan's notes, Fountain told the president that "he's probably committing [political] suicide but he's voting for us."[66] To further ratchet up the pressure on the Boll Weevils, Alabama's Democratic governor, Fob James, met with Reagan at the White House before embarking on a tour of six southern states to promote the administration's tax plan. In Raleigh, for instance, James derided his own party's tax proposals as "fine if you are only going to live for the next two years." Reagan's plan, he claimed, was "a truly bipartisan tax cut. . . . One great thing about the Democratic Party is that it's big enough for Boll Weevils."[67]

Some, however, would not be convinced. Alabama representative

Ronnie Flippo told Reagan that he "wants to be helpful in the direction we're going but no commitments."[68] One of several Boll Weevils who backed Reagan's budget legislation, he ultimately opposed the tax cuts, along with John Breaux and Billy Tauzin of Louisiana, Ken Holland of South Carolina, and Ed Jenkins of Georgia. On the day of the vote, Jenkins spoke against the Reagan tax cuts on the floor of the House. Observing that the "vast majority of my people make under $20,000 a year," he condemned tax breaks for the wealthy. "How you vote in respect to fairness and equity to all classes of society will be a decision which will be long remembered," Jenkins declared. "Let us serve the best interests of our people."[69] John Breaux made a similarly populist case, arguing Reagan's proposals would simply "give the break to the wealthy people because somehow they are going to invest it for the public good. I do not think that is a logical reasoning." Breaux announced he would instead support the Democratic tax bill because it directed cuts to "working people."[70]

Conversely, other Boll Weevils used the tax cut debate to reaffirm their support for President Reagan, highlighting just how distanced they had become from the Democratic Party leadership. "I can see no sense in approving the first two portions of the President's budget proposals, then balking at the underpinning of the proposals," said Florida representative Andy Ireland, who declared himself "proud" to support the administration's tax package.[71] In Buddy Roemer's view, "The spirit of the New Deal has become entombed in the programs of the Great Society." He had therefore decided to "vote with my conscience and for the dreams of my district. I will vote with the President."[72] The administration's intensive grassroots lobbying also swayed several votes. The White House had enlisted numerous industry organizations to campaign in support of its tax proposals. Aides observed that "groups with a southern orientation have been particularly active," notably including the Tobacco Institute, Cotton Council, and American Textile Manufacturers Association.[73] These efforts, when added to a deluge of constituent communications, proved difficult to resist. Florida representative Bill Nelson received around one thousand pro-Reagan calls, while an aide to Lawrence McDonald of Georgia described "the greatest outpouring of comment on any one issue we've ever received." The office of Georgia congressman Bo Ginn was likewise bombarded with telephone calls, leading an aide to comment, "The people of the district kicked the doors down."[74] Ultimately, after a few frantic days of lobbying and debate in late July, the House of Representatives approved the final major component of Reagan's economic program by 238 votes to 195.[75]

Reagan's tax bill was passed thanks to the votes of thirty-three southern Democrats, a dozen fewer than had supported his budget plan. The final bill bore evidence not just of Reagan's political compromises—his desired 30 percent income tax cut had been reduced to 25 percent—but also of the individual haggling required for victory. As the Democratic leadership and the White House each attempted to outdo the other, the struggle over Boll Weevil votes became, as one headline put it, "more auction than debate."[76] Alongside oil provisions aimed at winning the votes of Texan and Louisianan Boll Weevils, the Reagan administration promised to maintain a quota restricting the importation of foreign peanuts—a concession that helped to win the votes of seven out of nine Georgia Democrats.[77] As Rowland Evans and Robert Novak noted, there were numerous similar "Southern-flavored goodies" scattered throughout the bill.[78]

Some Boll Weevils found it necessary to justify their support of the tax cut to their constituents. Bill Nichols told a resident of his Alabama district, "Let me assure you that I consider myself a Southern Conservative Democrat, and have no intention of changing to another party." He confessed he had "real reservations about Supply Side Economics" but claimed he had received eight hundred calls to his office in the forty-eight hours preceding the vote, the vast majority of which "asked that I give the President of the United States a chance to try his plan." Nichols concluded, "The ball is now in his court."[79] In contrast, Ed Jenkins continued to make the case that Reagan's tax cuts were unfair and misguided. Writing to a constituent in March 1982, Jenkins argued, "I am still convinced that the tax cut is designed for the rich and discriminates against the working people of America. Its contribution to our astonishing deficit projections is a matter of record."[80] Many conservative southern Democrats were similarly uncomfortable about Reagan's tax cut legislation even if, like Nichols, they ultimately voted in favor.

Cutting taxes for the rich did not sit well with the white South's traditionally populist approach to economics.

The passage of Reagan's tax cut marked the apotheosis for his
administration's alliance with the Boll Weevils and, it would turn
out, the legislative highpoint of Reaganism. In the service of its economic agenda, the Reagan White House created a new variant of the
GOP-southern Democrat conservative coalition that had once held
sway in Congress. It was a coalition built through personal persuasion,
political horse-trading, and the shrewd exploitation of Reagan's southern popularity. Southern conservatives played a critical role in a series
of legislative achievements that quickly came to be mythologized as
the "Reagan Revolution," and the president's successes were celebrated
almost as much in the ranks of the CDF as they were in the White
House. Charles Stenholm spoke for many Boll Weevils when he acknowledged, "We had no earthly idea that things would work out this
well."[81] At the White House on 14 September, Stenholm, Kent Hance,
and Sonny Montgomery were among nineteen southern Democrats
who presented Reagan with a boll weevil tiepin and a bumper sticker
bearing the slogan "Thank Goodness for Boll Weevils."[82]

Even at the high point of their influence in September 1981, there was
media speculation that the Boll Weevil "phenomenon . . . may be evap-
orating even as it reaches the zenith of its power."[83] Many Boll Weevils
were aware that their position was untenable in the long term. Looking ahead to the 1982 midterms, Billy Lee Evans warned that if either
Republicans or Democrats made major gains in the House, "We could
wind up as a group without a party."[84] That was far from the only threat
to the CDF's position. Though Reagan had promised not to personally
campaign against anyone who voted for his economic package, White
House aides and GOP strategists were already planning an electoral
assault on Democratic incumbents across the South, identifying numerous districts as potential targets. An administration strategy report
argued that Republicans needed to exploit mistrust of the national
Democratic leadership among white southern conservative voters.
They should "keep hammering" the message that the "John Breauxs of
this world may seem like good ole boys back in the district, but when

they get to Washington they consort with the likes of Teddy Kennedy and Tip O'Neill, the liberal, venal Yankees that run the Democratic Party."[85]

Highlighting the dilemma facing the Boll Weevils, conservative Democrats from Georgia began telling journalists that although they were proud of their alliance with the administration, they were reluctant to support Reagan if he demanded further spending reductions.[86] The principal reason for the Boll Weevils' waning enthusiasm was a sharp downturn in the American economy that damaged Reagan's popularity, even in the South. Beginning in the autumn of 1981, the United States suffered a 2.9 percent fall in its GDP and around three million jobs were lost.[87] The South appeared to survive the recession better than other regions, but the prosperity of major cities in Texas and Florida served to distort the overall economic picture. Average wages in the region remained markedly lower than the rest of the United States and, as the *Washington Post* reported, there were "significant differences in the economic structure and prospects" of the southern states, with the likes of Alabama, Mississippi, Arkansas, Tennessee, and Kentucky lagging far behind. While unemployment levels were below the national average in most southern states, this was partly due to a tradition of "underemployment" in the rural South. "When jobs are hard to come by," the *Post* observed, "people will eke out a living on the family farm and wait for the labor market to pick up rather than register as unemployed."[88] Contrary to the positive headlines, many parts of the southern economy were hit hard by the recession of 1981–82.

Reagan's national popularity declined from a high of 68 percent in Gallup polls during the spring of 1981 to 49 percent by the year's end and plummeted to 40 percent by the autumn of 1982.[89] In the white South, widespread affection for Reagan was now combined with disapproval of his administration's economic performance, creating a political minefield for the Boll Weevils. Reagan's potential impact on the upcoming midterms was hotly debated at the 1982 meeting of the Southern Governors Association. His standing in the South remained "as high as it was when Dixie discovered him" and many attendees conceded that Reagan would carry the region again if he were running. But they also cautioned that "Reagan's personal popularity . . . should not be confused with political popularity." His approval ratings in North Carolina, for example, had slumped to 35 percent by August 1982, with voters citing the failing economy as the reason for their dissatisfaction. David Treen, Louisiana's Republican governor and a vocal Reagan supporter, argued that the president's "style, his personality, is attractive to the South." But Treen was also willing to acknowledge, "There's been some erosion, obviously. That's fundamental after a time." For the Boll Weevils, then, supporting the president no longer offered quite the same electoral advantage as it had a year earlier.[90]

The threat of censure by Democratic leaders was also growing. CDF members were largely excluded from the Democratic Party national conference in June 1982, but John Breaux and Kent Hance appeared before a party commission to defend the Boll Weevils' support for Reagan and to plead that no punitive action be taken against them. The possibility that committee assignments or campaign financing could be withdrawn was particularly worrying. "What is our crime?" Hance asked the commission, "Our crime is we represented the conscience of our district." Arguing that the Democrats risked committing "political suicide" by turning away from southern conservative voters, he went on to warn, "If I get beat, you're going to have an ultra-right-wing Republican." Hance also noted the electoral strength of conservatism across the South, observing that in the 1980 election Ronald Reagan won Boll Weevil districts by an average of 53 percent to 43 percent and Boll Weevil candidates outperformed President Jimmy Carter by an average of 35 percent overall. In the end, party leaders delayed a decision on punishment, meaning the threat of retribution hung over the Boll Weevils for the remainder of the 97th Congress.[91]

Consequently, many were rather less receptive to Reagan's personal appeals when he sought their votes for his budget in 1982. Georgia Democrat Doug Barnard warned Reagan of his concern that "we won't get as many Congressional [Democrats] as we need to." A few days later, after a call to Barnard's fellow Georgian Charles Hatcher, Reagan's frustration was apparent in his notes: "What is this—he won't commit either?"[92] On 11 June, though, enough Boll Weevils voted in favor of Reagan's budget that it passed the House by a narrow margin of 219–206.[93] Still, North Carolinian Bill Hefner told reporters he had supported the bill while "holding his nose" and, as the *Arkansas Ga-zette* noted, there was a feeling that many Boll Weevils had to simply "go along with a Republican budget or be accused of leaving the country with no budget at all."[94]

Boll Weevil enthusiasm for Reagan was clearly dwindling. Pushed into action by the faltering economy, the White House began seeking support for a tax bill which reversed some of the tax cuts of the previous year. The ensuing debate threw party affiliations in the House into flux, particularly among southern Democrats. The scale of the tax increases gave rise to vehement conservative opposition in both houses of Congress. A bipartisan group of conservatives even filed a lawsuit aiming to stop the legislation on the grounds that it was unconstitutional.[95] In August, when Reagan hosted a meeting at the White House with more than twenty Boll Weevils, aimed at soliciting support for his tax bill, aides warned him beforehand that political calculations were uppermost in Boll Weevil minds. Reagan was cautioned that many Boll Weevils were "hesitant to support the reconciliation tax bill because of the active opposition of conservative Republicans—opposition which they fear could cause difficulties in their home districts."[96] One attendee, Doug Barnard, acknowledged the pressure he and many other Boll Weevils were under from their constituents to oppose the bill: "My mail is 10-to-1 against the tax increase." Reagan's personal coaxing, which had proved so effective the previous year, had also lost some of its persuasive power. "I don't know how convincing the president was," Barnard said after the meeting. "If I had to estimate, very few minds were changed in there today."[97] Reagan himself was somewhat more optimistic, noting in his diary, "They are pretty much with us."[98]

Most of the Boll Weevils who had loyally backed Reagan in 1981 ultimately sided with conservative southern Republicans in opposing the president's proposals. Doug Barnard, Billy Lee Evans, and Lawrence McDonald joined their fellow Georgian, Newt Gingrich, in voting against Reagan's tax increase, along with Charles Stenholm and Sam Hall of Texas, Richard Shelby of Alabama, and around twenty-five others.[99] Having opposed Reagan's original tax cuts, Ed Jenkins also now voted against reversing them, fearing that taking money out of the economy would exacerbate the downturn.[100] However, many of Reagan's most prominent Boll Weevil supporters, including John

Breaux, Sonny Montgomery, Kent Hance, and Phil Gramm, were among around fifteen who voted in favor. They were motivated chiefly by concerns that the size of the federal deficit could impede any chance of economic recovery, while one Texan Boll Weevil also told journalists that he feared "some uglier options [for raising taxes] are waiting in the wings" if Reagan's bill failed.[101] The legislation—which became the Tax Equity and Fiscal Responsibility Act, or TEFRA—passed the House by 226 votes to 207 on 19 August 1982.[102] Boll Weevil votes had proved critical in another legislative victory for the Reagan administration, albeit one that was driven by economic circumstances. Nonetheless, the vote demonstrated just how far Boll Weevil support for the administration had diminished since its high point the previous year. As the 1982 midterm elections approached, the southern political landscape was becoming increasingly unpredictable.

Several midterm contests illustrated the growing fragmentation of partisan loyalties in the South. Bill Chappell, a Boll Weevil from northeastern Florida, faced a strong primary challenge from a moderate Democrat who condemned him for his support of the president. Despite his voting record showing 80 percent of his votes favored the Reagan administration, Chappell made awkward attempts to distance himself from the White House: "I vote with the president when I think he's right, and I vote against him when I think he's wrong."[103] Given that Chappell's re-election was viewed by the media as "a good test of the electorate's attitude towards the Reagan economic program," the narrowness of his victory indicated the ambivalence with which many southern conservatives regarded Reagan's economic record in late 1982.[104] In Georgia's 7th district, Boll Weevil Lawrence McDonald received the support of many of the state's leading conservative Republicans in his re-election, while his moderate Republican opponent was endorsed by large numbers of Democrats but not, notably, by President Reagan.[105] McDonald's fellow Georgian, Billy Lee Evans, was the only major casualty among the Boll Weevils. In the Democratic primaries, Evans lost a hard-fought race to a former physician, but not before he had accused his opponent of profiteering from abortions, described his own party as "irrelevant," and received the active support of the Republican mayor of Macon.[106]

Ultimately, though, with the advantage of incumbency and helped by an unfavorable economic climate for Republicans, few Boll Weevils found their campaigns for re-election problematic. Demonstrating the paradoxical nature of partisan politics in the South in the early 1980s, by returning the Boll Weevils to Congress southern voters were able not only to register a protest at the state of the economy and reelect trusted incumbents, but also to act in concert with their abiding affection for Ronald Reagan by reelecting the conservative Democrats who had provided him with crucial support. Reagan's popularity in the South was scrambling the region's political landscape, making white southern conservatives question their voting behavior and encouraging several Democratic candidates to become further detached from their own party and begin a gradual migration towards the GOP.

The wider success of the Democrats in the 1982 midterms—gaining twenty-six House seats nationwide—altered the political equation and ended the South's brief return to the center of legislative power in Washington. The Boll Weevils' initial hope was that newly elected Democrats from southern districts would be a fresh batch of recruits for their group, but this hope was misplaced. Most of the new southern Democrats were not conservatives but moderates elected with the help of increased African American turnout.[107] Conservative southern Democrats were now no longer a large enough bloc to provide the swing vote in Reagan's favor. "While they won their own battles," the *Washington Post* reported, "the nature of the war in the House has changed."[108]

In the short term, most Boll Weevils returned to the Democratic fold. Kent Hance had for weeks been "in the vanguard of those seeking reconciliation" with party leaders and had been raising funds for Democratic candidates in the South as well as voting with his party's leadership in an attempt to rebuild bridges. Consequently, he retained his seat on the House Ways and Means Committee.[109] Louisianans Jerry Huckaby and Buddy Roemer also tried to ingratiate themselves with Tip O'Neill and the Democratic House leadership, joining in their party's calls for Reagan to curb his administration's defense spending. Media reports had suggested Roemer might switch parties as early as the spring of 1981, and he openly speculated that he might defect to the GOP if he was refused a position on the Banking Committee. Roemer was one of several Boll Weevils regarded by House Republicans as potential defectors—Louisiana Republican Henson Moore told him "he'd be more at home with us, philosophically, than he is in the Democratic Party."[110] Yet once Roemer was granted his preferred committee assignment, he declared his loyalty to the Democrats and claimed there had only ever been a "slim chance" of him switching parties.[111] Most Boll Weevils likewise went unpunished by the Democratic leadership, but it was made clear that much greater loyalty was expected of them in future. Sonny Montgomery, who was re-elected as chair of the Veterans Affairs Committee despite many Democrats voting against him, told reporters he had "got the message."[112] Charlie Rose of North Carolina joked, "I will probably have more activity in my high school alumni association than I will in the Boll Weevil association this year."[113]

Though Jim Wright claimed the Democrats would "welcome the sinners back," some Boll Weevils were denied seats on their preferred committees.[114] After Doug Barnard was refused a position on the House Appropriations Committee, an angry editorial in the *Augusta Chronicle* claimed that "[Tip] O'Neill stabbed the Augustan in the back" because he "wouldn't play along with the Democratic leadership and its blind anti-Reagan strategy."[115] Unsurprisingly, the Boll Weevil who faced the harshest punishment was Phil Gramm. Leading Democrats regarded Gramm as particularly treacherous, not simply for his co-sponsorship of Reagan's budget bill, but because he had, according to the Texas Democratic Party chairman, acted as a "double agent" by providing information to the White House regarding Democratic strategy.[116] Gramm had relished working on Reagan's budget bill, telling journalists, "Was it hard for me? Bull—. It was the easiest thing I've ever done."[117] His notable lack of regret, and his refusal to campaign for fellow Democrats in the 1982 midterms, meant few were surprised when Gramm was voted off the House Budget Committee, nor when he subsequently resigned from Congress and announced he was switching parties. In February 1983, Gramm returned to Congress as a Republican after comfortably winning a special election in his district.[118]

Gramm's move to the GOP had been predicted for months. Even prior to the midterms, the *Fort Worth Star-Telegram* reported that he had been "written off as an undefendable casualty by some Boll Weevils," and his abrasive demeanor meant he had few friends in his party, even among fellow southern Democrats.[119] President Reagan, on the other hand, was eager to welcome a man who had been a more loyal supporter of the administration than many congressmen in the president's own party. Reagan had written to Gramm in December, saying, "I know what trying times these last few months have been for you and what a difficult political decision you face." But, Reagan reassured him, "I would welcome you into the Republican Party, where I believe you could more effectively continue your important leadership role in the rebuilding of our country's fiscal integrity."[120] At the time, Gramm appeared to be an isolated case. Most Boll Weevils returned to the backbench position they had occupied prior to Reagan's election, maintaining their opposition to the liberal Democratic leadership, particularly on budget issues. For some, however, the feeling of detachment from their own party would deepen over the coming months.

In March 1984, Florida representative Andy Ireland announced his own switch to the GOP, telling conservative supporters, "I do not see myself leaving the Democratic Party so much as I see the Democratic Party leaving me—and our state and its values."[121] The strength of the conservative vote in his district saw him easily win re-election later that year. Kent Hance would also ultimately join the GOP.[122] After resigning his House seat to seek the Democratic nomination for senator in 1984, Hance discovered that, even in Texas, a conservative voting record was a hindrance when fighting a state-wide Democratic primary. His loss to a liberal, Lloyd Doggett, would spur him to change parties in May 1985, while Doggett went on to lose the Senate election to Phil Gramm.[123] It is noteworthy that Gramm, Ireland, and Hance were closer philosophically to Reagan's anti-statism than many of their Boll Weevil peers. In his career as a GOP congressman and senator, Phil Gramm would mark himself out as more ideologically committed to the aims of Reaganism than even Reagan himself. All three men, moreover, represented largely suburban districts in Texas and Florida that had prospered in the Sunbelt boom, and where residents showed greater support for the Reaganite economic agenda than did lower-income voters in the rural South.

When interviewed by Nicol Rae in 1990, other Boll Weevils offered a variety of reasons for remaining in the Democratic Party. Ed Jenkins, for example, decided "to stay within the party and fight it out." Likewise, Marvin Leath argued, "it's important that the Democratic Party have a conservative wing to counterbalance the ultraliberal wing," while Doug Barnard claimed he would "never be tempted to switch" because "I'd lose my seniority and my subcommittee chairmanship."[124] For some, switching to the GOP became less likely as they grew increasingly disillusioned with Reagan's inattention to the budget deficit, particularly during the latter years of his presidency. It was not until Reagan had left office, and the trend in congressional elections in the white South was moving inexorably in the GOP's favor, that other Boll Weevil defections occurred. Buddy Roemer became Republican governor of Louisiana, defecting in 1991 after originally winning the governorship as a Democrat.[125] Richard Shelby and Billy Tauzin were among several southern Democrats who switched to the GOP in the wake of the Republican takeover of Congress in 1994, while Ralph Hall finally became a Republican in 2004.[126] Nonetheless, their support for Reagan's agenda during the first year of his presidency had signposted their future political direction, just as it did for millions of their fellow conservative southerners. Even those who remained Democrats throughout their careers found themselves swimming against the partisan tide. When Sonny Montgomery announced his retirement in 1996, for example, the GOP won his Mississippi seat in the subsequent election.[127] In Georgia, Ed Jenkins' successor, Nathan Deal, won election in 1992 as a Democrat but within months was already considering switching parties, eventually doing so in 1995.[128] Like Montgomery and Jenkins, many Boll Weevils would see their former districts turn Republican within a few years of leaving Congress.

The Boll Weevils' rise to prominence in 1981 may have been short lived, but their votes were unquestionably vital to the success of Ronald Reagan's presidency. Failure to enact the legislative cornerstones of his economic program would have fatally undermined the remainder of Reagan's time in office. Instead, the Reaganite agenda of cutting taxes and curbing the growth of federal programs became a dominant trend in US politics. The Boll Weevils were at the heart of that transformation, demonstrating that the South could still have a major influence on the political trajectory of the United States. Not since the late 1950s had southern conservatives been "the fulcrum of political power."[129] The coalition they formed with the Reagan administration and House Republicans acted as an important stepping-stone in pulling southern voters towards the GOP and aided Republican attempts to loosen the Democrats' century-long grip on the region at the congressional level. Once the Boll Weevil-GOP coalition had demonstrated that the economic interests of southern conservatism—whether it was shrinking federal welfare programs, increasing funding for the military, or simply winning concessions for regional industries—could be better furthered by allying with the national Republican Party, electing Republicans became a more logical and appealing option.

Yet the coalition also highlighted the divergence in economic agendas between the anti-statist conservatism of Ronald Reagan and the more populist conservatism of the white South. The former was radical and ideologically committed to shrinking the size and scope of the federal government. The latter, despite generations of overt antagonism towards federal power, was prepared to scale back government only when it did not have a negative impact on the interests of white southerners or important regional industries. As the Boll Weevils' negotiations with the Reagan administration illustrated, southern conservatives were willing to be openly transactional, even cynical, in advancing their region's economic priorities. In other areas of economic and trade policy, the populism of southern conservatives in both parties—and their determined defense of southern interests—would bring them to a point of outright opposition to the Reagan White House.

4. "Free Trade Will Destroy America!"
Reaganism Meets the Southern Economic Agenda

Even as they were helping to drive the "Reagan Revolution" through Congress, southern conservatives were fighting a separate legislative battle, this time against the Reagan White House. As part of its budget reductions, the administration proposed the elimination of almost all federal agricultural subsidies. The 1981 farm bill would see federal spending on agriculture reduced to less than $10 billion over five years, from approximately $30 billion spent under President Jimmy Carter. Given the importance of agriculture to their region's economy—particularly peanuts, tobacco, cotton, and sugar—this proposal met with unsurprising hostility from congressional southerners. Boll Weevils who backed Reagan's budget and tax-cutting legislation simultaneously joined forces with southern Republicans to oppose his plan to expose American agriculture to market forces. David Stockman, Reagan's OMB director, believed these southern conservatives preferred a "Soviet-style market" in agriculture by "having the government control production and marketing." Stockman recalled leading Boll Weevil Charles Stenholm telling him, "We'll hit your low budget numbers, but we're going to flush your free market ideology right down the commode."[1]

In Reagan's view, American farmers had become "too dependent on handouts and artificial price supports" and were "[harvesting] money from the federal pocketbook."[2] Indeed, federal assistance had been critically important to southern farmers in the years before Reagan came to office. The *Atlanta Constitution* reported in early 1981 that droughts, increased cost of production, and a "massive credit squeeze" had hit southern agriculture extremely hard. Over the previous decade, farm incomes across the region had plummeted, by 25 percent in Tennessee, 30 percent in both Florida and South Carolina, 32 percent in Georgia, and 36 percent in Alabama. North Carolina's farm income had fallen furthest, down by 45 percent, chiefly because tobacco and peanuts, the state's most important crops, were particularly vulnerable to drought.

Largely thanks to the heat-resistant nature of cotton, incomes in Mississippi were comparatively unscathed, falling only 16 percent.³ Similar issues were bringing farmers across the United States to crisis point. Reagan's solution was, he later explained, "to return farming to the free market. . . . The answer is unfettered free competition."⁴

However, conservative southerners in both parties were determined to resist any significant reduction in subsidies to their region. This was apparent when the Reagan administration proposed to force the Rural Electrification Administration (REA) to seek funding in the commercial marketplace. Established in the New Deal era with the aim of providing electricity to rural America, by the early 1980s the REA had morphed into a network of local cooperatives covering forty-six states and huge swathes of the rural South. Supported by federal loans and subsidies, it provided services to 98 percent of American farms and had branched out into building power stations, operating telephone systems, and providing cable television.⁵ Strom Thurmond was one southerner who resolutely opposed any changes to the REA. According to David Stockman, the South Carolina senator approached him with some friendly advice: "Now, we're all behind the President's program, yuh heah? But you take good care of those REAs. Them's some real *fine* people." This divide between Reaganite faith in free markets on one side and the economic populism of southern conservatives on the other became a persistent issue in the debate over agricultural policy. As the official primarily charged with overseeing cuts to the federal budget, Stockman became increasingly exasperated: "Even the most blatant boondoggles we proposed to cut or eliminate were producing stout champions."⁶

As the new chair of the Senate Agriculture Committee, Jesse Helms emerged as the stoutest champion of federal subsidies for both peanuts and tobacco. Helms had been instructing Ronald Reagan on the need for such federal largesse even before Reagan became president. Contradicting his expressed belief in unfettered free competition, Reagan had written to a North Carolina tobacco farmer in September 1980 describing tobacco subsidies as "an unqualified success." Reagan assured him, "I fully support this nation's tobacco price support program" and pledged to "seek Senator Helms' views on any decision my Administration makes concerning federal tobacco policy."[7] During the presidential transition, Reagan's nominee for Secretary of Agriculture, John Block, met with Helms and leaders of local farming organizations in North Carolina. Even as he was reiterating the incoming administration's commitment to a free market philosophy, Block was also quick to express approval of the tobacco price support program. It was, he suggested, "not a big user of federal money. The tobacco program stands on its own."[8] As commentator Mary McGrory wryly noted in the *Atlanta Constitution*, the episode served notice that Jesse Helms would "holler his lungs out if Reagan touches a leaf of the tobacco program."[9] Reagan's compromise with Helms frustrated David Stockman, who later wrote, "I had to chomp down on my tongue whenever its defenders said in public that the program didn't cost the budget 'anything much.'"[10]

In March 1981, just weeks into Reagan's presidency, North Carolina's Democratic governor Jim Hunt and Boll Weevil Charlie Rose joined forces with Helms to convince local farmers they were dedicated to preserving the tobacco program. At an event in Raleigh, Rose introduced Helms and praised him for his conservatism and influence in the Senate.[11] In return, Helms described Rose as "a remarkable young man" and "thoroughly dedicated to our people." Helms also reassured his audience that "the protection of the economic security of our tobacco growers, and all others who make their livings in tobacco, will always occupy a top priority with me—far above and beyond any partisan considerations."[12] North Carolina's eastern counties, Helms' political stronghold, were home to most of the state's tobacco growers. In these areas, as Helms asserted, "tobacco isn't a commodity, it's a religion."[13] In the face of strong resistance among congressional southerners, led forcefully by Helms, it was little surprise that when John Block outlined the Reagan administration's aims for US agriculture, tobacco supports were left largely untouched. Instead, Block proposed the abolition of a federal anti-smoking campaign.[14]

The tobacco program had long been governed by specific legislation and was not part of the farm bill the Reagan administration sent to Congress. Instead, the bill unveiled by John Block in late March focused on other commodities, and provoked immediate anger among

US farmers and their congressional representatives. Several southern crops came under attack. Drastic proposed changes to the peanut industry aimed to make prices more competitive by ending both the allotment system that licensed peanut production and restrictions on price supports. Charlie Rose complained that "the old peanut has been singled out for some special treatment," while Alabama's Democratic senator Howell Heflin condemned the proposals as "almost killing the peanut folks."[15] The administration's refusal to establish a sugar support program angered Louisianans including Democratic congressman Jerry Huckaby—described as "Sugarland's man" by the *Washington Post*—while Mississippi's Republican senator Thad Cochran criticized the proposal to eliminate deficiency payments for cotton producers.[16] The White House saw deficiency payments, a system which directly subsidized farmers by compensating them if crop prices fell below a certain level, as particularly incompatible with a market-driven approach to agriculture.

The food stamp program, despite coming under the auspices of the Department of Agriculture and consuming almost half the department's budget in 1981, was separated from the farm bill in the legislative process. In previous years, the program's inclusion in farm legislation had created a mutually advantageous relationship between urban representatives of food stamp recipients and congressmen from rural regions that benefitted from agricultural subsidies. Now, the political protection this relationship afforded to farmers was gone.[17] In a climate of hostility towards federal spending, southern conservatives were also demonstrating a greater willingness to prioritize their own region's crops at the expense of midwestern farmers. In March, Jesse Helms and other conservative southerners opposed an increase in milk price supports that would have aided dairy farmers in states such as Wisconsin.[18] A once solid congressional coalition was in danger of splintering under the strain of Reagan's budget cuts.

When it came to southern commodities, Helms took a very different approach. Though he had extolled Reagan's conservative values countless times on the campaign trail, in early April he announced a plan with strikingly different aims from those of Reaganite conservatism. Helms proposed raising the peanut price support level substantially to

$650 per ton—$200 per ton higher than the Reagan administration's desired level—and spoke vehemently in support of peanut subsidies in principle.[19] "To do away with any program because of a fine-line philosophical point would throw thousands of hardworking peanut farmers out of business," he argued. "I am not in favor of such a purist approach at the heavy expense of our farmers."[20] The Helms proposals triggered weeks of debate in congressional agriculture committees, with Georgia Boll Weevils Charles Hatcher and Bo Ginn adding their condemnation of the administration's assault on the peanut allotment system. Hatcher told John Block, "It's a shame to disrupt the economy down there simply to meet some philosophical need," while Ginn claimed the abolition of allotments would create a "calamitous situation" for southern farmers.[21]

Reagan's planned changes shocked many in the rural South. "The economy of south Georgia as well as many other areas has its life blood in the success of the farmer," a Georgia constituent wrote to Bo Ginn. "I feel that the abolishment of peanut allotments would cause further degradation of an already ill-healthed [sic] south Georgia economy."[22] Georgia's agriculture commissioner wrote to Republican Senator Mack Mattingly, "If we lose our peanut program, what's next???"[23] Alongside anger over the farm bill, fears for the future of the tobacco program remained widespread across the South. One South Carolina tobacco farmer wrote to Strom Thurmond urging him to "make whatever compromises . . . necessary with Northern and Western Senators in order to save our program." In response, Thurmond told him, "You may be assured that I shall do all I can to defeat any efforts to destroy the tobacco price support program."[24]

In the Senate, conservative southerners worked together to produce an alternative to Reagan's plans. During the spring of 1981, Mississippi Republican Thad Cochran and Alabama Democrat Howell Heflin were among members of the Senate Agriculture Committee who were, in the words of one commentator, "doing more violence to Reagan's budget than just about all the House Democrats put together."[25] In late April, the committee produced a bill that cost $6 billion more than Reagan's proposals, with most commodities receiving sizeable increases in price supports. Midwestern Republicans on the committee were alarmed at the result. Kansan Bob Dole complained, "We can't report out this monster," while Indiana senator Richard Lugar—a lone voice in support of Reagan's approach—warned his colleagues they were playing "a very dangerous game" by allowing farmers to believe the final farm bill would be so extravagant. Southern committee members were much more relaxed. Helms dismissed Lugar as pessimistic and Heflin suggested the proposals were simply "preliminary."[26] Nonetheless, southern conservatives in both chambers of Congress were staking out their positions in defense of their region's economy.

Haggling over the farm bill continued throughout the summer of 1981, with congressional committees showing a "bipartisan disregard" for Reagan's proposals.[27] Conservative Boll Weevils shrewdly used their leverage over Reagan's budget and tax cut legislation to win concessions for southern agriculture. In late June, the president dropped his previously adamant resistance to sugar price supports to win the votes of Boll Weevils from Louisiana and Florida.[28] Five weeks later, he reluctantly approved a significant increase in peanut price supports in return for Georgia Boll Weevils backing his tax cut legislation. As the summer progressed, John Block began to talk of a presidential veto if the farm bill's enormous cost was not reduced.[29] His threat, along with Reagan's deals with various Boll Weevils, placed further strain on the already brittle congressional farm coalition.

Divisions widened when the agriculture bill came up for Senate debate in September. Angered that southern commodities were receiving preferential treatment, midwestern senators attacked the deals struck during the bill's development. Minnesota Republican Rudy Boschwitz argued, "The administration's opposition to sugar and peanuts was traded away for the votes of Southern Democrats . . . [while] farmers of the Midwest who had supported the administration at the ballot box watched their crop support situation erode away."[30] The Reagan administration's spending cuts and horse-trading for southern votes had created an environment in which previously united farm state senators were now mutually hostile. "We all know . . . that the shape of the present farm bill that is before this body was shaped after the deals that the President made with certain people," complained Nebraska Democrat James Exon. "The President did not have to make deals with Northern

State Senators. He did not have to make deals with Congressmen from the North because most of them are Republican and they were locked in. Not so with the boll weevil Democrats from the South. I think that this bill is a bad bill."[31] Richard Lugar likewise described the Agriculture Committee's bill as "big, fat and ready to be shot down." Lugar may also have been the anonymous midwestern Republican committee member who criticized Jesse Helms's chairmanship to journalists, saying, "All he really cared about was peanuts and tobacco."[32]

Helms certainly mounted robust efforts to protect the crops most critical to his home state. Tobacco subsidies had been largely untouched by the Reagan administration, but the growing prominence of anti-smoking groups and repeated attacks by congressional liberals made the tobacco industry nervous. After one legislative assault on the program, Helms and John East circulated a letter to colleagues requesting their support for tobacco while also noting the amount of federal aid that farmers in their states received. It was widely interpreted, and probably intended, as a thinly veiled threat to reduce such aid if support for tobacco was not forthcoming.[33] On the Senate floor, Helms returned to a familiar refrain: "I just want to say over and over again, there is no tobacco subsidy."[34] Strom Thurmond also implored his colleagues, "How can Congress repeal a program that is costing so little and reaping such benefits to the economy, allowing small farmers to exist on the farm and make a living and allowing them to support their families?"[35] After several attempts to force the program's elimination were thwarted—one by just a single vote—both House and Senate voted to maintain it.[36] For all their vocal opposition to big government, Helms, Thurmond, East, and a significant number of conservative southern Democrats had succeeded in protecting federal support for a crop that was crucial to the South's agricultural economy.

Helms achieved similar success in protecting peanut subsidies. Working in concert with Boll Weevil Charlie Rose, he conducted a rear-guard action against legislative attacks on the peanut program led by Richard Lugar, who criticized it as "special interest agriculture policy at its least defensible."[37] Southerners on both sides of the Senate rose to the program's defense, including Strom Thurmond, John East, and Democrats Sam Nunn of Georgia, William Huddleston of Kentucky, and Howell Heflin of Alabama. East condemned what he regarded as "a frontal assault upon one of the vital commodity programs," while Heflin spoke in defense of the program's allotment system, a target of pro-free market senators. In Heflin's view, peanut allotments epitomized American enterprise: "What is an allotment? It is a franchise. Is there something un-American about franchises? Is there something un-American about McDonalds?"[38] Though the allotment system was technically abolished, senators voted to replace it with an amended peanut program which included higher price supports and offered farmers continued protection from competition. In the House, the peanut program faced an even greater challenge: a broad coalition of Reaganite free market Republicans and liberal Democrats seeking revenge against the Boll Weevils.[39] To the alarm of southern conservatives in both parties, an amendment abolishing the peanut program passed by a vote of 250–159. Not coincidentally, the sugar program suffered a similar defeat.[40] However, as the *New York Times* reported, when the process moved to a House-Senate conference to combine the two farm bills, "the South rose again" and the peanut and sugar programs were restored with only minor alterations.[41]

The Senate quickly approved the final farm bill, but debate in the House was heated, with midwestern representatives arguing that the Reagan administration had given the South preferential treatment and accusing southerners of betrayal.[42] Iowa's Neal Smith accused southern congressmen of "helping stick a knife in the back of principal commodities" such as grain and wheat.[43] A commentator in the *Lexington Herald* reflected the view of many on Capitol Hill that the outcome "amounted to a Southern farm bill."[44] Most of the region's commodities received sizeable increases in their federal supports, yet few southerners were entirely happy. Despite having supported Reagan's budget cutting agenda, leading Boll Weevils including Charles Stenholm and Kent Hance believed the subsidies in the farm bill were not generous enough.[45] Although fellow Boll Weevil Bill Nichols supported the legislation, he too was scathing about it, writing to a constituent, "The bill does virtually nothing for our Alabama farmers; however, it does contain the sections on tobacco, peanuts and sugar, all of which are skating on thin ice." He also admitted, "I am fearful that, if we came back in January to attempt to write a better bill, one or all of these commodities could be completely eliminated."[46] Similarly, Jesse Helms would have preferred even greater increases in southern crop subsidies but viewed the bill as "the best that could be hammered out" against a backdrop of budget constraints.[47]

The bill narrowly passed the House by 205 votes to 203 on 16 December, and a reluctant Reagan signed it into law.[48] While Reagan was able to say that the bill "recognizes the importance of the marketplace," it bore little resemblance to the proposals Agriculture Secretary John Block had announced the previous March.[49] A sugar price support program was established, subsidies for cotton remained broadly unchanged and, although the peanut program had seen alterations, farmers still had substantial protection from free market competition. Tobacco had survived a "long and bloody fight" in Congress and came through similarly unscathed.[50] The cuts which brought the farm bill more closely into line with Reagan's budget-cutting agenda fell predominantly on non-southern commodities, demonstrating how shrewdly and effectively congressional southerners had exercised political leverage. The stark contrast between southern conservatives' anti-government rhetoric and their willingness to fight tooth and nail to defend southern agricultural subsidies did not go unnoticed. "It must be, I would suggest, difficult for some people to get up and make these arguments given a long history of arguing for less Government, less interference, less cost," Massachusetts Democrat Paul Tsongas remarked during the Senate's farm bill debate. "But there is something to be said for fascinating turnarounds."[51]

The 1981 farm bill was a testament to the priorities of southern conservatives. For them, the South's interests took precedence over congressional alliances, personal affection for the president, and even reducing the size and scope of the federal government. Led by Jesse Helms, they angered many midwesterners in the formerly unified congressional farm coalition by creating a bill that was, in David Stockman's view, "a smorgasbord of everything."[52] They also severely dented the president's drive for a free market in agriculture. As political scientist Larry Schwab noted, "Not only did the Reagan administration end up supporting a huge expansion of most of the existing farm programs, his administration even added new ones."[53]

Nonetheless, over the following years US farmers continued to endure their deepest crisis since the 1930s. Their plight increasingly touched the national consciousness. In 1984, Hollywood produced three films—*River*, *Places in the Heart*, and *Country*—depicting the struggles of life on a family farm in hard times. Particularly in the Midwest, but also across the South, farmers suffered from droughts, high loan interest rates, spiraling debts, and falling property values, with farm foreclosures reaching record levels.[54] The farm program expansions that had provoked so much debate in 1981 did little to alleviate the crisis. In some cases, they exacerbated it. By maintaining a high sugar price, for example, federal assistance triggered a steady fall in consumption during the early 1980s. By December 1984, as one producer told the *New York Times*, the entire industry was "in trouble."[55] High price levels maintained by the tobacco program, combined with the strong dollar, also meant that the southern tobacco industry struggled to compete with foreign producers and America's share of the global market shrank.[56] Programs that had been vigorously defended by southern conservatives with the aim of protecting their region's farmers were proving increasingly counterproductive to the agricultural economy. A vicious circle had developed. Placing US farmers at the mercy of the marketplace would result in many losing their livelihoods, yet the federal subsidies they needed to survive were gradually crippling their industries. Consequently, when a new farm bill was required in 1985, many southern conservatives broadly accepted that price support reductions were needed. Again, though, they fought hard to keep the programs in place, fearing that fully opening agriculture to market forces could put large numbers of southern farmers out of business for good.

Speaking at a press conference in February 1985, Ronald Reagan's view of agriculture was unchanged from the start of his presidency: "Many of the problems [farmers] face today are the result of government's involvement." Once again, his administration would be "taking up proposals for, hopefully, getting the farm economy back into the free marketplace and government out of the agricultural business."[57] When the plans were revealed, they sparked outrage among farm state congressmen and senators. A proposal to abolish the allotment system that licensed the production of tobacco aroused the ire of Jesse Helms and other southern conservatives. The *News and Observer* reported that Helms reacted with "contempt" when shown the plan, theatrically "holding the page by one corner away from his body as if it were an object of disgust."[58] Helms had turned down the chairmanship of the prestigious Senate Foreign Relations Committee to remain chair of the Agriculture Committee. In doing so, he fulfilled a campaign promise that had helped him to win re-election in 1984 and prevented Richard Lugar, a vocal opponent of the tobacco program, from replacing him as chair of Agriculture. Though Helms accepted that some reductions in tobacco price support levels were necessary, ending the allotment system entirely was beyond the pale. The Reagan administration would need to drop their tobacco proposals "if they want a farm bill approved. I'm still chairman of the Senate Agriculture Committee, I'll put it that way."[59] Siding with Helms were Kentucky Republicans Mitch McConnell (newly elected to the Senate) and Larry Hopkins as well as North Carolina Democrat Charlie Rose. The latter described the plan as "stupid" and a "cock and bull set-up," while Hopkins declared, "The trenches have been dug. . . . If they persist in this then it's war."[60]

The administration's plans for the rest of US agriculture provoked a similar response. As part of a fifteen-year bill designed to guide US farmers through to the end of the twentieth century, all price support programs would be eliminated after a five-year transition. The aim, according to John Block, was to ensure that "farmers can make a profit out of the marketplace and are not dependent on the government for their income."[61] Farm state congressmen and senators disparaged the notion that US farmers could make a profit in the marketplace when competing against farmers in other countries who received subsidies. The resistance among both southerners and midwesterners was such that the administration's bill stood little chance of surviving without substantial alterations.[62]

The subsequent ten month-long congressional debate produced, as it had in 1981, a bill that was virtually unrecognizable from the Reagan administration's original proposals. Midwesterners again argued that the final farm bill favored the South. Led by Helms, southern conservatives forced the administration to back down over the tobacco allotment system but permitted small reductions in price support levels.

The administration's plan to phase out other price supports was also rejected, with cotton, peanut, and sugar supports remaining in place, albeit at a lower level. Instead of pushing American farmers towards the free market, what eventually emerged from Congress was—in terms of federal spending—the biggest farm bill in US history, with support for commodities costing at least $55 billion over the following four years.[63] Though Reagan had threatened to veto any farm bill which exceeded $50 billion, fears of a political backlash in the 1986 midterm elections pushed him into signing it.[64] At the signing ceremony, a frustrated Reagan did little to gloss over his "serious reservations" about the bill, stating pointedly that it "did not make all of the reforms we requested" and describing much of the legislation as "[representing] the worst in the way of policy."[65]

The Reagan administration's two attempts to reform US agriculture can only be viewed as outright failures. "Farm policy did not shift from a period of more government involvement to less government involvement during the 1980s. Just the reverse was true," Larry Schwab observes.[66] Ultimately, southern economic interests defeated Reaganite ideology. Reagan's plan to remove the federal government from US agriculture met determined resistance from southern conservatives who were beginning to re-assert their influence on Capitol Hill. A bipartisan group of southerners manned a legislative barricade around federal assistance to their region's farmers, against which the administration's attempts at fundamental reform repeatedly foundered. Their efforts ensured that the South's major commodities—tobacco, sugar, peanuts, and cotton—faced only minor reductions in federal subsidies and that their price support programs remained inviolate. These conservative southerners oversaw passage of farm legislation that was vastly more expensive than the Reagan administration's proposals and unquestionably favorable to the South. Yet these were the same southerners who had previously expressed support for the president and his small-government, budget-cutting agenda—Boll Weevil Democrats who were crucial in passing his spending and tax cuts, or southern Republicans who had lauded Reagan as a conservative savior on the campaign trail. Confrontations over agricultural reform showed that, if faced with a hard choice, southern conservatives would prioritize defending the economic interests and traditions of the South over their political loyalties and personal affection for Ronald Reagan.

Agriculture was not the only major southern industry to struggle during the 1970s and 1980s. Textile mills across the region were laying off workers in their thousands. Originally heavily concentrated in New England, much of the US textile industry had migrated to the South between the mid-nineteenth and early twentieth centuries, as mill owners were attracted by the prospect of a cheaper workforce (wages were around one-third lower than in the Northeast) and weaker labor unions.[67] By 1968, over a million workers were employed in textile and apparel production across eight southern states: Alabama, Florida, Georgia, Mississippi, North Carolina, South Carolina, Tennessee, and Virginia.[68] Textile mills were often the major employer in their local towns and were the lifeblood of thousands of rural communities. The *Atlanta Constitution* observed in 1984 that the textile industry "has knitted the entire economic, social and political fabric of towns like Burlington, Spring Mills and West Point—the names of which are more often spotted in white sale catalogs than on road maps."[69] The same year, the *New York Times* reported that mills remained "the dominant life force in many small towns, the source not only of paychecks but of civic energy." In the mid-1980s, the South accounted for around 75 percent of all textile jobs in the United States, and the industry was still the largest employer in Alabama, Georgia, Mississippi, North Carolina, South Carolina, and Virginia.[70]

After weathering several turbulent periods since World War II, however, the industry appeared to be in an irrevocable decline. Sales of American-made textiles had been falling steadily and the 1970s had seen the closure of 604 textile mills with the loss of over 113,000 jobs. Though a majority of these closures occurred at less profitable northeastern mills, most job losses came in the South. By 1984, textile employment in the Carolinas was at its lowest in thirty-seven years, with South Carolina having lost 50,000 textile jobs over the previous decade.[71] Mill closures were having a devastating impact on communities throughout the region. According to the *Christian Science Monitor*, when the local mill in Graniteville, South Carolina, was closed, over six hundred jobs were lost and the entire local economy suffered.[72] A mill closure in Ware Shoals, also in South Carolina, left around half the town's population unemployed and even impacted the water supply, as the local water treatment plant was owned by the textile mill. Few residents were confident of finding new jobs now that the foremost employer in the area had been liquidated.[73] Even in a larger city such as Augusta, Georgia, the closure of the Enterprise textile mill after one hundred years of operation "shattered" the order of the local community.[74]

Many in the industry believed these closures were the direct result of a surge in textile imports dating back to the early 1970s. Anger at the level of imports was widespread, with one mill worker in Augusta accusing overseas governments of "just [letting] us starve to death."[75] Emerging economies in Asia had established textile industries as a major element of their rapid industrialization. By the late 1970s, Asian textile production was expanding by 25 percent each year. US imports from Asia increased by 223 percent between 1973 and 1980. The Multi-Fiber Arrangement (MFA), established in 1974 to regulate exports by developing nations, governed the global trade in textiles. But political allies of the US textile industry repeatedly decried the MFA as ineffectual, accusing competitor nations in Asia of engaging in unfair trade practices. Both complaints were justified, but ultimately the issue facing American textile mills was a familiar one: Asian countries were producing textiles at a much cheaper cost.[76] The same undercutting which helped the South draw textile manufacturing away from the Northeast was now hurting the southern economy. As historian James Cobb told the *New York Times*, "The third world has out-Southed the South."[77] The sharp decline of the textile industry quickly became a contentious political issue. The industry and its congressional allies mounted a campaign demanding "regulatory relief"—legislation aimed at stemming the flood of textiles entering the United States.[78] A bill designed to prevent the United States from lowering trade tariffs on textiles was vetoed by President Jimmy Carter in November 1978 on the grounds that other industries would seek similar protection.[79]

On the 1980 campaign trail Ronald Reagan had pledged—albeit rather loosely—to tackle the issue of textile imports, a protectionist commitment that clearly ran counter to his faith in free markets and free trade. Nevertheless, appearing alongside Strom Thurmond in Columbia, South Carolina, Reagan declared that the textile industry provided "vitally needed American jobs. . . . As President, I want to make sure these jobs stay in this country, and are not exported overseas." He would work to "renew and strengthen" the MFA, as well as "[negotiating] aggressively with our trading partners."[80] Reagan was more specific in letters to both Thurmond and his fellow South Carolinian Carroll Campbell, suggesting that when the MFA expired at the end of 1981 it should be "strengthened by relating import growth from all sources to domestic market growth. I shall work to achieve that goal."[81] This was a substantial change, one strongly advocated across the textile industry. Southern conservatives expected Reagan to stay true to his commitment. They would be sorely disappointed.

During 1981 and 1982, the administration gave repeated assurances it would meet its target. Reagan's Chief of Staff, James Baker, told Carroll Campbell, "This Administration will make every effort to satisfactorily conclude an MFA that will allow us to relate total import growth to growth in the domestic textile and apparel market."[82] Reagan personally reassured Thurmond, "I have instructed all agencies and departments which have responsibilities related to the textile program to continue their efforts to work vigorously towards that goal."[83] Yet little was achieved. The strong dollar (a consequence of funding federal deficits with foreign borrowing) made importing cheaper and exporting more expensive, and so textile imports continued to increase. In late 1983, Secretary of Commerce Malcolm Baldrige bluntly informed Reagan just how far short of his commitment the administration had fallen. "You have pledged to Senator Thurmond and others to relate the growth of textile imports to growth in the domestic market," wrote Baldrige. "However, import growth continues at unprecedented levels. Since the beginning of your Administration, imports have grown by 49 percent while domestic production has grown only 1 percent."[84]

Relations between the White House and textile industry advocates—primarily southerners both inside and outside Congress—unsurprisingly soured. William Klopman, a textile magnate in North Carolina and loyal Reagan backer, wrote to the president: "I cannot help but think that the inconsistency between your commitment to our industry and your support of free trade . . . is being resolved in favor of the free trade advocates."[85] Demands for action also came from Roger Milliken, owner of one of South Carolina's largest textile companies. A hugely influential figure in the development of the southern GOP, having funded the expansion of the Republican Party in South Carolina and persuaded Strom Thurmond to switch parties in 1964, Milliken had a typically southern conservative antipathy for both labor unions and free trade.[86] Nonetheless, he had been an early backer of Reagan and was still an important Republican donor. Over several months in 1983, he repeatedly vented his fury to Reagan administration officials. In May, Milliken told Reagan aide Ed Meese that levels of imported textiles were "catastrophic" and "staggering compared with the President's oft-repeated commitment of an import growth of not more than the growth of our market." Unless action was taken, "the Republican Party in that part of the country which relies on jobs in the apparel and textile industries will have no remaining credibility."[87] Four months later, after attending a fundraising dinner in Columbia with Reagan, Milliken described the president's assurances to the textile industry as "very weak and totally unsupported. . . . There was a significant dead silence following his remarks on textiles."[88] By November, he was writing to James Baker of his increasing belief that "the Administration places a very low priority on the problem" and that 140,000 textile job losses could have been prevented "had the President lived up to his written and oft-restated commitment."[89]

Milliken's bitter complaints reflected rising anger throughout the textile industry. After a two-hour meeting with him in November 1983, a Reagan aide described Milliken's demeanor as "belligerent" and wrote of a widespread feeling that the administration had "abandoned" the industry.[90] Many of Reagan's most prominent southern supporters were equally unhappy. Strom Thurmond wrote to remind the president of the "vitally important commitment" he had made on textiles during the 1980 presidential campaign but expressed concern that Reagan was using "phraseology [that] creates a loophole which will essentially nullify your commitment."[91] Disgruntled messages arrived from Republicans right across the textile-producing areas of the South. Carroll Campbell warned Ed Meese that Republicans would "run into a buzzsaw in the South in 1984" because of Reagan's "empty political rhetoric in the face of skyrocketing imports."[92] A Republican member of the South Carolina state legislature told Reagan, "The alienation of the 'textile' South might conceivably destroy your solid base of support. . . . I urge and implore you to take immediate steps to protect your 'southern flanks' by protecting the textile industry."[93] Jesse Helms and Republican congressman James Broyhill, from neighboring North Carolina, also wrote to the White House. The latter cautioned that "the situation is bad and getting worse. This issue can be politically damaging to all those seeking reelection in 1984 if something is not done—and done quickly."[94] Some in the administration began to fear a damaging political confrontation over Reagan's broken pledges. In an internal memo, US Trade Representative William Brock wrote of the potential for an "unavoidable conflict" with the textile industry in the coming year.[95]

As Roger Milliken suspected, much of the counsel Reagan was receiving on the textile issue opposed restricting imports. Instead, Secretary of Commerce Malcolm Baldrige put it to Reagan in late 1983 that textile supporters' demands were "protectionist" and rejecting a proposal to impose quotas would "underscore our willingness to resist industry desires for protection."[96] In May 1984, a meeting of administration trade advisors reported its conclusions in a memo to the White House: "Acquiescing in a legislated solution involving quotas or some other restraint would simply make resisting similar measures for steel, footwear, and copper more difficult." There was, though, an awareness of the potential for political damage, especially in the South. "We can't simply leave our supporters with nothing to cling to," the group acknowledged, before recommending possible short-term measures designed to "buy us sufficient time to get past the November election."[97] The Reagan administration clearly understood the dangers the textile issue represented. But, like the president himself, Reagan's advisors were deeply resistant to employing protectionist measures to solve the problem. Despite a lack of White House action and an ongoing surge in textile imports, the issue ultimately did little damage to Reagan in the 1984 presidential election. The biggest confrontations over textile imports, however, still lay ahead.

Early in Reagan's second term, the campaign to limit textile imports brought together an unlikely national coalition of union leaders and industry bosses. In Congress, it created a bipartisan alliance across both House and Senate. Strom Thurmond led the charge in the Senate, backed by fellow Republicans Jesse Helms and John East from North Carolina, Georgia's Mack Mattingly, Mississippi's Thad Cochran, and Democrats Ernest Hollings of South Carolina and Sam Nunn of Georgia.[98] The scope of the pro-textile grouping in the House was even broader. In June 1985, southern conservatives from the GOP such as North Carolina's James Broyhill, Carroll Campbell of South Carolina, and Trent Lott of Mississippi, along with numerous Boll Weevil Democrats, including Marvin Leath of Texas, Doug Barnard of Georgia, and Bill Nichols of Alabama, signed a letter protesting the administration's failure to help the industry. Southern conservatives predominated, but the alliance also encompassed a smaller number of moderate southern Democrats and representatives from the Northeast, such as Connecticut Democrat Barbara Kennelly and Republican Bud Shuster of Pennsylvania, whose districts relied on what remained of that region's textile industry.[99]

The influential chair of the Congressional Textile Caucus, conservative Georgia Democrat Ed Jenkins, became the central figure in the congressional campaign to limit imports. Jenkins had acquired the nickname "Mr. Textiles" in his home state—his own mother had been a textile worker and his largely rural district was heavily dependent on the industry.[100] Softly spoken but a shrewd political operator, Jenkins preferred to work behind the scenes. His committee roles were especially advantageous when it came to forging congressional coalitions. "As a senior member of the Ways and Means Committee," the *New York Times* observed, "he can do many favors for many friends."[101] Like most congressional southerners Jenkins was adamantly opposed to free trade, and his stance on textile imports won him the admiration of influential Republican donor Roger Milliken. When he visited one of Milliken's textile mills in Gainesville, Georgia, Jenkins discovered a handwritten note had been left by Milliken himself saying, "Thank you for your leadership."[102] The textile legislation Ed Jenkins introduced triggered one of the toughest congressional battles of Ronald Reagan's presidency.

H.R. 1562, also known as the Textile and Apparel Trade Enforcement Act, was introduced to the House on 19 March 1985. Seeking to dramatically limit imports from twelve major textile-producing countries, mainly in Asia, it eventually garnered 290 cosponsors. Demonstrating that the campaign was a bipartisan effort led chiefly by southern conservatives, the House bill was coauthored by Ed Jenkins and North Carolina Republican James Broyhill and its primary sponsor in the Senate was Strom Thurmond.[103] Needing a broad range of support for his legislation, Jenkins purposefully avoided the language of protectionism. Not all his allies in the textile coalition were quite so strategic. North Carolina Republican Bill Hendon told journalists bluntly that the United States was "bleeding from a self-inflicted wound called free trade."[104] Given that Democratic Party leaders in the House—including Ways and Means Committee chairman Dan Rostenkowski—were opposed, the textile bill faced an uphill battle even to reach Reagan's desk. Ed Jenkins was forced to admit he was "not overly optimistic."[105] But all was not lost even if the bill failed. At the very least, a well-publicized bipartisan campaign against textile imports would, Jenkins reckoned, compel Reagan to follow through on his pledge to strengthen the MFA.[106]

While free-trade advocates and business groups were vehemently critical of the bill, the White House's response was surprisingly subdued. As the *Wall Street Journal* noted in late May, "To many, the Reagan administration has seemed adrift on trade issues."[107] Ronald Reagan was certainly not as outspoken on textile imports as he had been in his opposition to agricultural subsidies. This was partly because his own trade advisors accepted that high import levels were indeed harming the industry and that the administration bore some responsibility. William Brock and Malcolm Baldrige informed the president, "Imports have continued to increase despite our quota actions and bilateral agreements because only 60 percent of current trade is covered by quotas. Additionally, the strong dollar has impeded exports at the same time that it has attracted imports." Moreover, they warned, the issue carried "sharp political significance due to your commitment to relate import growth to growth in the domestic market."[108] Outspoken opposition to the Jenkins bill would make the administration seem uncaring to the hundreds of thousands of workers whose futures were in jeopardy—a majority of whom lived in deeply conservative, rural areas of the South. Such a response could damage Reagan's popularity in the region and, as Roger Milliken had warned, severely hurt the GOP's credibility at a time when the partisan loyalties of conservative southerners were in flux. Though it clearly did not favor legislation to limit imports, the Reagan administration was wary of pushing back too forcefully against the bill. "Relations with Capitol Hill are at a standstill," the *Journal* observed. "Nobody from the White House has gone to lobby for the administration's point of view on the textile legislation."[109]

The Reagan administration finally set out its opposition explicitly in mid-June. In a letter to all members of Congress, James Baker, Malcolm Baldrige, and other White House officials claimed the legislation would "impose a very high cost on U.S. consumers, invite retaliation against U.S. exports, spur inflation, violate our international obligations, and provide the domestic textile and apparel industry with an unprecedented level of protection."[110] In response, the textile bill's supporters intensified a campaign of letter-writing. James Broyhill and two of his constituents personally delivered seven thousand letters written by textile supporters in his district to the White House.[111] The campaign only served to strengthen Reagan's resolve. In mid-September the president told a news conference, "A mindless stampede toward protectionism will be a one-way trip to economic disaster."[112] A week later, without mentioning the textile bill directly, Reagan reiterated that "our trade policy rests firmly on the foundation of free and open markets —free trade."[113] This was not entirely accurate. That very month, September 1985, the Reagan administration negotiated a multinational agreement—the Plaza Accord—to bring down the value of the dollar by purchasing Japanese yen and German marks.[114] Two years later, it placed tariffs on selected Japanese imports in retaliation for perceived breaches of a US-Japanese trade agreement.[115] Neither action was consistent with a trade policy founded on free and open markets.

Yet the administration was unwavering on the textile issue. Throughout 1985 it became clear that little further action on textile imports would be forthcoming. In September, the *Greensboro News and Record* reported on anger among textile bosses in North Carolina, many of whom had strongly backed Reagan in 1980. "From my standpoint it [support for Reagan] has gone from 100 percent to zero," said one executive from Gastonia. "His record on textiles is pretty damn dismal."[116] Similar feelings prevailed among southerners in Congress. When Ed Jenkins' bill passed the House on 10 October by a majority of 262–159, the entire delegations from Alabama, Arkansas, Georgia, Mississippi, North Carolina, South Carolina, and Tennessee voted in favor, as did many other southern congressmen and every representative from Massachusetts. Several longstanding allies of Reagan— including Newt Gingrich and Trent Lott, both of whom had worked on his election campaigns—voted for the bill.[117] Though Jenkins demonstrated his political skill in guiding the legislation through, the margin of victory was short of the two-thirds majority required to override a likely presidential veto. The same was true in the Senate, where it passed by a majority of 60–39. Though many of the bill's supporters framed their rhetoric in terms of fairness rather than protectionism, some southerners were more overt in their opposition to free trade. Strom Thurmond highlighted the distance between his own southern conservatism and the ideology of Reaganism when, after casting his vote, he told the assembled media "Free trade will destroy America!"[118] After the Senate vote, Roger Milliken wrote to Thurmond, "If he [President Reagan] vetos [*sic*], he will be denying what he wrote to you when he was campaigning for the Presidency and made a commitment. . . . It would be devastating for the Republican Party and the control of the United States Senate if he vetos this bill."[119]

Nevertheless, a presidential veto appeared inevitable. The textile industry's supporters publicly called on Reagan to change his position. William Klopman told journalists, "It would be stupid to do it [veto the bill]," while Thurmond declared he was "hopeful that the president will see the light of day here and approve the bill. . . . It will enable the textile industry to survive."[120] On 5 December a group of southern Republicans, led by James Broyhill, Georgia senator Mack Mattingly, and

Alabama senator Jeremiah Denton, were granted a meeting with Reagan to plead their case. "We were given a very cordial audience," Broyhill told reporters afterwards. "He did not make any type of comment with respect to which direction he's leaning."[121] But in private Reagan's mind was made up. After the meeting he noted in his diary, "I listened but feel I must veto it. It is pure protectionism."[122] Reagan sent the bill back to Congress unsigned on 17 December with a message stating he was "deeply sympathetic about the job layoffs and plant closings that have affected many workers." He added, however, that it was also his "firm conviction that the economic and human costs of such a bill run far too high. . . . We want to open markets abroad, not close them at home."[123]

The veto provoked consternation in the textile caucus, as well as a resolve to continue the fight. "Congress has lost the battle but not the war," Strom Thurmond declared. Ed Jenkins, a Boll Weevil who had backed Reagan's budget cuts in 1981, pointedly noted that the president had not returned the favor. "I gave one to the Gipper, but he didn't give one to me." Jenkins was determined to override Reagan's veto but announced that an override vote would be delayed until the following August. The MFA was due for renewal in July 1986 and the textile caucus decided to give the administration a chance to "aggressively renegotiate" the agreement as Reagan had repeatedly pledged to do. But the delay was also a strategic one. "If they don't do what they say they will do at those talks," Carroll Campbell told reporters, "we'll probably be able to pick up additional votes and win the veto fight."[124]

The relationship between the Reagan administration and textile supporters, both inside and outside Congress, remained antagonistic. Suspicions among the industry's allies that presidential promises had been little more than expedient rhetoric were shared even by some Reagan advisors. "The most important point is there *must be some action actually taken*," wrote southern White House aide (and future Republican governor of Mississippi) Haley Barbour in an internal memo that illustrated his frustration with administration policy. "The textile industry's line is that Reagan has betrayed the industry because he has broken his word on enforcing the MFA. They are extremely cynical. . . . Some demonstrable action is critical to reviving any credibility."[125] The political risk for the president and his party was increasing. From the congressional perspective, James Broyhill told the administration that Reagan's veto was "a severe blow" and the GOP risked losing the trust of southern voters. "I am having a hard time convincing North Carolina textile workers that I can do more for them than my opponents, that I can get the President to help them." He added that "continued, aggressive action by the President" was required to "contain the political damage."[126] However, another White House advisor, Ed Stucky, was dismissive of textile supporters, complaining in a memo about "the textile and apparel people [coming] in bitching and moaning about their economic well-being."[127] As the date of a potential override vote neared, the dispute over textile imports remained bitter.

In early August 1986, the administration proclaimed victory in its efforts to renegotiate the MFA. The agreement was extended to cover a broader range of textiles and fibers, and now allowed the United States to negotiate stricter bilateral trade deals with major textile exporting countries. President Reagan hailed the new MFA as "stronger and more comprehensive," but the textile industry's congressional allies were far from convinced. Strom Thurmond was "disgusted and disappointed," while an industry spokesman accused the Reagan administration of "shameful deceit" in "attempting to disguise their failure as a success."[128] The House override vote was scheduled for 6 August, and the days prior were filled with bargaining and pleading from both sides. Southern conservatives implored their fellow congressmen to vote against the president. Writing to Texas Republican Tom DeLay, Carroll Campbell noted that DeLay shared "my support for President Reagan and his programs" but argued that the GOP needed to show solidarity with textile workers. "By hanging in with the worker on this vote, we can turn a political negative into a plus . . . by forcing the Administration legislatively to do what it should have been doing all the time."[129]

Ronald Reagan again called Boll Weevil Democrats to persuade them, but this time his appeals to Charles Stenholm and Buddy Roemer proved fruitless. Reagan noted after the calls that Roemer had changed his mind—initially unsure about the Jenkins bill, he had now decided to back it. About Stenholm, Reagan simply wrote, "I'm afraid the cotton lobby has him."[130] Carroll Campbell called on southern

House delegations to remain united. "The president cannot peel a vote away in North Carolina or South Carolina or Georgia or Tennessee or throughout our part of the country," Campbell said. "This thing is life or death, so as much as we admire and respect the president, we must be opposed."[131] Southern Republicans like Campbell found it particularly hard to oppose a president they had respected for years and who, despite his administration's stance on textile imports, was still personally venerated in the white South. In a letter to fellow Republicans rallying support for overriding the veto, Campbell wrote of his "reluctance to go against our President." However, he concluded, "I strongly believe that the Administration . . . has unnecessarily sacrificed jobs and plants on the altar of free trade."[132] Speaking in the House, Newt Gingrich likewise accused the White House of "fundamentally mishandling our trade policies" and argued it had shown "a record of indifference to American jobs that we must change. We must vote to override."[133] South Carolinian Thomas Hartnett directed some remarks at Reagan himself: "I think that your political consistency is wrong, Mr. President, and I, who have considered myself to be one of your most loyal soldiers, will leave you and urge my colleagues to vote to override your veto."[134] Mississippi Democrat Sonny Montgomery, once a key supporter of Reagan's budget cuts, described the effect the textile industry's decline was having on the South: "Small textile plants are the life-blood of many small communities in Mississippi. Layoffs and plant closures have a devastating impact on the economy of the entire region."[135]

In the end, the House supported overriding Reagan's veto by 276–149 but the Jenkins bill fell eight votes short of the all-important two-thirds majority. Ed Jenkins had worked tirelessly to win support for the override vote, but acknowledged the White House's superior bargaining power: "The President has a lot of power and a lot of chips. He had to play them all on this vote." According to the *Fort Worth Star-Telegram*, the Reagan administration offered beneficial trade deals to midwestern grain farmers and West Coast computer manufacturers, thereby shoring up support from their congressional representatives.[136] The congressmen and industry leaders who had fought hardest for the textile legislation understood that Reagan personally had made the decisive difference. Roger Milliken observed, "We had it won in the House of Representatives until the full force of the Administration and President Reagan himself came in and peeled off votes that we had during the last 24 hours."[137]

The narrow defeat of H.R. 1562 was a body blow to the campaign to limit textile imports. There were further attempts to pass legislation, but none came as close to success as the Jenkins bill. The next, in February 1987, was directed by Democrat Butler Derrick. The South Carolinian was a skilled politician and, like Jenkins, a close ally of Roger Milliken when it came to the textile fight. But his quiet southern drawl and repeated references to the concerns of workers in his own district made it easy for opponents to characterize him as acting purely out of regional interest. He was, as labor historian Timothy Minchin writes, "perhaps not the best leader to build a national coalition."[138] Moreover, as the wider economy improved during 1987 and 1988, it became harder to mount a powerful argument to rescue one industry. Persuading Americans that low-wage textile jobs were worth saving at a time when higher-paid job opportunities in the service sector were increasing proved a difficult task. Nonetheless, Derrick's bill attracted enough support to pass the House and Senate in September 1988 before being quickly vetoed by President Reagan, who described the legislation as "protectionism at its worst."[139] Again, the bill was defeated in the override vote—this time falling eleven votes short.[140]

In purely legislative terms, the administration successfully fought off two attempts to impose textile import quotas it regarded as damaging and protectionist. But the issue had been a constant strain on the relationship between the White House and southern conservatives in Congress. During its first term, many southerners believed the administration was ignoring an industry that was critical to their region's economy and that Reagan himself was betraying commitments he made to them in 1980. In Reagan's second term, as the trigger for two heated legislative battles, the textile issue created a rift between Reagan and southern congressmen that lasted until the end of his presidency. Yet his personal popularity in the South—as well as the electoral prospects of the Republican Party—suffered remarkably little. Clearly, broader motivating factors lay behind the GOP's increasing popularity among white conservative southerners, encompassing issues of cultural conservatism, race, and religion. The textile issue certainly did not hinder the Republican Party at the ballot box in 1984, 1986, or 1988.

To a surprising extent, Ronald Reagan also appeared immune to personal blame over textile imports. Some southerners even wrote to their congressmen urging both support for the president and a vote in favor of imposing import quotas. "On the ground, Reagan remained popular with voters," writes Minchin, "including mill workers who seemed unaware of the president's opposition to the textile bills."[141] Leading industry figures chose to believe Reagan had been led astray by his advisors. The inclination of southern conservatives to separate Ronald Reagan from the policies of his administration was "an interesting phenomenon" according to one textile executive in North Carolina. "A lot of folks blame Reagan, but they are more critical of his advisers," he continued. "They feel like he is a good fellow, and on many things, they agree with him. But on [textile trade issues] they are 180 degrees apart."[142] Likewise, in his many demands for action on textile imports, Roger Milliken often directed his anger towards White House staff rather than towards Reagan. After one meeting, a presidential aide reported that Milliken had "indicated that he personally believes that the White House inner circle is being too heavily insulated by staff on the textile and apparel issue" and Reagan was personally unaware of its "magnitude."[143] Strom Thurmond also preferred to think that Reagan had "heeded bad advice."[144] It is true that Reagan was somewhat cut off from direct involvement in the political furor over textiles, leaving negotiations with Congress to Commerce Secretary Malcolm Baldrige and Trade Representative William Brock. But Reagan's repeated vetoing of legislation, and his determination to prevent those vetoes being overridden, left no room for doubt about the president's beliefs on textile imports and free trade. The administration was simply following the president's lead.

Conservative southerners, for all their professed admiration of Reagan's political philosophy, were frequently infuriated when he and his administration stuck to that philosophy, particularly if it threatened to damage the southern economy. Yet largely due to the deep personal affinity he had built with white conservatives in the South over several decades, Reagan continued to escape significant personal criticism. His standing in the region seemingly outweighed policy matters, even when those policies jeopardized tens of thousands of southern jobs. With Ronald Reagan in the White House, many conservative southerners clung to the belief that their priorities would return to the top of the political agenda.

Legislative struggles over agriculture and textiles suggested that in terms of economic priorities, such faith was misplaced. The Reagan administration's tortuous and largely futile attempts to transform US agriculture demonstrated that the protectionist economic impulses of southern conservatives were regularly in direct opposition to the free market ideology of Reaganism. While its efforts to thwart the southern-led campaign on textiles were more successful, they also sparked intense struggles with conservative southerners. Southern conservatives, united in a bipartisan coalition, fought for and won concessions for their region's farmers in the face of opposition from free marketers, and came within eight votes of passing the most protectionist legislation the United States had seen in decades. These battles highlighted the divide between Reaganite conservatism and southern conservatism, an aspect of his presidency often obscured by the mythology that has surrounded the Reagan era and by the hagiographic way that many conservatives have regarded Reagan. But it was a divide that went beyond the politics of trade and economics. In the realm of cultural conservatism too, Ronald Reagan often failed to meet southern expectations.

III. Southern Priorities

5. "It Was Jesus That Gave Us This Victory"
Ronald Reagan and Southern Evangelicals

"God has used us in awakening the conscience of Americans," declared Texan pastor James Robison. "God has allowed us to touch millions of lives—like I've never seen before in my lifetime—and make them more aware of moral issues and their responsibility for voting."[1] To Robison and millions of his fellow Southern Baptists, Ronald Reagan's 1980 election victory heralded a moral rebirth in the United States. Reverend Jerry Falwell, Virginia pastor and leader of the Moral Majority, believed Reagan's election was "the greatest day for the cause of conservatism and American morality in my adult life."[2] During the late 1970s, Reagan's calculatedly pious language on issues such as abortion enabled him to convince Christian Right leaders that he shared their concerns and values. By the time he won the presidency, Reagan—a man who had not been a regular churchgoer since his youth and who had liberalized abortion laws as governor of California—was seen by conservative evangelicals as a spiritual savior.

The importance of evangelical voters to Reagan's election victory is hard to discern. At the very least, the Christian Right had become a powerful voting bloc that Republican Party leaders could not ignore. Jerry Falwell claimed Reagan owed him no political debt, saying simply, "I share many of his philosophical views, but I am just one citizen who voted for him and I don't expect anything from him."[3] This was disingenuous. Reagan's evangelical supporters, Falwell included, believed they had helped him win the White House and expected an administration aligned with their agenda. As political scientists Mark Rozell and Mark Caleb Smith have observed, "The major themes that define the Christian Right evolved out of the South's unique place in American history." The movement exemplified traditionally southern characteristics, including a "desire to preserve an imagined culture under external assault and a mistrust of concentrated federal power."[4] As much as it was guided by adherence to scripture, the Christian Right was driven by a determination to reverse the social transformation the United States had experienced since the early 1960s.

The Christian Right sought to spread the traditionalism of the white South, overturning many of the social gains made by women and imposing the region's deep-rooted illiberalism on the wider United States. The movement's leaders repeatedly linked federal efforts to protect abortion and promote equal rights for women with a wider sense of moral and political decline. Resisting such campaigns was vital to restoring American values. The day after Reagan's election victory, therefore, newspapers reported that "a human life amendment will be the Moral Majority's first legislative objective in 1981, followed by a war on pornography and drugs and a push for a return to traditional family values."[5] Reports also quoted evangelical leaders as cautioning the president-elect against any "backsliding from their demands."[6] James Robison warned that unless the new administration was staffed with "strong, competent, godly men," Reagan would "join the ranks of mediocrity."[7]

Following Reagan's inauguration, conservative evangelical leaders gathered in Washington to debate political strategy for the coming decade. Faith in the new president remained strong. For many, Reagan's election was a sign Americans were turning back to God. "It was Jesus that gave us this victory in November," claimed Bobbie James, wife of Alabama's Democratic governor Fob James and one of the most prominent women in Southern Baptist circles. "God in his mercy heard the prayers of Christians all over this country." Yet some appointments to the new administration were causing concern—as a Mormon, Education Secretary Terrel Bell was viewed with particular suspicion—and there was disgruntlement that no leading evangelical had been offered a White House position. Though evangelical groups "generally tried to smooth over their disappointment at not being included in the Reagan administration," signs of disillusionment with Reagan's actions were already starting to appear.[8]

The first major divide between Reagan and his Christian Right supporters occurred just five months into his presidency. When Associate Justice Potter Stewart retired in June 1981, it gave Reagan the opportunity to fulfil a campaign pledge to appoint the first female justice to the US Supreme Court. However, his choice of nominee enraged fundamentalist evangelicals and caused disquiet among conservative southerners in Congress. Judge Sandra Day O'Connor was described by Reagan as displaying "unique qualities of temperament, fairness, intellectual capacity and devotion to the public good."[9] Her history of judicial opinions on the Arizona Court of Appeals displayed a tendency towards caution rather than activism. To better understand O'Connor's views on major topics, it was necessary to look elsewhere. Many on the Christian Right therefore scrutinized her time as a Republican member of the Arizona state legislature. Alongside a reliably conservative voting history on issues like the death penalty, there were elements of her record that caused alarm. She had, for example, supported the introduction of the Equal Rights Amendment into the Arizona legislature in 1972. Even more worryingly for evangelicals, in 1974 she had voted in favor of the continued use of federal tax funds for abortions and opposed a resolution calling for an anti-abortion amendment to the Constitution.[10] O'Connor's record evinced an attitude towards social issues that was broadly typical of Sunbelt Republicans. She was "not your far-out Republican" one Arizona Democrat explained. "She might just surprise some people because I don't think she's out of the knee-jerk mold."[11]

In Congress, southern conservatives were at best noncommittal about Reagan's choice. Strom Thurmond, chair of the Senate Judiciary Committee, declined to comment. Jesse Helms, after speaking with Reagan, said, "The information he has about the lady and the information I have are not consistent." Helms's fellow North Carolinian John East and Jeremiah Denton of Alabama also refused to offer their support.[12] Outside Washington, opposition from southern evangelicals was more explicit. James Robison and Ed McAteer, a Memphis businessman and founder of the Religious Roundtable, organized an anti-O'Connor rally in Dallas.[13] Robison told journalists that O'Connor was "not a good choice" because "[all] evidence indicates that she stood for pro-abortion and was for the ERA."[14] He later recalled that he had "hollered and screamed" about the nomination to senior Reagan advisor Ed Meese.[15] Anticipating a Christian Right backlash, Reagan telephoned Jerry Falwell prior to the O'Connor announcement and persuaded Falwell not to publicly condemn her selection. The call was indicative of how Falwell's relationship with the White House differed from that of other Southern Baptist leaders.[16] Personally closer to Reagan than most, Falwell sought to maintain what he regarded as an advisory role, working with the administration to further the Christian Right agenda rather than loudly protesting from the sidelines. Unlike the firebrand Robison, Falwell decided against sacrificing his influence with the Reagan White House over O'Connor's nomination.

Six months into Reagan's presidency, *Chicago Tribune* columnist Jon Margolis observed a rift already emerging in conservative ranks, between southern evangelicals on one side and Reaganites who were "indifferent or hostile to . . . moralist concerns" on the other.[17] Notably, Sandra Day O'Connor's biggest advocate in the Senate was her fellow Arizonan Barry Goldwater, whose antipathy towards the Christian Right created headlines—particularly his blunt remark that "every good Christian ought to kick Falwell right in the ass." Goldwater's comments on the O'Connor nomination underlined the divisions between economic and cultural conservatives. "This abortion issue has gotten to be the biggest humbug issue in the United States," he told journalists. "The country is going to pot economically, militarily and every other way, and we spend all our time talking about busing and abortions."[18]

Many in the White House shared Goldwater's views. One unnamed Reagan advisor was dismissive of the Christian Right's anger, saying, "A little backlash from the kooks is good politics."[19] The nature of the backlash was made clear to Reagan aide Morton Blackwell at a meeting with conservative evangelicals. Blackwell reported in a memo that evangelical leaders threatened to campaign against Reagan's tax cut legislation, "feeling that only a defeat of the tax package will force the Administration to take social issues seriously." More explicitly, they warned Blackwell that "only we can hold wavering Boll Weevils in line because only we can put grass roots heat on them." A handwritten note in the margin of the memo pointed out that pro-life groups had endorsed a large majority of Boll Weevil Democrats.[20] Their threat proved to be an empty one, but it illustrated the influence Christian Right leaders felt they wielded over both southern politics and the Reagan administration.

Conservative voters in the South wrote to voice their anger with Reagan. "You made a fool of us," claimed one woman from Arkansas, who thought Reagan had "betrayed the people who trusted you and worked so hard for you." Another correspondent from Tennessee called the nomination "a shock" and implored Reagan to "please reconsider it."[21] Southern senators also received countless demands that they oppose O'Connor's nomination. A Baptist pastor in South Carolina told Strom Thurmond, "Those of us who have looked to President Reagan for moral leadership are stunned by this inconsistency."[22] A North Carolinian likewise wrote to Jesse Helms to complain that Reagan's decision was "a slap in the face" for southerners who "worked diligently to secure votes for this man who we thought was pro-life."[23] This grassroots anger led James Robison to call the White House and warn, according to Reagan aide Ed Thomas, that "there is a real likelihood that this is going to grow into a major issue, whereby the President will lose the support of those people who have backed him for years."[24]

But Thurmond, Helms, and other southern conservatives in Congress were more realistic. However unhappy they may have been with the choice of O'Connor, declaring war on the White House at such an early stage of Reagan's presidency would do little to benefit them in the long run. Breaking with Reagan would leave them with nowhere else to go and throw away any leverage they had over the direction of his administration. As the White House was aware, the threats coming from Southern Baptist leaders over the O'Connor nomination did not ultimately amount to much. "All they can do is moan and swear," said an unnamed Reagan advisor. "They can lead their troops but no one else will follow."[25]

Evangelical opposition did not derail Sandra Day O'Connor's nomination. In meetings with thirty-nine senators, O'Connor assuaged enough doubts among southern conservatives to smooth her passage to confirmation. Strom Thurmond, according to a White House memo, "raised the question of O'Connor being 'alright as long as Reagan is in,' implying she would vote liberal afterwards." O'Connor replied that she was "a conservative judge from a conservative state."[26] Reassured, Thurmond later stated his confidence that she would be confirmed to the Supreme Court. He had concluded that O'Connor "stands by the

Constitution" and declared, "I expect to support her."[27] Though he remained deeply skeptical, Jesse Helms also toned down his opposition. After a forty-minute meeting with O'Connor he told journalists, "I look forward to following this lady's career with great interest."[28] Weeks later, Helms still believed it was "disturbing that her legislative record is in direct opposition to the personal views which she expressed." Nonetheless, proclaiming his "faith in President Reagan's word," he voted in favor of confirmation.[29]

The most intransigent southerner was Alabama Republican Jeremiah Denton. During O'Connor's testimony before the Senate Judiciary Committee, Denton subjected her to a "tense and prolonged" period of questioning, telling the nominee he could not determine "where you're coming from philosophically" on abortion rights. Denton was the only committee member who refused to support O'Connor, instead voting "present."[30] Yet even Denton supported O'Connor in the Senate's unanimous confirmation vote on 21 September. President Reagan called Denton prior to the vote to allow him to express his concerns in person and ultimately won him over.[31] Pressure from fellow senators also prevailed over Denton's doubts about O'Connor. "Some colleagues said I'd be laughed out of the Senate if I voted against her," he told reporters. "I kept wondering, what would the President think of me, what would my colleagues think of me."[32] Personal loyalty to Reagan—along with a desire to afford him a historic political achievement early in his presidency—had clearly acted to focus the minds of Denton and other southern conservatives on Capitol Hill.

Outside Washington though, evangelical anger continued to simmer. A Religious Roundtable event in Dallas in early September was conducted with an air of "underlying fury," as praise for Reagan was mixed with condemnation of O'Connor. Pamphlets distributed to attendees described the nomination as a "broken promise," while James Robison warned that the United States risked approving a "death ethic" by appointing O'Connor. "I love and admire Mister Reagan," he continued. "I will be greatly surprised—shocked—if he doesn't help Americans to protect the unborn."[33] Yet by the time the Senate voted to confirm O'Connor, evangelical leaders' outrage had begun to abate. Jerry Falwell continued to shy away from overt criticism of the administration, but later maintained that the O'Connor hearings left him with "concerns regarding how she views the law relating to unborn life."[34] Falwell's Moral Majority released a guarded statement of neutrality on O'Connor. "Because of his [Reagan's] integrity, and because of his and the Republican platform's commitment to preserving unborn human life, and also because we do not believe the president would knowingly select a judge who did not share his own position on abortion," the statement read, "the Moral Majority has decided neither to support or oppose the confirmation of Judge O'Connor."[35]

At her confirmation hearings, O'Connor had been ambiguous on abortion. After admitting to supporting the decriminalization of abortion in 1970 (prior to the Supreme Court's 1973 *Roe v. Wade* judgement), she described that vote as a "mistake" and stated, "My own knowledge and awareness of the issues and concerns have increased since those days." She claimed a personal "abhorrence of abortion" but refused to express a view on the *Roe* decision, simply stating, "My personal views and beliefs have no place in the resolution of any issue."[36] Her subsequent Supreme Court career, however, showed that Christian Right concerns were justified. In almost twenty-five years as an Associate Justice, O'Connor's independent streak regularly made her the swing vote on the Court, and she repeatedly blocked efforts by conservative justices to restrict abortion rights.[37] Yet, at the time of her confirmation, few of those with reservations about O'Connor believed it was a wise battle to fight. Blocking her nomination would have placed both Christian Right leaders and conservative southerners in Congress in full-blown opposition to the Reagan White House, and for many social conservatives the administration still represented an exceptional opportunity to further their agenda at the national level.

During Reagan's first year in office, Christian Right leaders largely acquiesced to his focus on economic issues, even helping to enact the "Reagan Revolution" by lobbying Boll Weevil Democrats. Reagan aide Elizabeth Dole noted in a memo, "They went all out for Gramm-Latta and Hance-Conable although most of their hot button issues were not vitally affected by the economic bills."[38] But by the autumn, Christian Right demands for action were becoming hard to ignore. In a letter to

James Baker, Reagan's Chief of Staff, Moral Majority vice president Cal Thomas wrote, "The President said during the campaign, 'ask yourself if you are better off today than you were four years ago.' If we clean up the economy, but are still allowing the slaughter of one and one-half million unborn babies a year, I will not be able to say that we are better off at all." Thomas warned there would be a price to pay for inaction. "If a timetable hasn't been developed, it urgently needs to be developed. Without one, without something to share with our people, serious political consequences will develop, I assure you."[39]

As the year ended, there was relief among Reagan's advisors that they had delayed becoming entangled in controversial issues such as abortion. Elizabeth Dole observed, "In 1981 we managed to avoid major, national battles over most of the wide variety of issues which are near-and-dear to the hearts of grassroots conservative activists." However, with midterm elections approaching, the need to act was becoming more pressing. "We have just about reached the point where our passive support will be unable to hold many major conservative groups in line." Dole concluded, "Activists now require some signs from the Administration that it's worth continuing the fight in the next elections."[40] Even before Congress returned the following January, evangelical leaders and southern conservatives were expecting a shift in priorities. Strom Thurmond's press secretary told journalists, "We went along and spent most of 1981 on the economic issues. In return for that now, it is assumed that we'll be dealing with some of these social issues in 1982."[41] A Moral Majority spokesman claimed they had "waited patiently for a year" and now demanded movement from the White House: "We believe that all of our concerns, including the social issues, can be addressed by the administration at once."[42]

Rhetoric alone was no longer enough for Christian Right leaders. In March 1982, Morton Blackwell received a transcript of a forthcoming Moral Majority radio commentary from Cal Thomas, in which Thomas claimed the Reagan administration did not "seem to understand that our people are not motivated by Party, but by *principle*. Whether one wears a Republican or Democrat label is of less concern to us than the position the candidate or incumbent takes on important issues." Echoing Jesse Helms and Stanton Evans from the mid-1970s, Thomas warned, "We could form a third party so that we might still be able to vote and express our principles. . . . We need to change [the administration's] thinking to something more like this: 'If we don't do something soon for these conservatives, we're going to lose them and the back of the newly acquired Republican power will be broken.'"[43] Still the administration sought to delay. Blackwell replied to Thomas three weeks later, saying, "It's vital that we all keep the faith . . . and recognize that major progress can be made only through the accumulation of incremental gains." After seeing the urgency with which Reagan and his advisors had tackled their economic agenda, many southern conservatives regarded this incremental approach to social issues as insincere.[44]

The most pressing issue for the Christian Right was abortion. Alongside fundamentalist evangelicals, the broader pro-life campaign had long incorporated conservative Catholic and Mormon groups and had often been fraught with inter-denominational disagreements and disputes, tensions that reflected the increasing political power of conservative evangelicals. Prior to the late 1970s, Catholic groups had dominated the pro-life movement in the United States. However, the visibility of the Christian Right during Ronald Reagan's presidential campaign—and its work to elect anti-abortion candidates like Jeremiah Denton in Alabama—enabled Southern Baptist evangelicals to overtake the Catholic Church as the leading force in the movement by the start of the 1980s.[45]

During 1981, divisions in the pro-life movement triggered the emergence of two separate legislative attempts to roll back abortion rights. Jesse Helms, Congress's most high-profile champion of the Christian Right agenda, introduced the first to the Senate Judiciary Committee. The "Human Rights Bill" (known as the Helms bill) defined life as beginning at conception, effectively granting full legal rights to unborn babies and making anyone involved in conducting an abortion liable to prosecution for murder.[46] Unsurprisingly, the Christian Right regarded Helms' uncompromising legislation as the ideal way to achieve one of its foremost political priorities—the absolute reversal of *Roe v. Wade*. A second, more moderate, bill was a constitutional amendment designed to allow each state the right to formulate its own abortion laws. The Hatch Amendment (named after Utah Republican Orrin Hatch) was supported by a range of Catholic organizations.[47] In the view of one cardinal from New York, it was the option most likely to attract public support and seemed "capable of passage in Congress."[48] To conservative Southern Baptists, however, the Hatch Amendment was half-hearted and would allow abortion to remain legal in most states. There is a clear irony that a denomination consisting chiefly of conservative southerners should favor federal government action ahead of devolving rights to the state level, but this merely served to demonstrate just how inflexible many white southerners were on issues of social and cultural traditionalism.

Neither the Helms bill nor the Hatch Amendment had made any substantial progress by early 1982. Divisions in the pro-life movement allowed the Reagan administration to further delay its involvement. In January, for instance, Reagan sent a supportive statement to an anti-abortion rally outside the White House, demanding "greater protection for the most defenseless and innocent among us—the unborn child." Yet, at the same time, his press secretary claimed that pro-life disagreements were preventing the administration from acting: "Everyone agrees on the goal. They just don't agree on the way to get there."[49] A constituent of Kentucky Republican Larry Hopkins wrote to demand that he "contact President Reagan and ask him to concretely demonstrate his pro-life position by lobbying for this [Helms] bill with the same fervor with which he worked for his economic package."[50] Instead, the administration equivocated throughout the spring and summer. On 5 April, a letter from Ronald Reagan to Jesse Helms was released to the media. The president wrote, "Most important, it seems to me, is that the Congress consider one or more of the proposals in the near future."[51] But aside from offering lukewarm encouragement, Reagan did little to help resolve the differences of opinion over the two bills. Many pro-life campaigners suspected this was deliberate. An internal memo from the National Conference of Catholic Bishops observed that Reagan was "all too willing to seize on pro-life disunity as an excuse for inaction."[52]

In legislative terms, both measures were flawed. Jesse Helms's bill ostensibly required only a simple majority in both chambers. However, after Bob Packwood, a moderate Republican from Oregon, announced he would filibuster the legislation on the grounds that it was "a key civil liberties issue," sixty votes were required to break the filibuster—an unlikely target given the opposition of liberals and moderates in both parties.[53] Even if Helms' bill did pass, many legal commentators predicted that a federal court would deem it unconstitutional.[54] As a proposed amendment to the Constitution, Orrin Hatch's legislation faced the seemingly insurmountable task of winning two-thirds majorities in both House and Senate and then being approved by three quarters of all state legislatures. With polls showing popular support for abortion rights at almost 75 percent nationally, the chances of ratification were close to zero.[55]

By late summer, pro-life advocates had largely united behind a diluted Helms bill, after Jesse Helms removed definitions of life as beginning at conception and instead sought to end government funding for abortions. Debate in the Senate was "a contest of political wits and parliamentary maneuvering." Helms attached his legislation to a debt ceiling bill and then attempted to win over enough senators to overcome Bob Packwood's filibuster.[56] The pro-life movement now looked to Ronald Reagan. If the president was prepared to push for a cloture vote, there was a small chance the filibuster could be defeated and the bill could pass. The administration had reached "a critical moment in the relationship between the President and the pro-life activists," Morton Blackwell wrote in a memo. "Now that they are united, their attention is riveted on the White House to see if the President's actions speak as loudly as his words."[57]

Yet Reagan and his senior advisors remained circumspect about committing to an almost certainly unwinnable fight over a highly contentious issue. Publicly, the White House was determinedly evasive: "The President supports the Hatch Amendment, but not at the expense of, or in relation to, or instead of Cloture on the Helms Amendment."[58] Ultimately, this equivocation reflected the administration's profound indifference to any anti-abortion bill, but there was no longer a viable excuse not to support the Helms legislation. Reagan's powers of persuasion could prove crucial in encouraging sixty senators to vote for cloture. Administration officials suggested that "several Senators would probably be susceptible to quiet, private persuasion by the President on the merits of the measure."[59] Moreover, as media reports pointed out, with midterm elections a few months away this was opportune timing for White House strategists keen to "re-establish [President Reagan's] ties to the social-issue constituency."[60]

The debate over Helms' legislation came to a head in late summer, as the Reagan administration's ties to the Christian Right showed signs of fraying. The *Atlanta Constitution* reported that conservative evangelicals were doubting Reagan's commitment to their cause, with the administration's "lack of movement" being viewed as "immoral compromise and crass political expediency." Again, Cal Thomas of the Moral Majority voiced his organization's discontent. "There are no monuments in Washington to budget balancers; there are monuments to those who took a stand on principles," said Thomas. "I don't think he [Reagan] has come through at all for us." As was often the case, Thomas's boss, Jerry Falwell, struck a more encouraging tone, saying he retained "personal confidence" in Reagan. Still, even Falwell hinted at increasing disillusionment, admitting, "I'm a little anxious we haven't had some aggressive support."[61]

Reagan only intervened in support of Helms' legislation at the eleventh hour. Compared to his efforts on behalf of his budget and tax bills, his lobbying was perfunctory at best. In total, he telephoned seven senators and wrote a letter to six others which called on them to "stand and be counted on this issue. . . . It is vitally important for the Congress to affirm, as this amendment does, the fundamental principle that all human life has intrinsic value."[62] Such a half-hearted intervention was never going to be enough to convince the Senate to vote for cloture. After three votes failed during mid-September, with none coming close to the sixty-vote target, the Helms legislation was effectively dead. With an eye clearly on the midterms, Reagan's spokesman argued the president's efforts had demonstrated he was "very serious about the abortion issue."[63] Jesse Helms begged to differ, giving journalists a blunt assessment of Reagan's lobbying: "I'm not aware of any votes he picked up for us."[64] Helms' bill proved to be the closest anti-abortion campaigners came to achieving their goal at any point during Reagan's presidency. The probability of Democratic gains in the upcoming elections meant the chances of passing a pro-life measure in the next Congress were even more remote.

When Orrin Hatch's proposed constitutional amendment came up for a vote in the Senate in June 1983, it too fell a long way short of the required two-thirds majority. Though most supporters of the Hatch amendment had given their backing to Jesse Helms, Helms did not return the favor. He ultimately refused to support the amendment, instead voting "present" and arguing that giving states the right to set abortion laws "does not advance the principle that human life is inviolable. . . . It surrenders forever this principle in the illusory hope that some lives may be saved." Once again, Ronald Reagan's token lobbying had little effect on the outcome, with Hatch himself admitting he doubted Reagan's efforts "had much to do with it."[65]

The failure of both measures prompted a shift in strategy for pro-life campaigners, as they moved away from attempting to reverse the *Roe* decision through Congress and directed their focus towards the Supreme Court. In the short term, this actually served to bolster southern evangelical support for Reagan during his 1984 re-election campaign, despite his administration's obvious lack of enthusiasm for the anti-abortion cause. After the Hatch Amendment's defeat, a spokesman for a pro-life campaign group argued that it "makes abortion a key issue in the 1984 election. . . . President Reagan alone can add the fifth and decisive justice to the Supreme Court."[66] Jerry Falwell likewise declared his belief that a second Reagan term would see the appointment of at least two anti-abortion justices who would "make the court safe for the strict interpretation of the Constitution into the 21st century."[67] In the longer term, the appointment of conservative Supreme Court justices would become the chief political priority of the Christian Right, reinforcing its loyalty to the GOP well into the twenty-first century.

After the Hatch Amendment failed, angry southern conservatives criticized Reagan for his reluctance to become involved. To Stanton Evans, the Reagan White House was "business as usual, not much different from any other Republican administration of our lifetime. It has been an Administration populated by corporate executive types." In Evans' view, "People used to the decorum of the boardroom back off from controversy."[68] His critique was not far from the truth. Fears of a negative reaction from either side of the abortion fight certainly weighed heavily on an administration which placed far greater emphasis on economic priorities than on social issues. The White House's wary and detached attitude towards the anti-abortion campaign left many southern conservatives and Christian Right leaders feeling betrayed. Reagan had failed to live up to the promises he had made in 1980. His administration's evasiveness over anti-abortion bills reflected a deep reluctance to expend political capital on an issue which simply did not rank highly on the Reaganite agenda.

Alongside abortion at the very top of the Christian Right's list of political priorities was the issue of prayer in public schools. The battle over school prayer had profound constitutional implications. 1982 marked the twentieth anniversary of the *Engel v. Vitale* Supreme Court ruling, which deemed government mandated prayer in public schools to be a violation of the establishment clause of the First Amendment. Though it surprised many in 1962, *Engel* was nonetheless accepted by a broad spectrum of Christian organizations, including the moderate leadership of the Southern Baptist Convention. Unsurprisingly, resistance was strongest among conservatives and fundamentalist evangelicals in the South, where the practice of prayer in schools was most commonplace. In Congress, North Carolina senator Sam Ervin claimed the Supreme Court had "made God unconstitutional," while his colleague from Georgia, Herman Talmadge, argued the decision gave "aid to the disciples and followers of atheism." Arkansas pastor and televangelist Billy James Hargis proclaimed, "I do not think there has been a more serious blow against Christian freedom."[69] As the political influence and activism of fundamentalist evangelicals increased during the late 1970s, so, too, did calls for *Engel* to be overturned and prayer restored to public schools.

Action on school prayer, like the rest of the Christian Right agenda, was largely side-lined during the early months of Reagan's presidency. Predictably, it was Jesse Helms who ultimately triggered the legislative fight over school prayer by introducing a bill to the Senate which, by means of a simple majority vote, sought to remove the issue from the jurisdiction of US federal courts. Opponents condemned the measure as "court stripping," with Montana's Democratic senator Max Baucus saying the bill did "an end run around the constitutional-amendment process and thereby undermines the Constitution itself."[70] Though Reagan had declared his backing for a school prayer amendment, the White House refused to publicly support the legislation after the Justice Department expressed concerns it would prove unconstitutional. In the end, Helms' bill was voted down by the Senate in September 1982.[71]

Reagan had announced the previous May that he would submit a constitutional amendment to Congress reversing the *Engel* decision. "The law of this land has effectively removed prayer from our classrooms," he told attendees at a Rose Garden ceremony to mark the National Day of Prayer. "The amendment we'll propose will restore the right to pray."[72] Jerry Falwell was delighted by the announcement, declaring it to be "the light at the end of the tunnel we have all worked and hoped and prayed for."[73] There was a widespread view among Reagan's aides that, unlike anti-abortion legislation, a school prayer amendment would be the easiest way to keep conservative southern evangelicals happy. As one aide explained in an internal memo, "Unlike several of the other social issues, it has very little downside—there is not a large segment of the population likely to mobilize against us on the issue." Moreover, he argued, Christian Right groups "need our action on some issue to activate their members for the Congressional elections and for 1984."[74] While public opinion was firmly opposed to reversing *Roe v. Wade*, support for a constitutional amendment permitting prayer in public schools stood at 76 percent in 1980 and had remained largely constant for a decade.[75] Previous attempts at passing an amendment had failed during the 1970s, but with Republicans controlling the Senate and increased pressure from evangelical groups, a school prayer amendment now appeared to have a greater chance of success. Although public support had dropped slightly to 69 percent by March 1982, polling still indicated it was politically safer ground for the Reagan administration than any form of anti-abortion legislation.[76]

Nonetheless, moderate Protestant, Eastern Orthodox, and Jewish organizations released a joint statement opposing Reagan's proposal on the grounds it would "violate the constitutional separation of church and state and heighten religious tensions in the schools."[77] For Reagan's Christian Right supporters, the strength of this opposition emphasized the need for a powerful, unified campaign in favor of the prayer amendment. Religious Roundtable founder Ed McAteer—an influential figure in numerous evangelical groups—therefore spent the early months of 1982 working to win the support of the Southern Baptist Convention.[78] The SBC, representing a denomination which amounted to 6 percent of the US population, was the largest Protestant organization in the United States and the second-largest religious body behind the Catholic Church.[79] If McAteer won the SBC's backing for Reagan's amendment, it would add enormous weight to the campaign for school prayer.

An internal power struggle during the late 1970s and early 1980s had resulted in fundamentalist evangelicals regaining control of the Southern Baptist Convention. Despite a midcentury period of moderate leadership, during which the SBC had supported not only the Supreme Court's 1962 *Engel* ruling but also the *Brown v. Board of Education* decision in 1954 and *Roe v. Wade* in 1973, many of the organization's grassroots members were deeply traditionalist on social issues. Culturally-conservative white southerners remained its core demographic. In 1979, fundamentalist Memphis preacher Adrian Rogers was elected SBC president, riding the same conservative evangelical wave that saw the establishment of Jerry Falwell's Moral Majority.[80] Rogers' election signified that the SBC's longstanding adherence to the separation of church and state was over. Rogers and his successors during the 1980s—Bailey Smith, James Draper, and Charles Stanley—sought to follow Falwell's example by advancing a socially conservative agenda on the national stage, loudly protesting both abortion and the Equal Rights Amendment.[81]

In mid-1982, however, the SBC remained officially opposed to mandated school prayer, largely due to a residual belief among its membership that church and state should remain separate. A proposed resolution supporting a school prayer amendment had been defeated at the 1980 SBC convention—one of the moderates' last achievements as conservative leaders tightened their grip on the organization.[82] But at its June 1982 convention in New Orleans, Ed McAteer worked persistently to place conservative supporters of school prayer on the SBC's resolutions committee and directed them to frame their arguments in the context of religious liberty. Charles Stanley, pastor of the First Baptist Church in Atlanta, board member of the Moral Majority, and future SBC president, told the convention that the *Engel* ruling had been "one step in the demoralizing of America." Reagan's amendment would "protect our religious freedom," he argued. "If we continue to remain silent we will one day lose our freedom in our church houses as well as the school houses."[83]

Mcateer's maneuvering worked. On 17 June, SBC members voted by a margin of three to one to endorse Reagan's proposed constitutional amendment on the basis that it contained "no violation of those ideals inherent in the separation of church and state."[84] This was a radical shift. Once committed to the separation of church and state, the Southern Baptist Convention was now backing an amendment that would effectively imbue the legal and constitutional framework of the United States with the cultural traditionalism of the conservative South. According to Tom Wicker in the *New York Times*, theology was now "being sacrificed to the political (I refrain from saying secular) goal of a constitutional underpinning for religion."[85] Signaling that the conservative takeover of the SBC was now complete, Adrian Rogers wrote to Reagan aide Morton Blackwell in the wake of the vote, "The rank and file of Southern Baptists are solidly behind the Prayer Amendment proposed by the President."[86]

Following the SBC's endorsement, the campaign in support of Reagan's amendment came to be dominated by Southern Baptists—operating largely under the umbrella of the Project Prayer Coalition—and was therefore able to avoid the interdenominational disputes that handicapped the pro-life movement. The Christian Right's dominance of the campaign also gave rise to reports that Ed McAteer had collaborated with the White House to shift the SBC's stance on school prayer. Morton Blackwell, Reagan's liaison to religious groups, strongly denied any administration involvement. Writing to a Kentucky pastor, Blackwell claimed, "Neither I nor anyone else at the White House asked anyone to take any action regarding the New Orleans convention."[87] Nonetheless, the vote was a boost for Reagan's amendment. As a White House aide observed, "This is extremely significant and could be a major factor in the eventual passage of the proposal. (The Baptists have 13.7 million members and are a significant voting bloc throughout the South.)"[88] Tom Wicker also noted the importance of the SBC's reversal. "It's hard to imagine . . . Congress passing the school prayer amendment with the Southern Baptists opposing it, as they have in the past." SBC members could exert substantial pressure on Democrats "in Southern states or Congressional districts they need to hang on to or regain, but in which the Southern Baptists are a formidable force."[89]

Although White House aides were aware that the school prayer amendment was a comparatively safe way to demonstrate support for the Christian Right agenda, Reagan's senior advisors still remained doubtful about expending political capital on social issues. The president's announcement of the school prayer amendment in May 1982 was far later than many of his supporters had hoped. The fact that the administration had waited so long to address the issue meant that Congress had barely three months to pass legislation before campaigning started in earnest for that November's midterms. A vote in the Senate was likely, but a lack of time made the Project Prayer Coalition's efforts to lobby House members much more difficult. Gary Jarmin of Project Prayer told Morton Blackwell, "The primary reason we are in this predicament is because the White House waited much too long to get this legislation introduced. . . . Without some major backing from the White House, there will be no vote in the House."[90]

Throughout the summer of 1982, Reagan and his advisors were once again preoccupied by economic issues, most notably the passage of TEFRA. The school prayer amendment received scant consideration from either the administration or the Senate. Three days of poorly attended committee hearings brought the issue some media attention, but little action followed.[91] In August, Moral Majority executive Richard Godwin demanded to know, "If Reagan thought that his support for [social] issues would get him into office, why does he now think that only symbolic gesturing will keep him in office?" Godwin warned that the upcoming two years "could be the last two years of the Reagan administration."[92] By late 1982, with Jesse Helms's legislation defeated and the school prayer amendment stuck in committee, the issue was moribund on Capitol Hill. Yet Reagan continued to make rhetorical gestures towards the Christian Right agenda. In a radio address in January 1983 he declared, "I strongly support an amendment that will permit our children to hold prayer in our schools. . . . We didn't get that amendment through the last Congress, but I'll continue to push for it in the next Congress."[93] However, Reagan's State of the Union address three days later demonstrated that his real priorities lay in economics and foreign policy. In a 5,500-word speech, school prayer was dispensed with in just 21 words and mentioned as merely one element of the administration's education plan.[94]

The 98th Congress was scarcely more productive for the Christian Right. Wrangling over a school prayer amendment intensified after other versions were introduced to the Senate. One, proposing a form of silent group meditation or prayer, was viewed with deep suspicion by conservative evangelicals and was voted down after the administration opposed it. According to White House memos, the Moral Majority mounted a "substantial mailgram campaign" in support of Reagan's amendment, while the SBC undertook "large amounts of local activity directed at the Senators."[95] But still the campaign to restore prayer in schools suffered from a lack of White House leadership, despite Reagan's claim it was a "revered American tradition." The amendment finally died after a Senate vote on 20 March 1984. Despite being approved by fifty-six votes to forty-four and winning the backing of every southern senator, the bill failed to reach a two-thirds majority.[96] A greater effort from Reagan might conceivably have helped his amendment reach the required sixty-seven votes in the Senate, but the chances of success in the House—particularly after Democrats increased their majority in 1982—were slim.

Nonetheless, the distinct lack of presidential interest was noted by both senators and the media. "President Reagan was not willing to really get a prayer amendment," in the opinion of Arizona Democrat Dennis DeConcini. Christian Right leaders were coming to the same conclusion, as they repeatedly witnessed the Reagan administration fail to pursue social issue legislation with any great determination.[97] This may simply have been the consequence of the White House's preference to focus on economic and foreign policy issues. Over time though, it started to seem like a deliberate strategy. As sociologist William Martin has argued, the Reagan administration's attitude towards the Christian Right was to "give support to versions of their bills which would ultimately fail, or to support constitutional amendments that were sure to fail but would rally the troops."[98] These tactics were deployed once again in the run up to the 1984 presidential election. The GOP platform contained some of the most socially conservative language of any in the party's history, notably in calling for a "human life amendment" to ensure that unborn babies were protected by the 14th Amendment.[99] Similarly, passage of the Equal Access Act in August 1984, which enforced the right of students to assemble on public school grounds for religious gatherings, helped to rally Christian Right support. Jerry Falwell optimistically claimed that "'equal access' gets us what we wanted all along," though in reality the legislation's practical impact was minimal.[100] Still, after the failure of anti-abortion and school prayer legislation, the Equal Access Act was a small victory for the Christian Right. Importantly for the Reagan White House, it was something tangible they could point to when seeking to reassure conservative evangelicals.

Support for Reagan among southern evangelical voters remained solid as the 1984 election neared, despite his inattentiveness to their agenda.[101] This was chiefly because the Democratic ticket consisted of Walter Mondale and Geraldine Ferraro. Southern conservatives regarded Mondale—Jimmy Carter's vice-president and a former senator from Minnesota who was campaigning on a moderate platform—as typical of the Democratic Party's untrustworthy elite.[102] Likewise, as a liberal, a Catholic, and the first woman on a major party's presidential ticket, Geraldine Ferraro was not likely to win over traditionalist Southern Baptists. While Reagan did not need to fear his opponents in the South, the president's concern was whether disenchantment over his record on social issues would lead conservative southerners and evangelicals to not vote at all. Yet in the weeks before the election, Southern Baptist preachers were once again urging their congregations to vote for Reagan. With few legislative successes to show for their support during his first term, they focused instead on Reagan's rhetorical embrace of their agenda. "I think he's taken stands on some issues that have showed some Christian integrity," one pastor from Dallas told the *Boston Globe*. "He's been sensitive to religious groups. . . . I feel good about what he's done."[103]

After Reagan's reelection, Jesse Helms again introduced legislation to remove school prayer from the jurisdiction of the federal courts, but his second attempt at court stripping was quickly defeated.[104] The issue fell by the wayside once the Democrats regained control of the Senate in 1986. While Reagan's amendment was a legislative failure, the debate over prayer in schools acted as an important unifying factor between conservative southern evangelicals and the Republican Party. The GOP gained a valuable political weapon, as the Southern Baptist Convention became a powerful force in organizing and encouraging white southern conservatives to turn out in support of Republican candidates. Since 1982, SBC leaders have never endorsed a Democratic presidential candidate. Thanks to Ed McAteer, the school prayer issue confirmed the SBC's transformation into a loyal part of the Republican base.

After Reagan's landslide victory in 1984, the political power of conservative evangelicals appeared to be on an upward trajectory. Jerry Falwell claimed the Moral Majority and its Christian Right allies registered an additional three million voters in 1984 alone. It is hard to determine just how important the Christian Right's registration drive was to Reagan's re-election, but it certainly played a significant role in Republican victories further down the ballot. The Moral Majority worked particularly hard in North Carolina, where Senator Jesse Helms—whom Falwell described as "a national treasure"—narrowly won re-election, beating Democrat Jim Hunt by 52 percent to 48 after a record turnout. Helms' campaign was undeniably helped by Ronald Reagan's own popularity in the state, as the relieved senator underscored by thanking the president in his victory speech. But the Moral Majority's work to register 150,000 new voters for Helms also proved critical in a race decided by fewer than 90,000 votes.[105] Across the South, there were similar stories of the Christian Right's impact on congressional races. In Texas, Republicans won five House seats regarded as priorities by evangelicals, after Christian Right volunteers distributed tens of thousands of anti-abortion leaflets. Such efforts also helped to increase the number of conservative Republicans in the state legislature.[106]

On Capitol Hill, however, the influence of the Christian Right was already starting to wane. Debates over abortion and school prayer would effectively be side-lined during Reagan's second term. Arguably, the Christian Right's declining influence had been apparent even before his reelection. In late 1983, Reagan had sparked fury among conservative evangelicals when he proposed the establishment of diplomatic relations with the Vatican. The Southern Baptist Convention condemned the proposal, while Jerry Falwell—somewhat ironically given his support for school prayer—decried it as "a clear violation of the separation of church and state."[107] The most vociferous opposition came in an extraordinary letter Reagan received from Bob Jones Jr., the chancellor of Bob Jones University in South Carolina. Though not as media friendly as Falwell, Jones had long been one of the most zealous voices among fundamentalist Southern Baptists. He was scathing about Reagan's lack of attention to the Christian Right agenda. "Just exactly what has your administration accomplished toward fulfilling your election promises?" he asked. "Where have you lifted your hand to help God's people who are under attack?" The proposed appointment of an ambassador to the Vatican was, according to Jones, "a deliberate violation of your oath to uphold the Constitution" and "an insult to every Protestant church and every non-Catholic American. It will bring a curse upon our nation and make us, as a nation, the servant of Antichrist."[108]

By the time the Reagan administration established diplomatic relations with the Vatican on 10 January 1984, evangelical anger had largely subsided.[109] The Christian Right's ardent support for Reagan had, paradoxically, left it with little leverage over the administration's actions. It had become so apparent that conservative evangelicals had no other political home to go to that they had left themselves limited room for maneuver. The furor over relations with the Vatican demonstrated that Christian Right leaders would forgive almost any disloyalty Reagan showed to their cause. Their cries of betrayal gradually lost impact. Once Reagan won reelection, his administration felt able to push aside social issues and focus on foreign and economic priorities without fear of losing substantial support from southern evangelicals.

Internal power struggles and financial difficulties also damaged the Christian Right during the late 1980s, while personal scandals involving high-profile televangelists such as Jim Bakker and Jimmy Swaggart tarnished the popular image of evangelicalism.[110] Nonetheless, the Christian Right still had opportunities to advance its agenda. Reagan's appointment of Antonin Scalia to the Supreme Court in 1986, for example, was broadly welcomed. Despite his Catholicism, Scalia's originalist interpretation of the Constitution, particularly his opposition to abortion and dislike of gender- or race-based affirmative action, chimed with the views of southern conservatives.[111] Reagan's nomination of Robert Bork a year later, however, proved more problematic. Bork believed *Roe v. Wade* was unconstitutional, was a longstanding critic of an activist judiciary when it came to civil rights, and his appointment would have tilted the Court rightwards on social issues.[112] Unsurprisingly, conservatives in the Southern Baptist Convention were quick to support his nomination and Jerry Falwell's Moral Majority distributed a letter calling on evangelicals to contact their senators to demand that Bork be appointed. Falwell declared that evangelicals were "standing at the edge of history" and fighting for Bork's confirmation "may be our last chance to influence this most important body." The SBC and Moral Majority both kept the White House regularly informed of their intensive lobbying efforts.[113]

Yet, on 23 October 1987, the Senate rejected Bork by fifty-eight votes to forty-two.[114] His views on civil rights law, highlighted by his opponents in their own lobbying campaign, decided the outcome. Just over a year from the next election, even conservative southern Democrats were wary of appointing a Supreme Court justice who seemed eager to refight painful civil rights battles. Louisiana Democrat J. Bennett Johnston, far from a liberal when it came to affirmative action and civil rights, told journalists, "Maybe this is unfair to Judge Bork. . . . But we just cannot take a chance."[115] Conservative voters in Louisiana were quick to condemn Johnston's view. "A vote against Bork is a vote against the mandate President Reagan received in Louisiana," wrote one. Moreover, it was a vote against "an overwhelming majority that rejected the outmoded policies of the liberal Democrat Party in favor of a return to the family values we Southerners cherish."[116] Still, Johnston and his fellow southern Democrats were cognizant of the increasing importance of African Americans to the Democratic Party in their region and were wary of alienating a potentially crucial primary demographic. Responding to another disgruntled constituent, Johnston stated his fear that Bork's nomination could "reopen wounds that have long since healed" and said his preference was for a "Supreme Court nominee who maintains conservative principles yet does not prove so abhorrent to such a large segment of our society."[117]

Even Strom Thurmond, who voted in Bork's favor, told the media that next time "I would recommend [the White House] not send somebody as controversial."[118] The Bork defeat showed just how much the Christian Right's ability to exert political pressure had dissipated. The man ultimately confirmed to the vacant Supreme Court seat, Anthony Kennedy, was regarded as more moderate than Bork. Though he remained conservative on many issues, he often proved to be a swing vote on the Court alongside Sandra Day O'Connor, siding with her on abortion, school prayer, and marriage rights.[119] Overall, Reagan's record of appointing conservative justices to lower courts led Jerry Falwell to declare that his "chief legacy is what he has done with the federal judiciary."[120] But of Reagan's three appointees to the Supreme Court, only Scalia would prove a reliable ally for conservative evangelicals. During their time on the Court, the legal opinions of both Sandra Day O'Connor and Anthony Kennedy would regularly frustrate the Christian Right agenda.

With their influence in Washington steadily diminishing during Reagan's second term, Christian Right leaders were reduced to lobbying for the White House's foreign policy initiatives rather than their own social conservative agenda. As conservative southerners, Christian Right leaders had been closely aligned with Reagan's anti-communist rhetoric throughout his first term, enthusiastically supporting the administration's nuclear build-up and increases in defense spending. Whereas liberal religious organizations condemned Reagan for encouraging an arms race, the Christian Right publicly promoted administration foreign policy. "Realizing that evangelicals might be the only religious group that would endorse his policy," Daniel Williams observes, "Reagan made a concerted effort to use them as publicists."[121] While Reagan was denouncing the USSR as an "evil empire" to an audience of evangelicals in Florida in March 1983, for instance, the Moral

Majority was holding a "Peace Through Strength" rally in Washington to counter the campaign for a nuclear freeze.[122] But during his second term, Reagan pursued compromise with the Soviet Union and a global reduction in nuclear weapons—alarming many conservative evangelicals. Still, the Moral Majority's "Liberty Report" newsletter preferred to criticize the Democratic-controlled Senate for ratifying the INF Treaty in 1988 rather than reproach Reagan for negotiating it.[123] As they had demonstrated in the debate over textile imports, southern conservatives were quick to absolve Reagan of personal responsibility for policies they did not support.

Christian Right support for Reagan remained strong throughout the 1980s, despite the lack of administration effort when it came to social issues. As evangelical leaders like Jerry Falwell had repeatedly discovered, being close to power did not equate to being powerful. Yet the Christian Right's proximity to power during the Reagan administration, combined with rhetorical support from the president himself, moved conservative southern evangelicalism to the foreground of US politics. Reagan was, as a *Wall Street Journal* article suggested, the Christian Right's "entrée into the halls of political respect and power."[124] To many Southern Baptists, this alone was a substantial victory. The Christian Right's visibility during the Reagan presidency paved the way for more tangible successes, both in terms of electing allies to Congress and in pushing for the appointment of socially conservative justices to the Supreme Court. It also enabled the movement to develop into the most prominent vehicle for southern conservative identity on the national political stage.

In the late 1980s, as the Moral Majority became embroiled in legal and financial difficulties, the broader Christian Right appeared beleaguered and riven by internal disagreements. Jerry Falwell gradually withdrew from political activity as Reagan's presidency ended. In the summer of 1989, he announced the dissolution of the Moral Majority, claiming, "Our mission has been accomplished."[125] It was a clear indication of the decline in the Christian Right's political power. It may have gained precious little in policymaking terms, but it is unquestionable that the Christian Right's backing for Ronald Reagan was a vitally important factor in the rise to political prominence of conservative evangelicals—and thus crucial to the white South becoming a Republican electoral stronghold. Reagan's popularity among Southern Baptists filtered down to the congressional level, playing a decisive role in the campaigns of men such as Jesse Helms and Jeremiah Denton and helping to make GOP candidates across the region more competitive.

The conservative mythology that developed around Reagan after he left the White House has often portrayed his presidency as a golden age for southern evangelicals. This was far from the reality. After Reagan's death in 2004, Terry Mattingly, a commentator on religion and politics, summed up Reagan's relationship with the Christian Right. "Millions of Southern Baptists saw Reagan as a near-messiah," Mattingly wrote. "For Southern Baptist conservatives, Reagan offered hope that the cultural revolution of the Woodstock-Roe era might be overturned. They were wrong. Nevertheless, these conservative Baptists lost their historic fear of politics and jumped into the public square."[126] The Reagan administration was wary of expending political capital on social issues. Yet because he was the first president to openly embrace the Christian Right agenda, at least rhetorically, Reagan's status as a hero to conservative evangelicals was assured. Though it failed to make legislative progress and still lacked substantial congressional support, the Christian Right agenda became increasingly embedded into the Republican Party's identity during the Reagan era. It moved into the mainstream of American politics and, in the case of abortion, would remain there for decades to come. But the Christian Right looked to Ronald Reagan for active support in other areas too. When it came to issues of racial politics—be it school busing or civil rights legislation—southern conservatives and evangelicals viewed him as an ally in the White House.

6. "Affirmative Action Is Un-American"
Southern Racial Conservatism and the Reagan White House

Over six weeks in the spring of 1985, the *New York Times* ran a series of articles on race relations in "The Changing South." They served as a damning indictment of the region's failure to tackle racial injustice and inequality. In Dawson, a small town in rural Georgia, reporters found that "an unwritten code perpetuates what was once enshrined in law." Informal segregation persisted in many public restrooms, African Americans avoided certain restaurants, bars, or motels in which they knew they would not be served or allowed to rent a room, and one woman told of medical clinics that used separate entrances for blacks and whites. Similar stories were uncovered in Yazoo City, Mississippi, in Demopolis, Alabama, and in Augustine, Texas, as well as "countless" other small towns across the rural South.[1] Other forms of racial inequality were rife. The median income for white families in Mississippi was significantly lower than the white average nationwide, yet still almost double that of black families in the state.[2] Though the 1965 Voting Rights Act had increased black electoral participation, the race-based gerrymandering of districts and the manipulation of voting laws remained commonplace, as white conservatives sought to maintain their political power. White flight had left some public school districts in Little Rock, Arkansas, almost entirely African American, while thousands of white students attended private, all-white academies. Little Rock, the *Times* noted, was "not the only place in the South facing school resegregation. The phenomenon is widespread."[3]

Black and white southerners existed warily side by side with relatively little social interaction. As a black lawyer observed about life in Selma, Alabama, "There is a separation of black and white here to an extent almost as widespread as it was 20 years ago."[4] Likewise, an African American council member in Greensboro, North Carolina, claimed that while significant progress had been made since the time of Jim Crow, "that doesn't mean that white resistance has gone away. In many ways, it has just become more subtle, more institutionalized."[5] At times, white resistance remained shockingly explicit. In March 1981, Ku Klux Klan members in Mobile, Alabama, lynched a young black man—the first lynching in the South for twenty-two years.[6] In 1982, the *Christian Science Monitor* described Emory Folmar, the mayor of Montgomery, Alabama: "With a pistol strapped to his belt to symbolize his commitment to law and order, he defends 'honest, hard-working white men' against 'welfare blacks.' 'Affirmative action,' he concludes, 'is un-American.'"[7] Even southerners' contrasting perceptions of race relations carried echoes of the Jim Crow era. "Many whites say people want to stick with their own kind; blacks say they are discriminated against," the *Times* reported. "Whites also feel that race relations are good and that there are no racial problems; blacks say the opposite is true."[8] Many white southerners had yet to reconcile themselves either to racial integration or to increased black political strength. Millions more, even those accepting of integration, resented what they saw as excessive federal activism on behalf of African Americans.

Reagan's use of the phrase "states' rights" at the Neshoba County Fair in 1980 had encouraged many in the white South to believe he would be a formidable ally in Washington. So, too, did his declaration, two weeks after winning the presidency, that the longstanding use of court-ordered busing to integrate public schools was a "failure" and his promise to sign anti-busing legislation as soon as possible.[9] Likewise, the Republican platform had been unequivocal when it came to affirmative action: "Equal opportunity should not be jeopardized by bureaucratic regulations and decisions which rely on quotas, ratios, and numerical requirements to exclude some individuals in favor of others."[10] As he entered the White House, southern conservatives expected Reagan to take their side in a number of ongoing, racially-charged, political and legal battles.

The early weeks of his administration seemed to confirm their hopes. The Reagan White House inherited a legal dispute between the Department of Education and the state of North Carolina over the speed at which the University of North Carolina (UNC) was desegregating its college system. In a state where 22 percent of the population was black, African Americans comprised just 8 percent of students on historically white campuses and the number of white students attending the state's traditionally black colleges was similarly small.[11] Since 1970, the Department of Education had maintained that UNC had failed to sufficiently integrate its colleges. During the Carter presidency, Health, Education, and Welfare Secretary Joseph Califano threatened to cut $90 million from UNC's federal funding unless the situation was rectified.[12] University officials, backed by the state GOP's newly dominant conservatives, repeatedly condemned the legal action. Highlighting once again the white South's paradoxical approach to the federal government, they decried the threat to cut UNC's federal funding at the same time as defending North Carolina's right to run its education system free from Washington interference.[13]

With Reagan in the White House, UNC's supporters were optimistic the federal government would soften its stance. John East, North Carolina's recently elected Republican senator, raised the subject at confirmation hearings for incoming Education secretary Terrel Bell. East argued that North Carolinians felt "badgered" and "humiliated" by the legal case against UNC. In response, Bell promised "a dramatic change" in the federal government's approach.[14] The White House, the Education Department, and UNC undertook quiet negotiations, resulting in a compromise that reflected the new administration's relaxed stance on enforcing civil rights legislation. Guidelines were announced in June for UNC to increase white enrollment at black colleges and black enrollment at white colleges, but these encompassed lower targets than the Department of Education had previously demanded and set no firm quotas. The Reagan administration also declared that UNC had not been in violation of desegregation laws and the threat to its funding was dropped.[15] Civil rights organizations were quick to criticize the deal. A lawyer for the NAACP claimed the administration had "sold out civil rights," while a former Carter official argued that it showed Reagan and his cabinet were "not interested in enforcing the civil rights laws that prohibit segregation in education."[16] In contrast, Jesse Helms and John East were delighted. Helms—who had helped to instigate the negotiations—declared it "the end of a long ordeal that should never have occurred in the first place," while East credited Reagan's election to the presidency with bringing about a "dramatic change in attitude" at the Department of Education.[17]

In part, the swift settlement of the UNC case resulted from the White House's desire to prioritize its economic agenda and the wariness of Reagan's senior aides about becoming entangled in potentially controversial non-economic issues. Yet the resolution of the case so clearly in UNC's favor was indicative of Reagan's philosophical hostility towards the concept of big government. Rooted in his own interpretation of states' rights, Reagan believed control of education policy should lie with states and not with the federal government. In his memoirs, Reagan referred to officials in the Department of Education as "elite bureaucrats" who forced "ultimatums" onto schools and colleges about what should and should not be taught.[18] His anti-statism was such that on the campaign trail in 1980 he pledged to abolish the Department of Education entirely. This objective never came close to being achieved, but Reagan's opposition to federal involvement in education undoubtedly set the tone for the reversal over integration at UNC.[19]

The administration's handling of the UNC case also illustrated the disconnect between the way Reagan perceived his own approach to civil rights and the way he was viewed by black Americans. Reagan's personal views echoed colorblind conservative notions of equality of opportunity and a belief that civil rights laws should protect everyone regardless of race. But from the outset of his presidency, many African Americans regarded Reagan with deep skepticism. They suspected that his rhetoric of equal opportunity and personal liberty cloaked an intent to reverse years of progress in minority rights. The UNC deal—along with a similar case in which the Department of Education dropped a challenge to the Florida state university system—did little to quell those concerns.[20] In contrast to the Nixon administration, during which the Justice Department pursued a pragmatic, moderate approach towards civil rights and affirmative action (one rather at odds with Nixon's private views), it appeared the Reagan White House intended to withdraw the federal government from involvement in long-running legal battles to enforce civil rights laws.[21] At his confirmation hearing, Terrel Bell had suggested the Department of Education's new approach was representative of a shift in attitude right across the administration. The change was happening, he said, "not only because of my beliefs, but also because of the views of this administration and the views of President-elect Reagan."[22]

Alongside Bell, other administration appointees shared Reagan's views. Prominent among them was new Assistant Attorney General for Civil Rights, William Bradford Reynolds. Not long after his Senate confirmation, Reynolds told a conference on equal opportunity, "Racial and sexual preferences are at war with the American ideal of equal opportunity for each person to achieve whatever his or her industry and talents warrant."[23] His words alarmed civil rights groups. Weeks later, their concerns were compounded when Reagan appointed William Bell, a black conservative who opposed affirmative action, as chairman of the Commission on Civil Rights. The ousted chairman, Arthur Flemming—a liberal veteran of Eisenhower's cabinet who had been appointed to head the commission by President Nixon—accused the new administration of having "as an objective the weakening of civil rights laws."[24] Throughout 1981, statements by Reagan appointees appeared to justify Flemming's condemnation, and at the same time strengthened the hopes of Reagan's southern supporters. At first sight, the Reaganites' colorblind conservatism was a far cry from the unreconstructed racial attitudes historically associated with white southerners. But as the UNC case demonstrated, Reaganites and southern conservatives often found themselves in the same place when it came to civil rights and affirmative action, despite approaching such issues from different philosophical directions. Over the coming years debates over civil rights created a succession of political minefields for the Reagan administration. Conservative southerners regularly charged it with not acting swiftly enough to reverse affirmative action laws, while liberal critics accused it of callousness and insensitivity towards black Americans.[25]

Accusations of insensitivity on the part of the Reagan administration increased during the debate over renewal of the Voting Rights Act. Conservative southern senators regarded the enforcement sections of the Act as particularly unfair to the South. Under "preclearance" rules nine southern states—and parts of thirteen others, including California and Wyoming—required Justice Department approval for any change in their voting laws.[26] Jesse Helms opposed renewal of the Act outright, just as he had opposed the original legislation and all subsequent revisions.[27] Other southern conservatives, among them Strom Thurmond, chair of the powerful Senate Judiciary Committee, pledged to support renewal if the preclearance requirements were extended to the entire nation. Civil rights groups dismissed their stance as an attempt to undermine the law by making it too onerous to enforce.[28] There was, moreover, a clear majority in the House for extending the Voting Rights Act without changes, as demonstrated by an overwhelming 389–24 vote in October 1981.[29]

The House vote placed pressure on the administration to clarify the president's views. In terms of national public opinion, supporting the measure's extension would have been politically uncontroversial, a straightforward acknowledgement of the importance of the civil rights cause. Instead, Reagan sat on the fence. His ambiguity suggested to many that he shared the reservations of southern conservative senators.[30] Though he repeatedly asserted his support for voting rights, Reagan hinted his agreement with Strom Thurmond that enforcement provisions should cover every state. His instinct remained that civil rights protections must apply to every American. Shortly before his inauguration, Reagan had told *Time* magazine: "I was opposed to the Voting Rights Act from the very beginning, but not because I was opposed to the right to vote. I was opposed to the act being applied only to several states. I say make it apply to everybody."[31] But as recently as 1980, he had framed his opposition in less righteous language, claiming that the original Voting Rights Act had been "humiliating to the South."[32]

According to a June 1981 memo, several administration advisors were worried about potential political costs in the white South. Morton Blackwell argued that "a wrong decision here could be very damaging to the President and virtually all of his southern political support." At the same time, it was "highly unlikely to increase support for the President among groups which are already militantly opposed," namely African Americans and civil rights organizations. Alienating southerners in Congress, Blackwell feared, could harm the administration's economic agenda. "A wrong decision here would not only antagonize those conservative Republican leaders we have in the South, such as Trent Lott," Blackwell believed, "but it would also deal a devastating blow to our southern Democratic allies who are the key to most of our past and hoped for victories in the U.S. House."[33] His concerns proved unfounded—all but a handful of Boll Weevils backed renewal of the Voting Rights Act in October—but even the legislation's enormous margin of victory in the House did little to encourage the administration to publicly support it.[34] After the vote, White House aide Elizabeth Dole argued that Reagan should continue to avoid discussing the "nuts and bolts" of the bill and maintain a "take the high road" approach.[35]

White House advisors were right to be concerned that Reagan could lose southern support over the Voting Rights Act. To many conservatives across the South, the Act remained an egregious injustice. A Mississippian wrote to Jesse Helms declaring that blocking renewal would "prevent a Second Reconstruction," "reverse the leftward drift of national politics," and "save freedom and Americanism."[36] At the heart of white southern opposition to renewal was the belief that the law itself was prejudiced. Numerous southerners contacted their congressmen and senators to demand that they resist attempts at renewal. To one, the Act was "punitive" and "dangerous."[37] To another, it was "the worst discrimination against the South by our government since the disgraceful treatment inflicted upon us during Reconstruction."[38] One resident of Dalton, Georgia, asked Ed Jenkins "how can anyone justify application to only certain states?"[39] A constituent of Alabama Democrat Bill Nichols announced he was "sickened by the black attitude that their rights must be won—even at the expense of others! They feel . . . that their rights are tantamount to the rights of others. This is open, blatant discrimination."[40] Another demanded that Nichols oppose renewal of the Voting Rights Act and told him, "I appreciate your support of President Reagan . . . . I voted for President Reagan [because] of his promise to try to cure our country of too much FEDERAL interference." Nichols ultimately voted against renewal on the grounds that the Act should apply nationwide.[41]

While the House's renewal legislation sought to make the preclearance requirements—still chiefly directed at southern states—

permanent, it also included a mechanism for states to "bail out" of the provisions under certain circumstances. This did little to appease conservative southern senators, who maintained that the House bill reinforced the Voting Rights Act's unfairness. Their objections led to a lengthy legislative struggle. On 4 November 1981, junior policy advisor Mel Bradley, one of the few African Americans on Reagan's staff, argued that the politically wise course of action was to simply back the House bill. "A supportive position on the voting rights bill *as is* will gain for the president the good will and respect of many Americans who now question our agenda," Bradley wrote. "Technical reservations . . . will be viewed as a signal that this administration is trying to avoid protecting the voting rights of all."[42] Bradley's advice went unheeded. The White House's eventual stance on the legislation—advocating a ten-year extension of the Act and arguing for a simpler mechanism for bailing out of the enforcement provisions—largely satisfied the wishes of southern conservatives.[43]

The Reagan administration quickly found itself in troubled waters. A *Boston Globe* editorial argued, "Opponents of a strong Voting Rights Act see in President Reagan a possible ally, or at worst, a non-objector of efforts to seriously weaken the voting rights law."[44] The White House faced opposition from a huge majority of Representatives and almost two-thirds of senators who supported the House bill, as well as civil rights groups, who staged a symbolic 140-mile march to the Alabama State Capitol in Montgomery in support of voting rights.[45] In the end, the Senate compromised on a version of the House bill with a twenty-five-year limit which passed by eighty-five votes to eight in June 1982. Among those voting against were Jesse Helms and John East, Jeremiah Denton of Alabama, and Independent Virginia senator (and former Democrat) Harry F. Byrd Jr.[46] Helms and East even went so far as to stage a futile filibuster.[47] Significantly, Strom Thurmond supported the bill. As his biographer Joseph Crespino has written, Thurmond's vote represented "cold calculus." Given the increased importance of black voters in South Carolina, where they comprised a larger portion of the electorate than in Helms' North Carolina, there was "simply no political advantage . . . in playing the heavy."[48]

The Reagan administration ultimately reached the same conclusion. By the time the Voting Rights Act Extension was signed on

29 June 1982, the White House had publicly welcomed passage of the bill and even arranged a signing ceremony of the type normally reserved for the president's flagship economic legislation. Undoubtedly, this was an attempt to alleviate some of the criticism Reagan had encountered. The *Washington Post* noted that he "used the occasion to declare himself an unswerving defender of the right to vote . . . and to diminish the significance of his widely heralded differences with civil rights groups." But the ceremony also indicated anxiety among Reagan's advisors that accusations of racism were taking a political toll.[49]

The previous March, aide Edwin Harper had written to the president arguing that the administration's ambiguity on the Voting Rights Act, its stance on integration in education, a lack of minority appointments to government positions, and budget cutbacks which disproportionately hurt black Americans were having a "cumulative effect." When added together, these had "created distrust and bitterness within the minority community" and led to "a widespread sentiment that the Administration is 'anti-black' or engaged in a systematic effort to roll back civil rights achievements of the past." Harper added, "We have not helped ourselves. . . . A series of mishaps in timing and tactical judgment have strengthened the impression of insensitivity."[50]

The White House reinforced these perceptions in its response to the campaign for a national holiday in memory of Martin Luther King Jr. Despite overwhelming black support, the campaign had made little progress since King's assassination in 1968. Southern conservatives had been vocally opposed, arguing that the only men previously honored by a national holiday, Christopher Columbus and George Washington, were instrumental to the nation's existence in a way that King was not. But by 1981, King's birthday was established as a holiday in seventeen states and renewed debate over the Voting Rights Act gave the campaign further momentum.[51] Moreover, with black voter registration rising by more half a million between 1980 and 1982 and then passing ten million in 1983, the wishes of black voters could not be ignored.[52] Twenty states had voted to observe a King holiday by 1983, including several in the South. Recognizing the prevailing mood, even Strom Thurmond had quietly accepted the idea.[53] Legislation to create a federal holiday appeared increasingly likely.

When the House voted in favor of a King federal holiday by 338 votes to 90 in August 1983, Jesse Helms—its most vocal opponent on Capitol Hill—vowed to filibuster and defeat the legislation in the Senate.[54] In the chamber on 3 October, he condemned King's "calculated use of nonviolence as a provocative act" designed to trigger "overreaction by authorities," argued that "the legacy of Dr. King was really a division, not love" and asserted that King's "political views were those of a radical political minority that had little to do with racial minorities." King's opposition to the Vietnam War, Helms claimed, had sprung from his "Marxist" beliefs: "He and his principal vehicle, the Southern Christian Leadership Conference, were subject to influence and manipulation by Communists."[55] After his filibuster failed, Helms took legal action in vain to unseal documents from the FBI's surveillance of King.[56] When that was dismissed, John East joined Helms in trying to delay the King holiday legislation by proposing alterations to create additional federal holidays, supposedly designed to honor James Madison, Thomas Jefferson, Marcus Garvey, and Hispanic Americans. But Helms' provocative last-ditch tactics also failed, and the bill finally passed the Senate on 19 October 1983 by seventy-eight votes to twenty-two. Helms claimed the legislation had been passed in an "atmosphere of intimidation, political harassment . . . screaming and yelling and threats."[57]

Though Helms denied his actions were motivated by racism—claiming "I'm not a racist, I'm not a bigot"—an aide later admitted the senator had been "playing the race card." It certainly played well in North Carolina, where 83 percent of whites supported Helms's stance.[58] Racial overtones were evident in the views of many white southerners opposed to the King holiday. Some wrote to commend Helms for trying to block the legislation. Praising his "most gallant stand," one correspondent went on to claim, "Dr. King brought violence, hatred and division on a par unseen since Reconstruction." Another described King as an "infamous negro" and a "known Communist."[59] Strom Thurmond was condemned for supporting the bill, with one South Carolina resident claiming he had "sold out to the blacks." Demonstrating that race was a motivating factor for many white southerners in switching to the GOP, the constituent added, "There is a good possibility you will lose much of the white vote. . . . I have supported the Republican Party for many years, but if they are going to turn their backs on what we've stood for through the years, perhaps I will take another look." Thurmond was accused by another constituent of being so concerned about the black vote that he was "afraid to vote your true feelings."[60] The segregationist Democrat and former governor of Georgia, Lester Maddox, also chimed in to condemn the bill, saying the "cowards" who supported it should "give serious consideration to leaving the country on a permanent basis."[61]

Given its broad national backing, supporting the legislation was the wisest course of action for the White House, yet Reagan personally opposed it. He believed the economic cost of a King federal holiday was prohibitively expensive and warned, "We could have an awful lot of holidays if we start down that road."[62] Reagan also shared some of Helms's views on King. Even in the days after King's assassination in 1968, he had been skeptical of the motives of civil rights campaigners and had shown an inability to grasp King's importance to African Americans. Speaking on the day of King's funeral, Reagan claimed the murder was committed by "those who want dissent and insurrection." It was "a great tragedy that began when we began compromising with law and order and people started choosing which laws they'd break."[63] Fifteen years later, when former governor of New Hampshire Meldrim Thompson wrote to demand a veto of the King holiday legislation, Reagan replied, "I have the reservations you have but here the perception of too many people is based on an image not reality. Indeed to them the perception is reality."[64] Asked at a press conference whether he agreed with the claims made by Helms, he responded, "We'll know in about 25 years, won't we?" before adding, "I don't fault Senator Helms' sincerity with regard to wanting the records opened up." Yet Reagan grudgingly announced he would sign the bill: "I would have preferred a day of recognition for his accomplishments . . . but since they seem bent on making it a national holiday, I believe the symbolism of that day is important enough that I'll sign that legislation when it reaches my desk."[65]

By the day of the signing ceremony, Reagan's reservations about King had seemingly vanished. Instead, his remarks artfully linked King's legacy to his own administration's approach to civil rights and affirmative action. He claimed King "had awakened something strong and true, a sense that true justice must be colorblind." In a similar vein,

Reagan suggested that King's civil rights campaigning had fundamentally redeemed the United States from racial prejudice: "Across the land, people had begun to treat each other not as blacks and whites, but as fellow Americans."[66] On more than one occasion during his presidency, Reagan cited King's legacy to argue that civil rights laws should guarantee equality of opportunity for all and affirmative action programs and federal protections for black rights were no longer required. Each time, his interpretation of King's oratory was highly selective, focusing on the "I Have a Dream" speech while carefully ignoring King's more radical critiques of American inequality. In 1986, when criticizing the use of racial quotas in employment, Reagan argued, "We want what I think Martin Luther King asked for: We want a colorblind society."[67]

African American leaders were far from convinced by Reagan's attempts to coopt King into the cause of colorblind conservatism. To them, his initial stance on the King holiday legislation was further evidence of a callous approach towards civil rights. His lack of enthusiasm for the bill effectively offered tacit support to Jesse Helms' racially tinged condemnations of King. For varied reasons, the Reagan administration found itself taking the side of white southern conservatives in a series of civil rights debates. The anti-statist conservatism of senior administration officials had led Reagan's Education Department to side with both North Carolina and Florida in disputes over racial integration in their university systems. Reagan's deeply ingrained anti-communism meant he was quick to believe the worst accusations about Martin Luther King. When it came to Voting Rights Act renewal, political calculations had clearly been to the fore—the administration's fear of alienating white southerners engendered a cautious approach widely seen as racially insensitive. Yet these were far from the only race-related issues facing the Reagan administration. The White House was also drawn into a legal dispute that spoke even more viscerally to the story of southern racial prejudice. It involved one of the most racially conservative institutions in the South: Bob Jones University.

Based in Greenville, South Carolina, Bob Jones University (BJU) was a bastion of the white South's cultural traditions, both in terms of religious teaching (alumni included numerous fundamentalist preachers) and, most controversially, in terms of race. During the 1960s, BJU conferred honorary degrees upon ardent segregationists including Strom Thurmond, Lester Maddox, and George Wallace. Citing Scripture as a moral basis for racial separation, the university refused to admit black students until 1971, when it acquiesced after years of pressure from the federal government.[68] The reversal was prompted by the Nixon administration's decision in 1970 to overturn longstanding rules relating to tax exemptions for independent educational institutions. Under new guidelines, the Internal Revenue Service (IRS) could deny tax exemptions to organizations not deemed to be "charitable." To have charitable status, organizations were now required to abide by federal public policy—including the policy of nondiscrimination. Threatened with the loss of its tax exemptions, BJU opened its doors to African American students. Yet it still maintained a strict ban on interracial dating. In 1976, after years of legal wrangling, this ban prompted an effort by the IRS to revoke Bob Jones University's tax-exempt status. BJU stood accused of having continued to practice racial discrimination after the 1970 rule change and was therefore liable for payment of taxes dating back six years. After Bob Jones University challenged the IRS's case, the dispute gradually made its way through various tiers of the US legal system during the late 1970s.[69]

It was still doing so when Ronald Reagan made a campaign stop at BJU in January 1980. Declaring he was "delighted to be here" at a "great institution," he described the 6,000 white students and staff in attendance as a "most impressive audience."[70] A subsequent Harvard University report into the BJU case observed, "Whether Reagan knew that BJU practiced and advocated racial separation is unclear, but he seemed quite impressed by the University."[71] Bob Jones III, chancellor of BJU and grandson of the university's founder, did not offer an explicit endorsement, but multiple standing ovations attested to Reagan's longstanding popularity on the campus. In the mid-1970s, activists from Bob Jones University had been among the broader wave of conservative insurgents entering southern Republican parties with the intent to overthrow established party leaders. As part of their struggle for control of the South Carolina GOP, they had backed Reagan's primary challenge to Gerald Ford in 1976.[72] By 1980, the Republican Party platform gave BJU's supporters cause to believe that if he was elected Reagan would repay the favor by ending the IRS's legal challenge. The platform's position was unambiguous: "We will halt the unconstitutional regulatory vendetta launched by Mr. Carter's IRS Commissioner against independent schools."[73] It did, however, neglect to mention that the "vendetta" had begun under Richard Nixon and was continued by the Ford administration.

Still, the Reagan administration largely ignored the issue during 1981, thereby arousing the anger of southern conservatives in Congress. Mississippi Republican Trent Lott was particularly irate—several colleges in Mississippi had similar tax exemptions which were now in jeopardy. On 30 October, Lott told Treasury Secretary Don Regan that the administration's support for the IRS against Bob Jones University was "both legally and politically indefensible." Writing to Reagan's Solicitor General, Rex Lee, he declared himself "more than a little disturbed" that the White House's ambivalence conflicted with "a specific pledge of the President's platform." He continued, "Mississippians and many of their fellow citizens supported President Reagan simply to end this kind of unwarranted interference."[74] Lott was not alone in making such arguments. In December, Strom Thurmond—a trustee of Bob Jones University—also met with the IRS commissioner to underline his own objections.[75]

Apparently unrelated to these communications, the Reagan Justice Department reviewed the federal government's position in the expectation that the case would reach the Supreme Court in early 1982. BJU's argument had now been combined with a similar case involving Goldsboro Christian School in North Carolina, which still refused to admit black students. Both colleges claimed that because their racial policies were founded in religious belief, the actions of the IRS were a violation of the First Amendment. Justice Department officials were initially inclined to maintain government support for the IRS, but the involvement of more senior figures prompted a policy reversal. Deputy Attorney General William Bradford Reynolds believed the Nixon administration's 1970 decision had been misguided, and unelected bureaucrats (namely the IRS) did not have the power to determine whether an organization was conforming to public policy. However, there was also a second, more political, line of thinking. If the administration supported the IRS in a Supreme Court battle against BJU and Goldsboro, it would be reneging on Reagan's campaign pledge to end federal interference in the affairs of private Christian schools. The Justice Department settled on its position by early January: it was outside the remit of the IRS to judge whether organizations were abiding by public policy. The administration would therefore ask the Supreme Court to render the case moot.[76]

Ronald Reagan was intentionally absent from this debate. In December, a memo written by Peter Wallison, General Counsel in the Treasury Department, emphasized the administration's desire to "preserve the President's position of non-involvement in this matter, whichever way it goes."[77] Reagan's personal view was, however, jotted succinctly on an aide's log of incoming mail. Next to an entry informing him of Trent Lott's view that the White House must intervene in the Bob Jones University case, Reagan wrote, "I think we should."[78] His four-word note would prove important in finalizing the administration's position, as it indicated that the Justice Department's decision to no longer support the IRS chimed with the president's instincts.

When the administration's new stance was announced on 8 January 1982—at 4:00 p.m. on a Friday to keep it "low key"—it met with immediate hostility from civil rights groups and much of the national press.[79] According to the leader of the NAACP, Benjamin Hooks, the shift was "nothing short of criminal" and gave "encouragement to racist and reactionary groups in this country."[80] The head of the organization's Georgia branch accused the White House of "attempting to turn back the clock by instituting segregation of the races."[81] The administration's decision was "not in the tradition of conservatism, nor in the tradition of Republicanism," claimed the *Baltimore Sun*. "It is in the tradition of racism."[82] Likewise, the *Los Angeles Times* called it a "reprehensible reversal" which "shows contempt for the attempts of minorities to participate fully and freely in American society."[83] *Boston Globe* columnist Robert A. Jordan argued that the White House's "deliberately weak posture on civil rights enforcement has given a clear signal to certain constituents that efforts to keep some blacks out of the mainstream of American society may draw nothing more than a blink from the Administration's eye."[84]

Among conservative southerners—surely foremost among the

"certain constituents" Jordan had in mind—the reaction bordered on delight. The Moral Majority claimed, "BJU has every right to operate according to religious convictions, whether they are unpopular or not."[85] The administration's reversal was "a vindication of the correct position."[86] Bob Jones III said the decision "in effect gives us a clean bill of health." It had answered "the prayers of God's people. Nobody has put any pressure on the administration." BJU's congressional allies similarly reveled in what was, from their perspective, a major victory. For Strom Thurmond, the administration had brought "an end to a decade of trampling on religious and private civil rights by the Internal Revenue Service." He concluded, "Freedom of religion will no longer have to take a back seat to bureaucratic determinations of public policies. President Reagan has kept another campaign promise."[87]

The administration's decision combined legal conviction and political pragmatism. Southern conservatives like Trent Lott had undoubtedly pushed the White House into action, but at the same time the case was already being considered by the Justice Department. Still, when details of Lott's communications and President Reagan's handwritten note leaked to the media, the story became one of cynical calculation. The Reagan White House appeared to have shifted policy simply to appease conservative southerners. Once again, the administration found itself aligned with southern conservatives in an apparent rejection of African American rights. When political opponents seized on the president's note to demonstrate that he personally approved of the racial discrimination at BJU and Goldsboro, Reagan felt it necessary to defend himself. "I am opposed with every fiber of my being to discrimination," he declared at a press conference on 19 January. "I have been on the side of opposition to bigotry and discrimination and prejudice— and long before it ever became a kind of national issue under the title of civil rights." He took personal responsibility for the political firestorm, saying, "I'm the originator of the whole thing, and I'm not going to deny that it wasn't handled as well as it could be." Yet Reagan also disingenuously claimed that the administration's intention had simply been to encourage Congress to act. Exemplifying just how much the administration had painted itself into a corner, Reagan's attempted justification was so convoluted it barely made sense. He insisted, "What we set out to do was to change that procedure and stop the Internal Revenue Service from doing this and then to have Congress implement with law the proper procedure . . . and to have set in law the fact that tax exemptions could be denied to schools that—and educational institutions that practiced discrimination."[88]

That had clearly not been the motivation of Lott or Thurmond. However, it did now become administration policy. After a White House meeting in which two black policy advisors outlined African American perceptions of Reagan as personally racist, a strategy was devised to defuse the issue. The administration introduced hastily drafted legislation to Congress that gave the IRS authority to withdraw tax exemptions from discriminatory schools and colleges. Despite Reagan's claim, this had never been the original intention, and the move failed to assuage the anger of liberals and civil rights campaigners who correctly saw it as an attempt to escape a political crisis of the administration's own making.[89] Although BJU and Goldsboro would both keep their tax exemptions until the bill passed, the proposed legislation angered southern conservatives. Jesse Helms told journalists, "If President Reagan or anybody else proposes to confer on some bureaucrat the power to decide whether a tax-payer is violating the law, then I shall oppose."[90] Bob Jones III urged BJU students to campaign against the bill, telling them, "You know very well there is no discrimination at this school. There is absolute racial harmony at this school."[91] Ten days later, Jones described Reagan's proposal as "an abomination and a sell-out."[92]

Across the South, there was fury among grassroots conservatives and evangelicals. A correspondent from the Church of God in Lexington, Kentucky, told Republican Larry Hopkins that the bill was "a contradiction to the division of rights between church and state."[93] A couple from Georgia wrote to Democrat Ed Jenkins, "We do not consider a school that prohibits interracial dating and marriage to be racially discriminatory, but to be a matter of religious conviction." According to member of the Smyrna Baptist Church in Union, Mississippi, the bill was "a 'green light' for the IRS to commit flagrant abuses of power against *all* churches."[94] Others directed their ire towards Reagan personally. "Mr. Reagan has a funny way of getting government off our backs," wrote one North Carolinian. "He's turning the IRS loose to plunder and destroy our churches. Mr. Reagan has betrayed some of his best friends." A member of the Moral Majority wrote that they had been "delighted" by Reagan's original decision but described the new legislation as "a tragic threat" to religious freedom. "Mr. President," he concluded, "this is not a racial issue, but a 'freedom of religion' issue. I sincerely hope that you will again rise to the occasion and 'get the government off the people's backs' as you so often stated during the campaign."[95]

In Congress, the legislation was doomed. Christian Right organizations vowed to lobby against it, and they were joined in opposition by congressional liberals who claimed the IRS already had the authority to withdraw tax exemptions. Unnamed Reagan allies were variously slamming the phone down on senior White House aides and offering predictions of "an unbelievable bloodbath."[96] According to records of White House phone calls, even the most supportive congressmen had reservations. Georgia Republican Newt Gingrich's response was cautious at best: "Have we talked with Christian conservatives? [He is] with us but doesn't want to offend our friends." His fellow Republican Bill Dickinson of Alabama was more critical: "Matter handled poorly. . . . From our point of view it hurt us."[97] Few in Congress wanted to get involved in such a contentious issue. "Bipartisan opposition to pursuing any legislation is still strong," reported Reagan aide Nancy Risque in mid-February 1982. "It seems that many on the Hill are hoping that the Administration will file a second brief that would allow the Supreme Court to pursue the issue."[98]

After the bill quickly died in both chambers of Congress, the issue returned to the Supreme Court. Somewhat farcically, both the Reagan White House and the Justice Department were now in legal opposition to the Internal Revenue Service. When hearings began in April 1982, the administration maintained its view that the IRS did not have authority to withdraw tax exemptions to BJU and Goldsboro.[99] When the ruling was finally announced a year later, however, the court disagreed. By a margin of eight to one, the Supreme Court rejected the arguments put forward by Bob Jones University, Goldsboro, and the federal government and concluded that the IRS did have the necessary authority. Notably, Reagan appointee Sandra Day O'Connor sided with the majority. The decision was, as the *Los Angeles Times* proclaimed, "a stinging rebuke to the Reagan Administration." Chief Justice Warren Burger's majority opinion declared that "racial discrimination in education violates deep and widely accepted views of elementary justice." The Supreme Court also rejected arguments by BJU and Goldsboro that the IRS was infringing on their religious freedom.[100]

Asked for comment by journalists, President Reagan responded to the humiliating outcome by saying simply, "We will obey the law." Predictably, Bob Jones III was less docile. He expressed "pity for the heathens who sit on the Supreme Court, pity for their damned souls and their blighted minds." Religious freedom, he said, had been "murdered" by "eight evil old men and one vain and foolish woman."[101] Since the case began, relations between the White House and Bob Jones University had deteriorated. By December 1983, Jones was writing to tell Reagan he felt "betrayed, deceived, and used by a man in whom he put his confidence. . . . You have not fulfilled your promises to your Christian supporters, and you have been a party to the betrayal of religious freedom in America." Accusing Reagan of being a president who "while promising much, basically does nothing at all," Jones concluded, "why should we vote to reelect a man who has broken every promise he has made to protect and preserve religious freedoms and Christian schools?"[102]

A memo written by White House aide (and future Chief Justice of the Supreme Court) John Roberts illustrated the administration's increasing exasperation with the demands being made by southern conservatives and fundamentalist evangelicals. Roberts believed the "audacity" of Jones was "truly remarkable, given the political costs this Administration has incurred in promoting the interests of Fundamental Christians in general and Bob Jones University in particular." In response, Roberts prepared a "restrained reply to his petulant paranoia . . . telling Jones, in essence, to go soak his head."[103] The BJU episode highlighted the Reagan administration's difficulties in satisfying some of the more extreme elements of its southern conservative support. It also underlined the risks involved in pursuing the Reaganite aim of reducing federal involvement in education, particularly when it impacted on an issue as profound as racial segregation. A combination of misguided legal thinking, a desire to appease congressional southern conservatives, and a significant lack of political acuity led to humiliation for the Reagan administration. The episode also demonstrated that education remained a vital battleground in the struggle over the rights of black southerners.

One of the most divisive issues of the 1970s reared its head once again during Reagan's first term: the debate over using court mandated busing to desegregate public schools. In late 1980, a federal judge had ordered the imposition of busing to desegregate the school system in Rapides Parish in Louisiana's rural heartland, an area with a long history of resisting racial integration. The defiant response of white residents—particularly local Louisiana state judge Richard Earl Lee—received national media attention. Among hundreds of children affected by the busing order, three white girls from the rural community of Buckeye became the focus of the dispute after their parents challenged the order and their case developed into a cause célèbre.[104]

The three were pupils at an all-white high school but were among those instructed to attend a predominantly black school fifteen miles away, with black students being bused in the opposite direction. Their parents petitioned Judge Lee, who vowed to defy the court busing order and in doing so became a hero to the local white population. Over the next two weeks, Lee escorted the girls to school, always making sure to pass by crowds of journalists and photographers on the way.[105] Every hour, radio stations in the area played "The Ballad of Judge Lee," a specially composed country song that included the refrain, "Judge Lee, he will set the people free."[106] The Ku Klux Klan announced their intention to protest outside Buckeye school and, some months earlier, a burning cross had been placed opposite the offices of a black attorney campaigning for the integration of local schools. When the "Buckeye Three" case came before a district judge in Alexandria, hundreds of white demonstrators gathered on the steps of the city's federal courthouse to support Judge Lee, alongside a much smaller, and entirely black, group of civil rights protesters.[107] Though the families involved maintained their complaint was solely about their daughters' right to attend the local school, the issue was inextricably bound up in the racial history of the South.

The dispute was eventually resolved when Judge Lee accepted the busing order under threat of legal action for contempt of court. But instead of attending the black school, the three girls and many other white pupils from Buckeye eventually enrolled in a local, all-white, private academy.[108] Georgia Democrat Lawrence McDonald later demanded the impeachment of the federal judge who imposed the busing order on Rapides Parish, but his crusade was short-lived.[109] The day before Reagan's inauguration, the principal of Buckeye high school, Charles Waite, wrote to the president-elect calling for action to curb the power of federal judges. Telling Reagan that it was "imperative that this letter be read by you personally," he said, "I can think of no more important a matter than the one of which I am writing you—that of the threat of lost rights of the majority of individuals in this country." Waite declared, "We are losing control over local government more and more each year. . . . If something isn't done to stop this abuse of power, the idea of 'government of the people, by the people, and for the people' will be a thing of the past."[110]

Few busing disputes received the widespread media coverage given to events in Louisiana, but the Buckeye case showed that school desegregation remained a source of anger in the white South. For many white southerners who had helped make Reagan president, busing remained an intolerable federal incursion into their lives and communities. One couple from Louisville, Kentucky, reflected the views of millions of conservatives in the South: "We think forced busing should be done away with since it was forced on our community by the Supreme Court. . . . To us this looks like dictatorship."[111] Having listened approvingly to Reagan's states' rights rhetoric on the campaign trail, southern conservatives were expecting quick action to end court busing orders.

To Reagan's aides, the issue appeared politically advantageous. Polling suggested large numbers of Americans—even African Americans—believed the policy had outlived its usefulness. In March 1981, around half of black respondents agreed that the policy "has caused more difficulties than it is worth."[112] Later that year, an unattributed

White House memo advised, "Of all the highly emotional so-called social issues, busing is probably the most universally attractive from the standpoint of this Administration." With some exaggeration, the memo asserted, "A majority of blacks and a whopping majority of whites agree with the President on this issue."[113] Yet, with Reagan showing scant interest in the subject, the Justice Department did little to alter its stance on busing. Though the head of the Civil Rights Division, William Bradford Reynolds, clearly shared Reagan's skepticism of affirmative action, the department was staffed by long serving attorneys reluctant to oppose busing orders that had been imposed under the Carter or Ford administrations.[114] Southern state governments became increasingly agitated by the new administration's lack of urgency. The Democratic attorney general of Texas, Mark White, wrote to inform Reagan of his "extreme disappointment" that the administration was still requesting busing orders be used to desegregate public schools. Texan conservatives had been incensed when the Reagan administration advocated mandatory busing in the school systems in Portland and Port Arthur. "I had hoped that when you took office," an embittered White told Reagan, "the country would see a new policy in the Justice Department in which busing was no longer recommended by our highest leaders in government."[115]

In 1981, the Senate saw the introduction of two legislative attempts to ban busing. One, inevitably, was led by Jesse Helms and sought to allow students to choose which school they attended without the involvement of the federal government.[116] The other was crafted Louisiana Democrat J. Bennett Johnston, a prominent opponent of busing in the 1970s. Johnston crafted a stringent anti-busing amendment to the Justice Department's appropriations bill which was then also introduced to the House of Representatives by Louisiana Republican Henson Moore. With Judiciary Committee chair Strom Thurmond acting as cosponsor, it was clear the congressional anti-busing drive was a bipartisan—and principally southern—initiative. Johnston's bill prevented courts from adding over ten miles or thirty minutes to a child's round trip to school and permitted the reopening of cases in which a court had imposed a journey greater than ten miles. Furthermore, it forbade the Justice Department from initiating any case in which it intended to impose mandatory busing.[117]

Though Johnston insisted it was "not the intention of this bill to turn back the clock," his work met with approval across the white South.[118] Richard Earl Lee, the state judge in the Buckeye case, wrote to praise Johnston's efforts: "The people are certainly proud of you for the action you have taken to abolish busing." Similarly, the Superintendent of Schools in Charleston, South Carolina, wanted "to commend you for taking this initiative. . . . It certainly should have the effect of minimizing busing."[119] Over the coming months, the Johnston and Helms proposals were combined into one legislative push, with Alabama Democrat Howell Heflin also joining the anti-busing drive by adding a provision allowing the Justice Department to seek the repeal of existing busing orders. Media reports observed that Heflin's addition was "intended primarily for the South." After overcoming determined filibuster attempts by liberal senators, their amendment to the Justice Department bill was approved in March 1982 by fifty-seven votes to thirty-seven.[120]

Yet, as with so much of the southern conservative social agenda, the legislation received lackluster public support from the Reagan administration. Instead, it served to highlight divisions between the Justice Department and some of the more conservative White House advisors. Assistant Attorney General Theodore Olson's ambivalent testimony on the bill before a House Committee outraged Reagan aide Morton Blackwell. "This testimony could have been expected from the Justice Department during the Ford and Carter administrations," Blackwell fumed. "He suggests misleadingly that the current widespread practice of forced school busing is an old wound which is healing and must be left alone. . . . The opponents of busing worked hard to elect President Reagan and surely have reason to expect some leadership from his Administration in their behalf."[121] But little leadership was forthcoming. The Democrat-controlled House quickly stripped the bill of its more stringent anti-busing measures, though it did approve an amendment preventing federal funds being used on legal cases that sought to impose busing.[122]

After the Johnston-Helms amendment failed, southern conservatives again pinned their hopes on the White House, but once more in vain. In November 1983, Moral Majority leader Jerry Falwell offered his advice: "President has not spoken out strongly on busing legislation., Strategy appears to hinge on begging the Courts to reconsider. President did not support Johnston-Helms Amendment in time for any action." He concluded that Reagan "must have a higher profile on busing."[123] But it was not until Reagan was seeking re-election that he and his Justice Department showed greater urgency. Campaigning in Charlotte, North Carolina, in October 1984, Reagan gave his most explicit denunciation of busing since 1980. Democrats, he claimed, "favor busing that takes innocent children out of the neighborhood school and makes them pawns in a social experiment that nobody wants. We've found out it failed."[124] In reality, as a *Charlotte Observer* editorial pointed out, Charlotte had been one of the first cities required to employ busing to desegregate its school system in the 1960s, and for many the policy's success was a source of local pride.[125] Nonetheless, the fact that the president finally appeared to be showing interest in the issue, even if it was largely for electoral reasons, offered hope to conservative southerners.

By the mid-1980s, Reagan's Justice Department was indeed beginning a gradual shift from legal neutrality on busing towards outright opposition, most obviously in cases concerning schools in St. Louis, Missouri, and Bakersfield, California. The shift came about partly, William Bradford Reynolds later claimed, because long-serving attorneys "either left or got on board."[126] It was also likely spurred by the upcoming election, particularly given the Reagan administration's failure to act on his 1980 campaign pledge to bring busing to an end. Following Reagan's reelection, Attorney General William French Smith—who had led the Justice Department in his typically "quiet and undramatic manner"—was replaced by Ed Meese.[127] Previously one of Reagan's most bullish senior aides, Meese's leadership gave the Justice Department greater impetus. Where Smith and William Bradford Reynolds had a distant working relationship, Ed Meese's arrival meant Reynolds found himself newly empowered to tackle busing cases.[128]

Reagan's southern conservative supporters even began to see legal efforts to overturn existing busing orders, something his administration had previously been highly reluctant to attempt. The most prominent case related to the school system in Norfolk, Virginia. Like Rapides Parish, Norfolk was an area that fought hard against desegregation during the 1950s and 1960s. After the imposition of busing in the early 1970s, Norfolk's schools had gradually integrated, to the point that the city began a legal case arguing the order was redundant. For the first time, a legal judgment was required to decide how long busing should continue after a school system had been desegregated. Given that many school systems across the United States could potentially make a similar argument, the case had enormous significance. However, civil rights groups and local African American leaders were skeptical, viewing the case as attempting to "legalize segregation in public education again" and to safeguard white political power in the city. Media reports also pointed out that the progress made in integrating Norfolk's school system would be quickly undone by ending busing, because "10 of 35 elementary schools would become more than 96 percent black."[129]

Nevertheless, under Ed Meese's leadership, the Justice Department's view was that busing in Norfolk should stop. After a lengthy legal struggle, in November 1986 the Supreme Court decided not to rule on the case, instead allowing an Appeals Court judgment to stand, effectively permitting education officials in Norfolk to end school busing. According to William Bradford Reynolds, the decision suggested "the Court was comfortable" with an end to mandatory busing.[130] The case proved to be a high-water mark in the Reagan administration's belated push to overturn court ordered busing. As the Justice Department, and Ed Meese in particular, became distracted by the Iran-Contra scandal in the last years of Reagan's presidency, the issue slid back down the political agenda. The administration had gone some way to fulfilling the GOP's 1980 platform pledge and appeasing the demands of southern conservatives, but at the end of Reagan's presidency over six hundred public school systems remained under court busing orders. Still, after more than two decades in which liberals had led the way on busing—making it a vital tool in federal efforts to integrate public schools—his administration had tilted the debate in a conservative direction. While many Americans were already uneasy about the policy at the start of the 1980s, as historian Lawrence McAndrews writes, Reagan's "ritualistic denunciation of forced busing had helped persuade a majority of blacks as well as whites." The Reagan administration also pushed Washington's perception of busing closer to that of public opinion. It remained a feature of life in numerous school districts across the country, but where possible the federal government's priority was now to end busing orders. What had been an intense civil rights battleground in the 1970s had largely ceased to be a major issue by the end of Reagan's presidency.[131]

More practically, Reagan's judicial appointments altered the legal landscape when it came to busing and other affirmative action programs. In his eight years as president, Reagan made 346 appointments to the federal judiciary, around 47 percent of all judges. These appointees were overwhelmingly aligned with Reagan's anti-statism and, as legal scholar Sheldon Goldman observed in 1989, "compatible with the president's judicial philosophy." During Reagan's second term, Ed Meese sought to appoint younger judges who would push the federal judiciary in a conservative direction for decades to come.[132] When it came to busing, southern conservatives were initially frustrated by Reagan's nonexistent leadership. As with other racial issues, his administration's position generated anger on both sides of the argument. Reagan's lack of personal involvement was deeply unsatisfactory to southern conservatives, while the Justice Department's anti-busing rhetoric alienated civil rights groups. As McAndrews' puts it, "These issues, which inflamed his most ardent supporters and his most fervent critics, hardly seemed to interest the president at all."[133] Yet his administration's impact on the issue was substantial. It was apparent in a Justice Department that eventually supported the repeal of existing busing orders and in a federal judiciary that became more hostile to affirmative action policies. Both transformations would endure long after Reagan left office.

"Whites are not afraid because they're not under any Federal pressure. It used to be Federal this and Federal that, but where's the Federal Government now? We're slowly going back to where we were."[134] The views of an African American civil rights worker in Mississippi in April 1985 summed up the way Reagan was perceived by black southerners. They had witnessed his reluctance to renew the Voting Rights Act and to honor Martin Luther King Jr., as well as his administration's acceptance of racial separation in Christian colleges and attempts to end the use of busing to desegregate schools. When added to spending cuts that disproportionately affected African Americans nationwide, and increased racial disparities in poverty and employment, it seemed obvious the Reagan administration was instinctively attuned to the wishes of the white South and cared little for those of the black South.[135] Many southern whites shared this view, something which helped Reagan to sweep the southern states in 1984 and to receive a higher portion of the white vote in the South—almost three quarters—than he did in any other region. As a Duke University professor told the *New York Times,* whites in the South had for years "bought the argument of reverse discrimination, that blacks have gotten more than they deserve."[136] Reagan's opponent, Walter Mondale, won 90 percent of the South's black vote as the southern electorate split along starkly racial lines.[137]

Voting rights and busing fell down the political agenda during Reagan's second term, but arguments over diplomatic relations with South Africa and a Supreme Court judgment on civil rights kept racial issues close to the center of political debate. By 1984, it was apparent the administration's strategy of 'constructive engagement' with the white South African government was failing. Notionally designed to encourage the moderation of apartheid, constructive engagement was instead aggravating the situation in South Africa by "encouraging and indulging the white regime's divide-and-rule tactics," argued Sanford Ungar and Peter Vale in *Foreign Affairs.* It seemed to the rest of the world that "American prestige is on the side of the Pretoria government."[138] The Reagan White House rejected pleas from anti-apartheid campaigners—including Nobel Peace Prize recipient Archbishop Desmond Tutu—to impose economic sanctions. When a bipartisan group of congressmen and senators proposed sanctions legislation in 1985, Reagan vowed to veto the bill.[139]

Prominent southern conservatives joined Reagan in opposing sanctions. Jesse Helms announced he would filibuster the sanctions bill, claiming it would be "very harmful to blacks in South Africa. . . . They don't need fewer jobs. They need more jobs." California's Democratic senator Alan Cranston suspected opposition to sanctions was motivated by "a dirty undercurrent of racism" and condemned Helms' argument as "like suggesting we shouldn't have abolished slavery in the South because it would result in some unemployment."[140] Other conservative southerners sided with Helms and claimed sanctions would undermine US interests. "South Africa is a government friendly to the United States in a troubled area of the world," argued Strom Thurmond, "and this country should take care to ensure that it does nothing that would jeopardize its own security interest in that region."[141] Returning from a five-day visit, Moral Majority leader Jerry Falwell maintained Americans were being misled about South Africa and that apartheid was being reformed. Falwell described Archbishop Tutu as "a phony . . . as far as representing the black people of South Africa" and warned of civil strife and a communist takeover if the country's social order was disrupted.[142]

For some, Falwell's claims of communist influence in the anti-apartheid movement were a throwback to segregationist accusations that the civil rights campaign was a communist conspiracy. But Ronald Reagan agreed, saying it was "innocent, naïve" not to think that communists were "stirring the pot" and stoking opposition to apartheid in South Africa.[143] After Congress passed sanctions legislation, Reagan vetoed the bill on 26 September 1986. While acknowledging that apartheid was "an affront to human rights and human dignity," Reagan argued in his veto statement, "America's power to deepen the economic crisis in this tortured country is not the way to reconciliation and peace."[144] However, Reagan's veto was overridden by large majorities in both houses of Congress, 313–83 in the House and 78–21 in the Senate. Prominent southern Republicans, including senators Jesse Helms, Strom Thurmond, Jeremiah Denton, Thad Cochran, and James Broyhill, voted to sustain the president's veto.[145] Once again, Jesse Helms argued that imposing sanctions through "absurd legislation" would stir "violent, revolutionary change and, following that, lasting [communist] tyranny" in South Africa.[146] Helms' provocative language, as well as the presence of Martin Luther King's widow, Coretta Scott King, watching from the

Senate's public gallery, served as powerful echoes of the civil rights struggle in the Jim Crow South.[147]

Civil rights once again came to the fore during Reagan's final year in office. Eight years after declaring his support for states' rights to a cheering white audience in Mississippi, he became the first president to veto a civil rights bill since Andrew Johnson in 1866. In the 1984 case of *Grove City College v. Bell*, the Supreme Court had decided that antidiscrimination laws applied only to programs and departments in receipt of federal funding, and not to the wider institution in which the discrimination had occurred. The case centered on sex discrimination, but the decision also encompassed discrimination against the disabled and minority groups. Congress passed legislation in early 1988 which sought to reverse *Grove City* and apply discrimination laws to whole institutions.[148] Reagan vetoed the bill, making the anti-statist argument that it would "vastly and unjustifiably expand the power of the Federal government over the decisions and affairs of private organizations."[149] Numerous southern conservatives supported Reagan, but on rather more culturally traditionalist grounds. Jesse Helms raised the specter of transvestites demanding to work with children in federally-subsidized daycare centers, while the Moral Majority described the bill as "perverted" and claimed it would leave churches at the mercy of "militant gays, feminists and others who have no respect for God's laws."[150] Still, their opposition did not prevent Congress from overriding Reagan's veto. The Civil Rights Restoration Act became law on 22 March 1988.[151]

During his second term, Reagan's record deepened the belief among black Americans that he was not serving their interests. His administration's internal decision-making was often tortuous when it came to issues of race and civil rights. Its positions resulted from a mixture of Reaganite commitment to anti-statism, the president's own personal beliefs and suspicions, and sometimes simply an absence of wise political judgment. President Reagan frequently tried to convince the public—as he had convinced himself—that he lacked any form of racial prejudice, whether by coopting the legacy of Martin Luther King or repeatedly insisting that his vision of the United States was entirely colorblind. But, overall, the evidence suggested a presidency that instinctively sided with the views of white conservative southerners and, at the very least, had no understanding of the acute problems facing black America. This applied not only to issues directly affecting the South, such as voting rights or the integration of schools and colleges, but also to those which were profoundly symbolic for all black Americans, like apartheid in South Africa or the commemoration of Martin Luther King's birthday. African Americans certainly did not perceive Reagan as an ally. In 1984, he received only 11 percent of black votes nationwide. In 1986, polls showed that 56 percent of black Americans believed Reagan was personally racist, while 49 percent felt his administration's anti-statist policies had actively held them back.[152] Shortly before Reagan left office, black political commentator Juan Williams wrote, "Eight years of Ronald Reagan as president have left many blacks feeling scorned and many neglected, and whites feeling far less inclined—or morally obliged—to lend a helping hand to the black community."[153]

As Williams implied, white conservatives, particularly in the South, viewed Reagan's record rather differently. His administration's conservative rhetoric on affirmative action and civil rights met with approval from those southerners who were yet to fully accept the changes their region had undergone. Reagan had often demonstrated a lack of consideration for the economic and social priorities of white southerners, whether in his opposition to agricultural subsidies or his inattention to the demands of the Christian Right. But during his presidency the white South had gravitated steadily towards the Republican Party. Though his administration repeatedly tied itself in knots trying to navigate controversial debates on race and civil rights, and was occasionally forced into embarrassing reversals that enraged many in the white South, Reagan's overall record in this area arguably encouraged southern conservatives to forgive, or at least overlook, his lack of action on other parts of their agenda. From the Ed Brooke leaflet in 1976, to his Neshoba speech in 1980, and through to his veto of a civil rights bill in 1988, Reagan had repeatedly signaled an instinctive alignment with racially conservative southerners. Their affection only grew for a man who appeared to share their reservations about the changes wrought by the civil rights revolution. Yet, politically, Reagan often succeeded in having it both ways. As his landslide national victory in 1984 suggested, moderate voters did not view him as a bigot. His colorblind rhetoric, focus on equality of opportunity for all, and insistence on his own racial innocence largely insulated Reagan against charges of personal prejudice. Nevertheless, in a region still marked by historical, and often overt, racial tensions, millions of white southerners regarded him as a man who was on their side.

Epilogue

In the wake of Ronald Reagan's 1980 election win, one of Strom Thurmond's closest friends and advisors, Robert Figg, observed that he had long believed that "someday, somebody's going to run for president on the platform that this is a white man's country." While acknowledging "I never heard Reagan saying that," Figg concluded, "the election turned out that way didn't it?"[1] More than any previous Republican, Reagan's presidential campaigns offered southern conservatives a political home and a path to increased power in Washington. Thanks to Reagan's primary challenge in 1976, the white South gained a foothold in the Republican Party and began to reorient the national GOP agenda. Four years later, his presidential victory was perceived as a breakthrough for southern conservatism. Its influence on the party was evident in the Republican platform, in the high profile of the Christian Right, and in Reagan's pledges to act on a range of issues that were close to the hearts of conservative southerners. Over the next eight years, the long-established affection for Reagan among white southern voters translated into robust electoral support throughout his time in office, as demonstrated by his strong performance in the region in the 1984 presidential election.

Yet, considering his legislative record, Reagan's southern popularity was paradoxical. In many policy areas white southerners saw relatively little practical benefit in return for backing him. For the millions who lived in rural areas and small towns, the economic impact of the Reagan Revolution of 1981 was far from positive. During Reagan's last year in office, journalist Jerry Hagstrom observed that the South "is now so divided between its prospering metropolises and its poor countryside that it is impossible to reach a conclusion about the effects of Reagan policies in the region." Cities and suburbs that had flourished as part of the Sunbelt boom enjoyed further prosperity thanks to lower taxes, reduced inflation, and the administration's massive increases in military spending, but for many already poor communities in the region Reagan's retrenchment of federal programs was damaging. When deep funding cuts to organizations such as the Appalachian Regional Commission started to bite, education and healthcare suffered, and underfunding and unemployment increased markedly across an area covering several southern states.[2] Reagan's federal spending reductions had the support of both southern Republicans and Boll Weevil Democrats, particularly in the case of welfare cuts. But while many of them gave their support to Reagan in exchange for concessions designed to aid regional industries, from a wider perspective the budget cuts they worked to enact did as much to harm the southern economy as to help it.

When it came to agricultural policy, southerners felt compelled to defend price support programs and other subsidies against two major Reaganite attempts to slash US farm spending. Dogged resistance from southern congressmen and senators, who often resorted to tactics that would have been familiar to their predecessors—obstructing legislation and bartering with, cajoling, and occasionally threatening their fellow congressmen—meant the Reaganite ambition to push American agriculture towards the free market met with outright failure during the 1980s. The only notable subsequent attempt to end farm subsidies came with the 1996 farm bill, which replaced them with a system of fixed payments that would gradually decline over the next seven years. Even then, the so-called Freedom to Farm Act still bore the hallmarks of big government and won the support of some southern senators who had fought bitterly against Reagan's attempts at agricultural reform.[3] One free market advocate derided it as "'Freedom to Farm'—with other people's money."[4] Following passage of the 1996 Act, American farmers took advantage of the reduced restrictions on planting and flooded the market with crops, leading prices to collapse. As the 2000 presidential election approached, low crop prices led Congress to pass several farm bailout packages restoring most of the subsidies that had been eliminated.[5]

The story for southern textile manufacturing, however, was very different. In 1990, conservative Arkansas Democrat Marilyn Lloyd led one final attempt to protect the industry, but the Textile, Apparel, and Footwear Trade Act met with another presidential veto, this time from President George H. W. Bush. Once again, the House failed to reach the two-thirds majority required to override.[6] In a broader context, the Reagan administration's ideological commitment to free trade and deregulation triggered a rightward turn in US economic discourse. During the 1990s, a major product of that rightward turn, the North American Free Trade Agreement (NAFTA), ultimately sounded the death knell for southern textiles. Resistance to NAFTA once again united southerners from both sides of the aisle. In South Carolina, Democrat Ernest Hollings and Republican Strom Thurmond banded together in opposition, fearing the damage the agreement could inflict on their state's already ailing textile industry. Jesse Helms and his fellow North Carolina Republican Lauch Faircloth joined them, along with Democrats Howell Heflin and Richard Shelby of Alabama.[7] In the end, southern-led efforts to defeat NAFTA proved futile. With its implementation in 1994 came the outsourcing of manufacturing jobs and the removal of import barriers between the United States and Mexico, which rapidly combined to create a "tidal wave drowning whole communities," in the words of one report on the southern economy. The consequences were catastrophic for textile workers across the South. The report estimated that "between 1986 and 2000, textile employment in the southern states fell from 549,000 to 418,000. Apparel jobs plummeted even faster, from 536,000 to 259,000." In North Carolina, "a third of layoffs during 2001 were in textiles, and 69 percent of these were in the state's rural counties."[8] Despite occasional foreign investment, the South continued to hemorrhage textile jobs into the twenty-first century, until the industry was reduced to a fraction of its previous scale.

The fate of the textile industry epitomized the decaying of the South's traditional economy. This trend was, of course, not solely a consequence of Reaganite policies or ideology—technological advances and an increasingly globalized marketplace swept away manufacturing jobs in most western nations during the latter decades of the twentieth century. But while the southern textile industry had been facing difficulties since the 1970s, Reagan's veto of two attempts to impose stricter limits on textile imports accelerated its decline, as well as the decline of thousands of small-town communities. Likewise, the tax cuts and spending reductions implemented by the Reagan Revolution had the overall effect of aiding wealthier metropolitan southerners and hurting those in rural areas. During the 1980s and into the 1990s, Reagan's ideology of deregulation, small government, and free markets effectively became the center ground of economic debate. This shift only served to entrench the poverty of millions of rural southerners, further widening the already substantial urban-rural economic divide in the South and cementing its status as America's poorest region.

Still, despite the negative impacts of his economic policies in the South and numerous heated confrontations over textile imports and farm policy, Reagan's standing in the region remained high. As former Democratic governor of Mississippi William Winter remarked in 1988, "Reagan remains personally very popular despite his failure to perform to the benefit of many in the South."[9] Reagan's time in the White House was instrumental in pulling the partisan loyalties of white conservative southerners—particularly those rural, working-class whites who had seen little economic gain from his presidency—away from the Democratic Party and towards the GOP. Long after he left office, southern Republicans continued to credit this shift to Reagan personally. After Reagan's death in 2004, former Georgia Republican Party chairman Rusty Paul went so far as to claim, "For however long the South is going to be Republican, it will be because of Ronald Reagan."[10]

This view cannot be based on his legislative record. Aside from cuts to welfare and increases in military spending as part of his 1981 economic program, Reagan repeatedly neglected the political agenda of the white South. Alongside disputes over agriculture spending and trade, his administration's failure to act on social issues regularly fostered impatience and rancor among his southern supporters, particularly among those fundamentalist evangelicals on the Christian Right who had backed him so enthusiastically in 1980. Repeatedly, legislation designed to restrict abortion or restore prayer in public schools foundered because of a lack of effort on the part of the Reagan administration—in turn stemming from Reagan's own disinterest in such issues. Similarly, the Reagan administration's clumsy attempts to navigate through controversial debates over the Martin Luther King holiday, Voting Rights Act renewal, or the charitable status of southern Christian colleges often resulted in humiliating climbdowns that frustrated southern conservatives.

Instead, as we have seen, the reasons for Reagan's popularity in the white South were always somewhat intangible—rooted more in emotion than any detailed legislative agenda. Affection for him grew when he showed understanding and acknowledgement of white southern fears and anxieties during the turmoil of the 1950s and 1960s, and it intensified when he embraced the social and cultural concerns of conservative southerners during his political campaigns in 1976 and 1980. Through their support for Reagan millions of white southerners, many of them disillusioned and disaffected Democrats, were persuaded that the GOP could be their new political home. That feeling only deepened during his presidency. Despite the frustrations and disputes of the Reagan era, southern conservatives made significant gains in advancing their agenda. Reagan's supportive rhetoric—though it often proved to be empty—thrust social issues from the fringes of political debate towards the center. The priorities of southern conservatives came to be woven into the fabric of the Republican Party and the tone of national political discourse began to shift, particularly when it came to abortion and increased resistance to affirmative action. Such gains were subtle, and the progress made by southern conservatives was often obscured by legislative failures on Capitol Hill, but this ultimately goes a long way to explain Ronald Reagan's enduring personal popularity in the white South and the role it played in holding together an uneasy coalition of Reaganites and conservative southerners. After feeling abandoned and betrayed by the Democrats, white southerners saw their support for Reagan as a route to acceptance and influence in the Republican Party and as a way to begin restoring southern conservative political power. From that perspective, Reagan delivered as president. For all the legislative disappointments and conflicts over economic ideology and political priorities, the Reagan era saw the white South return to the center of events in Washington for the first time in a generation.

Ronald Reagan's impact on the partisan realignment of the white South is unquestionable. Polling in 1988 showed that 60 percent of conservatives in the South identified as Republican, up from 40 percent in 1980.[11] As southern historian Wayne Flint has observed, "The Reagan era forced the level of change well beneath the veneer of presidential politics."[12] Yet the legacy of the South's realignment in the Reagan era proved to be a mixed blessing for the Republican Party. During the 1990s, even as the GOP's new southern base was lifting the congressional party to levels of electoral success it had not seen since the early 1950s, the increasing power of the white South continued to cause internal party strife and to drag the Republican Party's identity in an ever more culturally conservative direction. Within a decade of Reagan leaving office, some political commentators were bemoaning what they regarded as the wholesale capture of the GOP by conservative southerners. In 1995, Michael Lind wrote, "The South [has] finally conquered Washington. . . . The stereotypical reactionary Southern senator with a drawl is more likely to be a member of the Republican congressional leadership than a Dixie Democrat."[13] Three years later, the *Atlantic* observed that so extensive was southern conservative influence on the national GOP's character and agenda, Republican leaders had "narrowly defined 'values' as the folkways of one regional subculture [the white South], and have urged their imposition on the rest of the country."[14]

The campaign to be Reagan's successor in the Oval Office illustrated the growing power of southern conservatism in the GOP. In 1988, Republican strategists sought ways to compensate for both an uncertain economic climate and a candidate seen by grassroots conservatives, especially southerners, as a moderate establishment figure.[15] Vice President George H. W. Bush's loyalty to Reagan had been enough to win him southern primary contests and to secure the nomination. "Pulling the lever for Bush was a sentimental action," observed one journalist during the primaries. "It was the closest Southerners could come to voting for Mr. Reagan."[16] But more was required to energize white conservative voters in the presidential election. Bush's national campaign manager was Lee Atwater, the South Carolinian whose "southern blitz" had been instrumental in persuading Boll Weevils to vote for Reagan's budget in 1981 and a strategist steeped in the traditionally brutal political culture of the Deep South.

Atwater planned to use cultural and social issues to paint Bush's Democratic opponent, Massachusetts governor Michael Dukakis, as an extremist liberal. After accusing Dukakis of lacking patriotism for vetoing a bill that would have required students in Massachusetts to recite the pledge of allegiance, the Bush campaign released an advertisement blaming him for the crimes committed by black convicted murderer Willie Horton. It became one of the most controversial in presidential campaign history. As governor, Dukakis had supported a rehabilitation program under which Horton had been granted a weekend furlough from prison. Horton subsequently absconded and went on to commit further violent crimes including assault, rape, and robbery.[17] The Horton story effectively became the core of the Bush election message. "By the time we're finished," Lee Atwater declared, "they're going to wonder whether Willie Horton is Dukakis' running mate."[18] It was, an anonymous Republican campaign official triumphantly added, "a wonderful mix of liberalism and a big black rapist."[19]

Along with the strategic decision to focus on cultural issues and personal attacks on the character of Dukakis and his wife, the Horton ad exemplified Atwater's influence on the Republican Party's campaign—and the increasing influence of southern conservatism on the party. George H. W. Bush went on to a resounding victory in November, including winning every southern state, as his campaign's fearmongering about Dukakis' liberalism hit home with voters who had previously regarded Bush with skepticism. The 1988 campaign illustrated a new reality for the GOP: mobilizing an emerging base of culturally and racially conservative whites, particularly in the South, was crucial to winning a national election. As the *Washington Post* noted after Bush's win, "The crushing of Dukakis represented the application in a national contest of the theory Atwater has used to win in the South."[20] As the chief strategist for a presidential nominee who had neither Ronald Reagan's natural charisma nor his longstanding relationship with the white South, Atwater decided instead to resort to unsubtle appeals to white anxiety and grievance. While Reagan had certainly been willing to indulge in dog whistle politics if he believed electoral circumstances demanded it, Atwater's strategy ventured even further into the political swamps. It reflected the exploitation of racial fear that had long been central to southern conservative campaigning and would increasingly become a Republican weapon in the post-Reagan era. Another important step on that journey came in 1990, with Jesse Helms' use of a campaign advertisement depicting a white man being rejected for a job because of racial quotas. The ad, clearly designed to energize racially conservative white voters in North Carolina, helped Helms win re-election to the Senate against a black Democratic challenger, Harvey Gantt.[21]

As president, Ronald Reagan had expended relatively little energy on trying to overturn federal policies such as those imposing minority employee quotas on government contractors. But within a few years, even moderate Republicans had become more openly hostile to affirmative action. Following the success of Helms' tactic, and reflecting a steady increase in the power of southern Republicans, by the mid-1990s the *Los Angeles Times* was noting that party leaders had become "much less squeamish" about the prospect of reversing federal affirmative action programs.[22] Senator Bob Dole, the GOP's 1996 presidential candidate, was a Kansas moderate who had a long history of supporting civil rights legislation, including voting for the Civil Rights Act in 1964 and leading efforts in the Senate to extend it in 1982. Yet on the campaign trail he condemned attempts to "fight the evil of discrimination with more discrimination" and described affirmative action as a "blind alley in the search for equal justice."[23] Reagan's opposition to affirmative action had manifested itself predominantly in conservative judicial appointments, but the legacy of his colorblind, anti-statist language was to give impetus to southern racial conservatism in the GOP and to provide legitimacy for later, more explicit Republican attacks on affirmative action and appeals to racial fear.

While southern racial politics was becoming an ever more visible part of the Republican Party's identity, other southern conservative priorities appeared to slip down the political agenda. Following repeated failures to pass school prayer or anti-abortion legislation during the Reagan presidency, Jerry Falwell's decision to disband the Moral Majority in 1989 suggested the Christian Right's time in the spotlight had passed. The impression was reinforced when southern evangelicals supported George H. W. Bush only to discover he was even more reluctant to pursue social issue legislation than Reagan. Under Bush the Christian Right endured a spell in the political wilderness, during which the movement's core priorities largely disappeared from view.[24]

By the mid-1990s, however, southern evangelicalism was staging a dramatic resurgence. Pat Buchanan's challenge to President Bush in the

1992 Republican primaries, and particularly his claim that the United States was experiencing a "cultural war" in which white Christian identity and values were under attack, provided an enormous boost to the Christian Right. Though born in Washington, DC, Buchanan was proud of his family's Mississippi heritage and his ancestors' service in the Confederate army and was an active member of the Sons of Confederate Veterans.[25] His rhetoric exemplified old-style reactionary southern conservatism. According to Buchanan, the most profound threats to American society were radical feminism, gay rights, and "discrimination against religious schools." At the very top of his list, however, was "unrestricted abortion on demand."[26] Though controversy over school prayer had waned since the mid-1980s, abortion remained one of the most divisive cultural issues in the United States. Buchanan's primary challenge placed the issue back at the center of political debate and forced a reluctant Bush to run on a strict anti-abortion platform in his unsuccessful reelection campaign.[27]

Two years later, voter turnout efforts by the Christian Right played an important role in the GOP takeover of the House of Representatives in the 1994 midterms, as the party won a majority of southern House seats for the first time since Reconstruction and conservative southern Republicans assumed senior leadership positions in Congress. However, when Republican control of the House failed to generate any new impetus on Capitol Hill for anti-abortion legislation, conservative evangelicals shifted their focus completely towards the Supreme Court, recognizing that the appointment of pro-life justices was now their most likely route to overturning *Roe v. Wade*. When faced with the alternative of a Democratic Party that was developing an increasingly liberal social agenda, voting Republican in presidential elections was ultimately the only way for the Christian Right to get anti-abortion justices—or at the very least justices who were not pro-choice—appointed to the Supreme Court. Thus, the abortion issue bonded socially conservative southern evangelicals ever more closely to the GOP. Republican Party platforms came to advocate the kind of uncompromising anti-abortion stances that had been well outside the mainstream of the party during the 1970s and were still regarded as politically unpalatable by the Reagan White House in the 1980s.

As the Republican Party's hold on the white southern electorate became ever stronger during the 1990s, southern evangelicals increasingly used the political experience they had acquired as allies of the Reagan administration to strengthen their control over the GOP apparatus across the South. Southern evangelical churches effectively became local party offices, distributing GOP leaflets and registering Republican voters.[28] In the words of Ralph Reed, head of the Christian Coalition (effectively a successor organization to the Moral Majority), by the mid-1990s conservative evangelicals had become "thoroughly integrated and enmeshed into the machinery of the Republican Party."[29] A study conducted in 1994 supported Reed's claim. It rated the Christian Right's influence over the Republican Party leadership as "dominant" in every southern state. Significantly, it also found that state Republican Parties around the rest of the United States were also seeing "substantial" Christian Right influence, trending towards dominant, with the notable exception of those in the Northeast.[30]

Less than a decade after the end of the Reagan presidency, the seemingly unstoppable transformation in the GOP's identity demonstrated just how far southern conservatism had expanded its reach. Further evidence came in early 1995. Following midterm elections in which the Republican Party won the House of Representatives for the first time since the 1950s, conservative southerners came to occupy some of the most influential leadership positions on Capitol Hill. An editorial in the *Atlanta Journal* claimed the midterms had "swept into power the governing philosophy of Southern conservatives."[31] In the House, southern Republicans held the roles of Speaker, majority leader, majority whip, and chair of the Appropriations Committee. Conservative southerners also occupied important positions in the Senate, including majority whip, president pro tempore, and the chairs of both the Armed Services and Foreign Relations committees. The composition of the new Congress marked a significant watershed in US political history. Not only were both House and Senate under Republican control for the first time in four decades, but a tipping point had been reached in the balance of power between Reaganism and southern conservatism. "What happened today," the *Journal* excitedly proclaimed, "is that Southern conservatives now write the rules, define the debate, set the agenda." The swearing-in of the 104th Congress on 5 January 1995 was "an extraordinary moment for a Southerner."[32]

Though these southerners were elected on an economic program that largely resembled a Reaganite agenda—the "Contract with America," which promised tax cuts, welfare reform, and job creation through deregulation—and the popular image of the GOP remained synonymous with that of Reagan himself, in reality Republican conservatism was undergoing what Nicole Hemmer has called "an evolutionary leap."[33] Led by Newt Gingrich, the Georgia congressman who became Speaker of the House, newly ascendant southern Republicans brought an antagonistic and intensely partisan style to the GOP leadership. Many were deeply socially conservative, but this now manifested itself in tougher policies to tackle crime and pornography rather than futile legislative efforts to ban abortion.[34] Much of the legislation passed by the House of Representatives during 1995 was voted down in the Senate, where some Republicans were less than convinced by the confrontational approach of the House leadership.[35] Nonetheless, the so-called Republican Revolution of the mid-1990s had an enduring impact on the tenor of political debate, most obviously in forcing government shutdowns during late 1995 and early 1996 and in the push to impeach President Bill Clinton over the Monica Lewinsky scandal. Thereafter, threatening government shutdowns or presidential impeachment— previously radical acts that indicated a profound national crisis— became a more frequent refrain among many Republicans in Congress. "With a Democrat in the White House," Hemmer observes, "congressional Republicans adopted a politics of destruction, concerned less with legislation than with investigation and obstruction."[36] It was a shift in character that would ultimately prove impossible to reverse.

As a party, the GOP remained riven by splits between Reaganites and southern conservatives. Political scientist A. James Reichley told the *Washington Post* in early 1996 that "the closer the Republicans get to being a majority the more the divisions appear." The major disputes, as they had been during Reagan's presidency, were over "moral and social issues," "the priority of budget cutting and economic stimulus," and a "recurrence of the isolationism and protectionism which have been dormant for quite a few years."[37] This time, there was no Ronald Reagan at the top of the party to unify Republicans and temper the belligerence of conservative southerners. Instead, southern conservatives in Congress were driving the GOP down a road of aggressive partisanship. In doing so, they were reflecting a shift in the Republican base. Throughout the 1990s the locus of power in the party moved inexorably towards the white South, and the antagonism of the GOP leadership echoed the mood of the party's increasingly influential southern voting bloc. Writing in 1996, Godfrey Hodgson noted, "Much of the steam behind the Republican victories [in the 1994 midterms] came not from converts to conservative ideas, but from those who wanted to punish insiders and Washington politicians generally."[38] The reactionary populism displayed by the millions of southern whites who had been drawn to the party during the Reagan era was pervading the party's grassroots—spreading out from the South to rural whites across the nation. By the late 1990s, its influence was clearly visible. "Southerners," the *Atlantic* perceptively argued in 1998, "now wag the Republican dog."[39]

If Ronald Reagan's enduring popularity in the white South was paradoxical given his record in office, so, too, was its legacy for the Republican Party. Many of the conservative southern Republicans who were leading the GOP away from Reaganism in the 1990s owed a significant political debt to Reagan himself. In 1981, Newt Gingrich had been asked to lead a House task force designed to help push Reagan's tax cuts through Congress.[40] Dick Armey and Tom Delay—who in 1995 became House majority leader and House majority whip respectively—had won their Texas congressional seats in the Reagan landslide of 1984. In the Senate, two of Reagan's longstanding southern allies, Jesse Helms and Strom Thurmond, became chairs of the Committee on Foreign Relations and the Armed Services Committee respectively, with Thurmond also acting as president pro tempore.

But it is Trent Lott's ascent in the Republican Party that best illustrates the rise to power of the white South during Reagan's presidency and into the post-Reagan era. As a young man Lott had been a segregationist Democrat, before switching parties in 1972 and winning election to Congress.[41] Acting as Reagan's Mississippi campaign chairman in 1980 he had encouraged Reagan to appear at the Neshoba County Fair, and four years later told a Sons of Confederate Veterans convention that the 1984 Republican platform contained "the spirit of [Confederate President] Jefferson Davis." Lott also proudly declared, in a subsequent interview, that "the South's sons, Jefferson Davis' descendants, direct or indirect, are becoming involved with the Republican Party." Throughout the 1990s, even as he reached the position of Senate majority whip, Lott maintained close links to groups that promoted racial separation, particularly the Council of Conservative Citizens, a successor organization to the segregationist Citizens Councils of the 1960s.[42] In 2002, by which time he had become Senate majority leader, a speech Lott gave in honor of Strom Thurmond's hundredth birthday sparked a national furor. He declared, "I want to say this about my state. When Strom Thurmond ran for president [on a segregationist platform in 1948], we voted for him. We're proud of it. And if the rest of the country had followed our lead, we wouldn't have had all these problems over all these years either." Though Lott apologized and claimed the comments were "lighthearted," he was forced to resign as majority leader.[43]

Lott's politics embodied southern conservatism. Alongside his record on race, he was deeply conservative on social issues and had "fought strenuously and effectively to bring federal money to Mississippi."[44] As the GOP's base of white southerners expanded, they brought into the party an aggressive political style, a history of racial resentment and division, a predilection for economic populism, and a profound resistance to social change. As political scientist Stephen Schaffer told the *New York Times* in 1994, Lott's story "represents as well as anything how the conservative element in the South has moved firmly into the Republican Party."[45] Trent Lott's rise to leadership of the Senate by the turn of the twenty-first century epitomized both the transformation of the GOP's character and the white South's return to power in Washington. Not since the late 1950s had the white South wielded such influence on the direction of national politics.

This was the outcome many white southerners had envisaged when they first supported Ronald Reagan for president. Reagan had convinced them that the Republican Party was the only viable home for their conservatism, and they viewed his presidency as an ideal vehicle through which to expand southern conservative power and protect their region's social and economic traditions. But for the Republican Party, as political scientist Joseph Aistrup noted, attempting to forge an electoral coalition of economically focused suburban voters with culturally conservative white southerners had "inadvertently opened a Pandora's Box of intraparty strife." After joining the GOP, southern conservatives quickly sought to exert their influence and advance their region's economic, social, and cultural priorities. During the Reagan presidency, conflicting agendas in the party created "new sets of problems for Republicans" and the focus of the White House was pulled in different, often incompatible, directions.[46]

While Reagan was in the Oval Office, his popularity in the South repeatedly led to him being absolved of blame for pursuing policies that southerners vehemently opposed. Similarly, it helped the GOP to remain united through frequent battles caused by the divergent philosophies of Reaganism and southern conservatism. But once Reagan's presidency was over, the coalition he forged began to fragment and the South's ascendance in the GOP gathered pace as Reaganism waned. The party's base became ever more influenced by the social and cultural conservatism of the white South. The 1990s saw the culmination of the southern partisan shift that Reagan had done so much to encourage. Between 1994 and 1998 more than fifty southern Democratic officials switched to the GOP, including prominent figures on Capitol Hill such as Alabama Senator Richard Shelby.[47] By the end of the twentieth century, conservative southern Democrats were a rare species. The white South was unquestionably a Republican stronghold. When Newt Gingrich was forced from the Speaker's office after the GOP's poor showing in the 1998 midterms and George W. Bush was elected in 2000 on a Reaganite domestic program of tax cuts and immigration reform, it briefly appeared that Reaganism was going to reassert itself as the dominant force in the Republican Party. But, as the first two decades of twenty-first century would prove, at the grassroots level the cultural conservatism of the white South was steadily tightening its grip on the GOP.

"In the South the Reagan realignment of the 1980s was a momentous achievement," observed Earl and Merle Black in 2002. "By transforming the region's white electorate, Ronald Reagan's presidency made possible the Republicans' congressional breakthrough in the 1990s."[48] Yet the complex relationship between the Reagan White House and

southern conservatives also created a succession of political problems and disputes, at times leading to outright confrontation. Conservative southerners demanded action on social issues, exhorted the
administration to roll back advances in civil rights, fought to protect
the economic status quo in their region, and ultimately became frustrated by Reagan's lack of interest in their agenda. The heated disputes
of the Reagan years laid the groundwork for the South's rise to power
in the 1990s and presaged a full-blown intraparty civil war in the early
twenty-first century. The white South's transformation into the heartland of the Republican Party, which Ronald Reagan did so much to
bring about, ultimately precipitated the decline of Reaganism and
proved to be a double-edged sword for the GOP. Barely a decade after
he left office, the "Party of Reagan" was becoming the party of the white
conservative South.

Afterword
Republican Civil War in the Age of Trump

When Donald Trump won the Republican presidential nomination and then the White House itself in 2016, several journalists drew comparisons with Ronald Reagan.[1] Some similarities were apparent. Before Trump, Reagan was the only man with a background in the entertainment industry to become president. Trump's "Make America Great Again" slogan—which became ubiquitous when it was emblazoned on millions of red baseball caps—was adapted from one used by Reagan on the 1980 campaign trail. Trump's mantra, however, lacked the positivity of Reagan's "Let's Make America Great Again" message, and there was very little of Reagan's innate optimism to be found in Trump's exploitation of white anger and grievance.[2] Indeed, everything about Donald Trump's political persona and campaigning style suggested that, far from being the new Ronald Reagan, his rise to power was instead the culmination of the southern conservative takeover of the Republican Party.

During the 2000s, the rift between Reaganites and southern conservatives had festered. The 9/11 terror attacks and the Bush administration's subsequent War on Terror acted as a temporary unifying force in the GOP, but discontent in the Republican base simmered throughout George W. Bush's presidency. White House attempts to pass a compromise immigration reform bill, its self-proclaimed commitment to "compassionate conservatism," and an economic approach that positioned Bush as the heir to Reagan all meant that support for the president among the grassroots was hesitant at best.[3] Southern conservatives were placated by the appointment of two pro-life justices to the Supreme Court, but as Bush's national approval declined in his second term—a result of the quagmire in Iraq, the administration's poor response to Hurricane Katrina, and particularly the near collapse of the US economy in 2008—grassroots Republican anger boiled over. It manifested itself in the Tea Party, initially an inchoate, largely libertarian movement that quickly morphed into a vehicle for white rage.

By 2010, eighteen months into the administration of Democrat Barack Obama, the issues that most stirred the anger of Tea Party members were deeply entwined with white identity and racial resentment, including supposed voter fraud among ethnic minorities and conspiracy theories claiming that Obama had been born in Kenya. If Tea Party activists had a consistent political agenda, it was strongly reminiscent of southern conservatism. Traditionalist cultural and social priorities, including opposition to gun control, abortion, and immigration, were combined with contradictory views on federal spending.[4] Echoing the traditionally southern approach to economic policy, Tea Partiers condemned government welfare as "handouts" while at the same time demanding protection for Social Security, Medicare, and other federal programs from which they personally benefitted.[5]

The GOP leadership harnessed this grassroots anger for electoral gain in the 2010 midterms, which saw scores of right-wing Republicans elected to the House of Representatives. These newcomers—whose districts were on average 75 percent white and only 27 percent college educated—coalesced into the Freedom Caucus and formed the congressional arm of a populist insurgency within the GOP.[6] The divide between Reaganism and southern conservatism erupted into intraparty civil war. Republican leaders who were broadly in the Reaganite tradition, such as House majority leader Eric Cantor of Virginia and Speaker of the House John Boehner of Ohio, were ultimately brought down by the movement they had encouraged. Cantor stood accused of pursuing an immigration "amnesty" and wanting "open borders," while Boehner's efforts to win Democratic support for legislation were viewed as treacherous by the Freedom Caucus. Cantor was defeated in a 2014 primary election, and a year later John Boehner resigned from office after five years of battling Republican colleagues he regarded as "legislative terrorists." A senior aide to Boehner astutely observed, "We fed the beast that ate us."[7] At the heart of this insurgency were the white southerners who had been drawn to the GOP under Reagan and had steadily expanded their influence over the party's base. In 2015, a Pew Research Center report noted that more than half of Freedom Caucus members represented districts in the South.[8] As columnist Michael Lind lamented in *Politico*, "Working-class white Southerners who are heirs to paranoid and sullen Dixiecrat conservatism" had become increasingly powerful among the Republican grassroots.[9] In Donald Trump, they found a new national leader.

Support for Trump was unsurprisingly strongest in the white South and those rural parts of neighboring states—such as western Pennsylvania and southern Ohio—that have long exhibited southern characteristics.[10] More than any other major political figure since George Wallace, Trump personified the aggression, anti-establishment anger, and willingness to stir racial resentment that had been key elements of southern conservative politics since the nineteenth century. In 2016, *USA Today* asked southern academics to place him in the context of their region's political culture. Trump's excoriation of mainstream politicians and journalists was "music to a lot of Southern ears" according to one, while another noted that he spoke to the white South's "fighter ethos and an anti-establishment mentality." The kind of "entertainment value" Trump provided on the campaign trail was a "staple of Southern politics" going back to the days of "Pitchfork" Ben Tillman in the late nineteenth century and Huey Long in the early twentieth century. Put simply, Trump was "screaming at people in power, which is what they [conservative white southerners] would like to do."[11]

Rather than offer a positive agenda, Trump followed the southern campaigning tradition of defining himself and his candidacy in opposition to external forces. In Trump's case, these included a weak GOP leadership, Mexican migrants, the supposed corruption of the Democratic Party, and Wall Street elites. He resembled an old-style Dixiecrat in other ways too. His anti-intellectualism ("I love the poorly educated"), his less than subtle threats of violence towards protesters at his rallies, and his economic populism—including pledging to bring back blue-collar jobs and claiming that foreign nations were taking advantage of the United States—would all have been familiar to those who attended George Wallace events in the late 1960s.[12] But it was Trump's divisive rhetoric on race and immigration that recalled the darker periods of southern history. He was, a former Republican strategist suggested, "the rightful heir to Lester Maddox's ax handles and George Wallace standing in the schoolhouse door."[13] Notably, polling subsequently found that 75 percent of Trump supporters across the

United States regarded the Confederate flag as a symbol of heritage and pride.[14] Trump's emergence as the leader of the right-wing GOP insurgency confirmed that it was predominantly southern conservative in character: culturally and racially focused, economically populist, and rooted in white grievance.

In office, much of the Trump administration's agenda demonstrated that Reaganism was a thing of the past in the Republican Party. At the 2017 Conservative Political Action Conference, Trump received a rapturous response with a speech that, as Tim Alberta has observed, "made no mention of 'liberty' or 'constitution' and instead championed 'our movement' as one that would embrace protectionist, cronyist, big spending policies in the name of shielding Americans from the menace of a global economy." 80 percent of those in attendance believed that Trump was "realigning" conservatism.[15] Be it enforcing draconian anti-immigration policies, imposing import tariffs and launching damaging trade wars with China (which created the need for a huge bailout for US farmers), or attacking globalist institutions such as the World Trade Organization, Trump's actions illustrated that southern conservatism was in the ascendance and the Reaganite agenda had been pushed firmly to the margins. The remaining Reaganites in the congressional GOP found themselves having to compromise with Trump and refrain from criticizing his erratic and controversial behavior to stand any chance of pursuing their preferred policies. Even when they did succeed, such as in passing a significant reduction in corporate tax rates in November 2017, polls showed that such policies generated little approval or interest in the Republican base. "All the polling we get back shows the fiscal issues are a complete wasteland," remarked the director of the conservative lobbying group Heritage Action in 2018.[16]

The mood of the GOP base was very different when it came to race and social issues. Throughout the early twenty-first century, opposition to abortion had continued to be a powerful motivator for grassroots Republicans, particularly in the South. Trump's previous pro-choice statements on abortion—along with a history of personal behavior that was anything but pious—meant he had to overcome the suspicions of conservative evangelicals even as he repeatedly promised to appoint pro-life Supreme Court justices. The vocal backing Trump ultimately received from evangelical leaders like Jerry Falwell Jr. suggested that an aggressive, populist political style was rather more impressive to southern evangelicals than a commitment to Christian values or a record of opposing abortion.[17] Still, in appointing three deeply conservative, pro-life justices to the Supreme Court in just four years, Trump richly rewarded evangelicals for their backing and certainly fulfilled his campaign pledge. In doing so, he shifted the balance of the Court rightwards in a manner that southern conservatives in the GOP had desired for decades.

A southern-led resistance to the protection of minority rights had also become entrenched in the Republican Party, one that was ultimately a legacy of the Reagan era. Ronald Reagan's campaign dog whistles about states' rights, his aversion to approving a national holiday for Martin Luther King, and his reluctance to renew the Voting Rights Act—along with Jesse Helms' fervent opposition to renewal—had all helped to encourage the growth of southern racial conservatism in the GOP. By 2016, it was in full bloom. On the campaign trail, Donald Trump did not need to make loaded references to affirmative action programs or states' rights. Events such as Reagan's 1980 Neshoba appearance—with its subtextual appeal to "George Wallace inclined voters"—became redundant in an era when Trump could announce his presidential candidacy by describing most Mexican immigrants as "rapists" and "criminals."[18] Racially conservative whites, in the South and elsewhere, did not need to read between the lines to understand that the man at the top of the GOP shared their views.

After his inauguration, Trump's Justice Department, under the leadership of former Alabama senator Jeff Sessions, embarked on a mission to overturn affirmative action policies. In 2017, it announced plans to sue universities and colleges that undertook "intentional race-based discrimination," effectively challenging any institution that employed affirmative action in recruiting students.[19] A year later, the Justice Department rescinded guidelines instigated by the Obama administration that encouraged the consideration of racial diversity in the makeup of student bodies in both schools and universities. Such actions led minority groups to fear the Trump administration was undoing the progress that had been made on issues of racial equality over the previous decade.[20] The sight of a Republican president regularly using provocative and reactionary language about minorities and immigrants to energize his party's overwhelmingly white base served to deepen those fears.

The influence of the white South had likewise pushed the party towards more extreme positions on civil rights, with accusations of voter fraud being used to justify restricting the voting rights of minorities. In 2006, the renewal of the Voting Rights Act had followed weeks of debate in which conservative southern Republicans once again opposed the preclearance section of the law.[21] Seven years later, in the case of *Shelby County v. Holder* (2013), the Supreme Court struck down the preclearance section as outdated and unconstitutional. In a five–four decision, justices appointed by Republican presidents formed the majority.[22] The 2016 elections became the first since 1964 to take place without federal protection of the right to vote in many southern states. Republican-controlled legislatures in Alabama, North Carolina, and Texas, among other states, purged voter registration lists and passed laws imposing stringent ID requirements on voters. Such laws would previously have required federal preclearance prior to their implementation. Federal appeals courts subsequently overturned a number of these voting provisions on the grounds they were discriminatory— new laws in North Carolina were said to have targeted African Americans "with almost surgical precision."[23] Nonetheless, the passage of such laws marked the beginning of a new and concerted effort on the part of numerous state Republican Parties across the United States, but particularly in the South, to restrict the voting rights of minorities. They did so with the tacit, and sometimes explicit, support of the party's national leadership. In December 2019, a Democratic majority in the House of Representatives passed a restored Voting Rights Act, including a new preclearance process. The Republican Senate majority leader, Mitch McConnell of Kentucky, refused to bring the legislation to a vote, and President Trump vowed to veto the bill even if it were to pass Congress.[24]

Donald Trump's emergence as GOP leader epitomized the extent to which, over the previous four decades, southern conservatism had transformed the identity of the Republican Party. The continued unity and strength of the white conservative vote, and its overwhelming loyalty to the Republican Party, meant southern conservative power in the party only increased during the Trump era.[25] Likewise, white voters in the mountain states of the West, the farm states of the Midwest, and formerly Democratic, postindustrial small towns in Michigan and Pennsylvania were increasingly turning towards the same protectionist and culturally conservative agenda that southerners had instilled in the GOP. This was a shift driven in part by the legacy of Reaganism. In the South and elsewhere, voters in agricultural and postindustrial regions had suffered disproportionately from Reaganite cuts to government programs and a federal emphasis on free trade and free markets around the turn of the twenty-first century. The political disenchantment and anti-establishment rage they expressed formed the basis of the GOP's populist insurgency and was expertly tapped by Donald Trump. By the beginning of the 2020s the Republican Party was, in essence, the party of rural, small town, and non-college-educated white Americans. In contrast, the belligerent southern conservatism of Trump's GOP turned off affluent, college-educated suburbanites who had benefitted most from Reaganite tax cuts and deregulation.[26] Reaganite former House Speaker Paul Ryan put it in more personalized terms: "The Reagan Republican wing beat the Rockefeller Republican wing. And now the Trump wing beat the Reagan wing."[27]

Yet the white South and the Republican Party have a grip on each other that will outlast Donald Trump's time as leader of the party. Even following significant demographic shifts in some states, conservatism still dominates the South. As Anthony Badger has observed, "There is little evidence in North Carolina, Tennessee, Mississippi, Alabama, Florida, Texas, and South Carolina that the fundamentals of conservative control have changed."[28] That conservative control is now exercised solely through the Republican Party. In electoral terms, the modern GOP is moving towards an ascendancy in the white South akin to that which the Democratic Party enjoyed in the 1950s. As a result, many of the party's most prominent, and often controversial, figures are southerners. As Republican leader in the Senate since 2007, Kentuckian Mitch McConnell has proved to be one of the most influential and ruthless political operators of recent decades, particularly during his time as Senate majority leader from 2015 to 2021.[29] In the House, a succession of outspoken southerners have established national platforms by espousing a provocative and fervent brand of social conservatism, creating the impression that the Republican Party is travelling in an ever more extremist direction.

This was very apparent in the wake of Joe Biden's victory over Donald Trump in the 2020 presidential election and the shocking events of 6 January 2021, when a mob of Trump supporters stormed the Capitol building to prevent certification of the election result. White southerners were disproportionately represented among the demonstrators subsequently arrested as well as among those charged with organizing the riot.[30] Even after the attack on the Capitol, most southern Republicans in the House opposed certifying Biden's victory and falsely claimed that the election had been stolen from Trump. Of the 139 Republicans who voted against certification, well over half represented districts in the South.[31] Among them, representatives such as Matt Gaetz of Florida, Marjorie Taylor Greene of Georgia, and Steve Scalise of Louisiana have become some of the most well-known, or notorious, figures in the contemporary GOP. Scalise, who had previously denied accusations of racism after it emerged he had spoken at a white supremacist conference in 2002, rose to become House majority leader in 2023.[32]

On the national stage, white southern influence on the GOP continues to have a dramatic impact on US political discourse. The two front-runners in the battle for the 2024 Republican presidential nomination are, at time of writing, Donald Trump and the man regarded by many as his obvious successor, Florida governor Ron DeSantis. As governor since 2019, DeSantis' record has been one of hardline cultural conservatism—including opposition to abortion and hostility to immigration, gay rights, and "wokeness" in education—as well as populist attacks on large corporations and attempts to limit the electoral strength of minority voters.[33] In the 2024 primaries, therefore, the contest for leadership of the Republican Party will likely come down to two men who exemplify the political character of the white conservative South. Republican presidential candidates will invoke Ronald Reagan's name just as they have in every election since 1988. But many of the core principles of Reaganism—such as a belief in free trade and the benefits of immigration—will be nowhere to be seen.

Perhaps the most dramatic indicator of the white South's political power occurred in June 2022, when the Supreme Court voted six–three to overturn *Roe v. Wade*. In the wake of Donald Trump's appointment of three pro-life justices, such a decision had become increasingly likely. By ruling in *Dobbs v. Jackson Women's Health Organization* that the Constitution does not grant the right to an abortion, the Court fulfilled a core political ambition that conservative southern evangelicals had harbored for almost half a century.[34] Within weeks of the judgment, numerous southern states had implemented draconian anti-abortion laws. Arkansas, Alabama, Mississippi, Louisiana, and Tennessee were among those banning abortion in all circumstances, while other Republican-controlled legislatures across the South were in the process of introducing similarly harsh restrictions.[35] This historic victory is unlikely to mean any lessening of southern conservative demands when it comes to other areas of their political agenda. At grassroots, state, and national level, southern Republicans continue to push back against any restrictions on gun ownership, seek to limit the economic and electoral strength of minorities, and to resist the changes brought to American society by immigration. Notably, a 2020 poll by PRRI found that 66 percent of conservative evangelicals regarded immigrants as "invaders." Such views now comprise the mainstream of the GOP.[36]

The modern Republican Party is, therefore, a very different institution to the GOP of the Reagan era. As Jesse Helms and other southerners demonstrated during Ronald Reagan's presidency, the southern strand of conservatism has long prioritized its own identity and interests over party affiliation. It has always been, as political commentator Jonathan Rauch has noted, "a political third force—anti-establishment in its credo, disruptive in its influence, and opportunistic in its partisan attachments."[37] As affluent, college-educated voters have steadily drifted away from the GOP over the last decade, the power of southern conservatism in the party has only become more entrenched. For better or worse, southern conservatives have essentially gained control of one of America's two major parties, and Reaganite conservatism—at least for the time being—has been eclipsed as a political force. The GOP of the 2020s would likely be far more recognizable to Jesse Helms than to Ronald Reagan. Indeed, it is questionable whether Reagan, with his displays of political pragmatism and his dedication to free markets and free trade, could even find a place in today's Republican Party. The angry, reactionary character of the Trump-era GOP makes for an inescapable conclusion: the South won the Republican civil war.

Notes

ARCHIVAL COLLECTIONS AND ABBREVIATIONS

1980 PCP   1980 Presidential Campaign Papers, Ronald Reagan
Presidential Library, Simi Valley, California

AHF   Anne Higgins Files, Ronald Reagan Presidential Library, Simi
Valley, California

BGC   Bo Ginn Collection, Georgia Southern University Special
Collections, Statesboro, Georgia

CCP   Carroll Campbell Papers, Clemson University Libraries
Special Collections, Clemson, South Carolina

CFRC   Citizens for Reagan Collection, Hoover Institution Library
and Archives, Stanford University, Palo Alto, California

CHC   Charles Hatcher Collection, University of Georgia Special
Collections Libraries, Athens, Georgia

CLP   Charlton H. Lyons Papers, Louisiana State University
Libraries, Baton Rouge, Louisiana

CR   *Congressional Record*. Washington, DC: US Government
Printing Office.

CSF   Carolyn Sundseth Files, Ronald Reagan Presidential Library,
Simi Valley, California

DNF   David Neuman Files, Ronald Reagan Presidential Library,
Simi Valley, California

DWF   David Waller Files, Ronald Reagan Presidential Library, Simi
Valley, California

EDF   Elizabeth Dole Files, Ronald Reagan Presidential Library,
Simi Valley, California

EJP   Ed Jenkins Papers, University of Georgia Special Collections
Libraries, Athens, Georgia

EMF   Ed Meese Files, Ronald Reagan Presidential Library, Simi
Valley, California

ESF   Edward Stucky Files, Ronald Reagan Presidential Library,
Simi Valley, California

FMF   Frederick McClure Files, Ronald Reagan Presidential Library,
Simi Valley, California

GP   Governor's Papers, Ronald Reagan Presidential Library, Simi
            Valley, California
JBJP   J. Bennett Johnston Papers, Louisiana State University
            Libraries, Baton Rouge, Louisiana
JEJF   James E. Jenkins Files, Ronald Reagan Presidential Library,
            Simi Valley, California
JHP   Jesse Helms Papers, Jesse Helms Center Archives, Wingate,
            North Carolina
JJF   Jerry Jones Files, Gerald R. Ford Presidential Library, Ann
            Arbor, Michigan
JPF   Jim Pinkerton Files, Ronald Reagan Presidential Library, Simi
            Valley, California
JRF   John Roberts Files, Ronald Reagan Presidential Library, Simi
            Valley, California
LAF   Legislative Affairs Files, Ronald Reagan Presidential Library,
            Simi Valley, California
LHP   Larry Hopkins Papers, University of Kentucky Libraries
            Special Collections, Lexington, Kentucky
MBF   Morton Blackwell Files, Ronald Reagan Presidential Library,
            Simi Valley, California
MDF   Michael Driggs Files, Ronald Reagan Presidential Library,
            Simi Valley, California
MLBF   Melvin L. Bradley Files, Ronald Reagan Presidential Library,
            Simi Valley, California
MLP   Marvin Leath Papers, Baylor University Libraries, Waco,
            Texas
MOF   M. B. Oglesby Files, Ronald Reagan Presidential Library, Simi
            Valley, California
STC   Strom Thurmond Collection, Clemson University Libraries
            Special Collections, Clemson, South Carolina
PHP   Peter Hannaford Papers, Hoover Institution Library and
            Archives, Stanford University, Palo Alto, California
PPP-RR   *Public Papers of the Presidents of the United States: Ronald
            Reagan (1981–1989).* Washington, DC: Office of the Federal
            Register, National Archives and Records Administration,
            1981-1989.
PTC   Presidential Telephone Calls, Ronald Reagan Presidential
            Library, Simi Valley, California
SGF   Stephen Galebach Files, Ronald Reagan Presidential Library,
            Simi Valley, California

WBA	Warner Brothers Archives, University of Southern California Libraries, Los Angeles, California
WHORM	White House Office of Records Management Files, Ronald Reagan Presidential Library, Simi Valley, California
WLF	William Lacy Files, Ronald Reagan Presidential Library, Simi Valley, California
WNP	William Nichols Papers, Auburn University Special Collections, Auburn, Alabama

PROLOGUE

1. "Reagan, Wallace Talk to Alabama 'Faithful,'" *Miami News*, 22 March 1975; Marcia Kunstel, "Reagan's Visit Wins Welcome," *Montgomery Advertiser*, 22 March 1975.

2. Richard Bergholz, "Reagan, Wallace Meet in Alabama," *Los Angeles Times*, 22 March 1975; "Reagan, Wallace Talk to Alabama 'Faithful.'"

3. "Wallace, Reagan Talk at Alabama Motel," *Fort Worth Star-Telegram*, 22 March 1975; Baxter Omohundro, "Reagan, Wallace Share Platform at Southern Grassroots Banquet," *Washington Post*, 23 March 1975.

4. Numan V. Bartley, *The New South: 1945–1980* (Baton Rouge: Louisiana State University Press, 1995), 1.

5. Matthew Lassiter, "Big Government and Family Values: Political Culture in the Metropolitan Sunbelt," in *Sunbelt Rising: The Politics of Space, Place, and Region*, ed. Michelle Nickerson and Darren Dochuk (Philadelphia: University of Pennsylvania Press, 2011), 86–87.

6. Lassiter, "Big Government and Family Values," 87.

7. James C. Cobb, *The Selling of the South: The Southern Crusade for Industrial Development, 1936–1980* (Baton Rouge: Louisiana State University Press, 1982), 5–63.

8. James C. Cobb, *The South and America Since World War II* (New York: Oxford University Press, 2012), 61–63.

9. Bruce Schulman, *From Cotton Belt to Sunbelt: Federal Policy, Economic Development, and the Transformation of the South, 1938–1980* (Durham, NC: Duke University Press, 1994), 116–117, 183–184.

10. Lassiter, "Big Government and Family Values," 88.

11. Ira Katznelson, *Fear Itself: The New Deal and the Origins of Our Time* (New York: Liveright, 2013), 427.

12. Schulman, *From Cotton Belt to Sunbelt*, 149.

13. William Faulkner, "On Fear: The South in Labor," *Harper's Magazine*, 1 June 1956.

14. Schulman, *From Cotton Belt to Sunbelt*, 146–147.

15. Rowland Evans and Robert Novak, "The South in Space," *Washington Post*, 25 August 1964.

16. Sean Cunningham, *American Politics in the Postwar Sunbelt* (New York: Cambridge University Press, 2014), 5–7.

17. Cobb, *The South and America*, 55.

18. Stephen F. Lawson, *Running for Freedom: Civil Rights and Black Politics in America since 1941* (Malden, MA: Wiley-Blackwell, 2009), 35.

19. Lawson, *Running for Freedom*, 25.

20. Cobb, *The South and America*, 9–10.

21. Lawson, *Running for Freedom*, 27–28.

22. Jason Sokol, *There Goes My Everything: White Southerners in the Age of Civil Rights, 1945–1975* (New York: Knopf, 2006), 14.

23. Michael Honey, "Operation Dixie: Labor and Civil Rights in the Postwar South," *The Mississippi Quarterly* 45, no. 4 (Fall 1992): 445–446.

24. "14 Klan Crosses Burned In 4 Southern States," *Atlanta Constitution*, 27 July 1951.

25. George Lewis, *The White South and the Red Menace: Segregationists, Anticommunism, and Massive Resistance, 1945–1965* (Gainesville: University Press of Florida, 2004), 53–54.

26. Sokol, *There Goes My Everything*, 84.

27. Sokol, *There Goes My Everything*, 42.

28. "The Press: The Hot Middle," *Time Magazine*, 16 May 1955.

29. William A. Link, *Southern Crucible: The Making of an American Region* (New York: Oxford University Press, 2015), 520.

30. Anthony Badger, *Why White Liberals Fail: Race and Southern Politics from FDR to Trump* (Cambridge, MA: Harvard University Press, 2022), 78, 111.

31. Bartley, *The New South*, 198.

32. Lewis, *The White South and the Red Menace*, 41.

33. Lewis, *The White South and the Red Menace*, 40.

34. Robert Penn Warren, *Segregation: The Inner Conflict in the South* (London: Eyre & Spottiswoode, 1957), 46.

35. William Martin, *With God on Our Side: The Rise of the Religious Right in America* (New York: Broadway Books, 1996), 33.

36. Martin, *With God on Our Side*, 39–44.

37. Daniel K. Williams, *God's Own Party: The Making of the Christian Right* (New York: Oxford University Press, 2010), 26–27.

38. Edward H. Miller, *Nut Country: Right-wing Dallas and the Birth of the Southern Strategy* (Chicago: University of Chicago Press, 2015), 23.

39. Sokol, *There Goes My Everything*, 101.

40. Sokol, *There Goes My Everything*, 100.

41. Paul Harvey, "Religion, Race, and the Right in the South," in *Politics and Religion in the White South*, ed. Glenn Feldman (Lexington: University of Kentucky Press, 2005), 109–110.

42. Curtis W. Freeman, "'Never Had I Been So Blind': W. A. Criswell's 'Change' on Racial Segregation," *Journal of Southern Religion* 10 (2007): 1–4.

43. Miller, *Nut Country*, 26–27.

44. Williams, *God's Own Party*, 4–5.

45. Harvey, "Religion, Race, and the Right in the South," 105.

46. Harvey, "Religion, Race, and the Right in the South," 104–105.

47. Michael Bowen, *The Roots of Modern Conservatism: Dewey, Taft, and the Battle for the Soul of the Republican Party* (Chapel Hill: University of North Carolina Press, 2011), 5.

48. Lewis L. Gould, *Grand Old Party: The History of the Republicans* (New York: Random House, 2003), 314.

49. Robert Mason, *The Republican Party and American Politics from Hoover to Reagan* (New York: Cambridge University Press, 2012), 119.

50. Katznelson, *Fear Itself*, 221, 389–398.

51. Mason, *Republican Party and American Politics*, 116.

52. Gould, *Grand Old Party*, 319.

53. Godfrey Hodgson, *The World Turned Right Side Up: A History of the Conservative Ascendancy in America* (London: Houghton Mifflin, 1996), 50.

54. Bowen, *Roots of Modern Conservatism*, 172–173.

55. Ronald Reagan, *My Early Life or Where's the Rest of Me?* (London: Sidgwick & Jackson, 1981), 139.

56. Ronald Reagan, *An American Life: The Autobiography* (New York: Threshold, 1990), 115.

57. Iwan Morgan, *Reagan: American Icon* (London: I.B. Tauris, 2016), 50–53.

58. David Farber, *The Rise and Fall of Modern American Conservatism: A Short History* (Princeton: Princeton University Press, 2010), 168.

59. Thomas Evans, *The Education of Ronald Reagan: The General Electric Years and the Untold Story of His Conversion to Conservatism* (New York: Columbia University Press, 2006), 11–12.

60. Evans, *Education of Ronald Reagan*, 66.

61. Bowen, *Roots of Modern Conservatism*, 173.

62. Farber, *Rise and Fall of Modern American Conservatism*, 62–66.

63. Farber, *Rise and Fall of Modern American Conservatism*, 41.

64. Lee Edwards, *Goldwater: The Man Who Made a Revolution* (Washington, DC: Regnery History, 1995), 50–51.

65. Bowen, *Roots of Modern Conservatism*, 198–199.

66. Cunningham, *American Politics in the Postwar Sunbelt*, 17–18.

67. Lisa McGirr, *Suburban Warriors: The Origins of the New American Right* (Princeton: Princeton University Press, 2001), 4–6.

68. James Salt, "Sunbelt Capital and Conservative Political Realignment in the 1970s and 1980s," *Critical Sociology* 16, no. 2–3 (May 1989): 148.

69. Elizabeth Tandy Shermer, *Sunbelt Capitalism: Phoenix and the Transformation of American Politics* (Philadelphia: University of Pennsylvania Press, 2013), 3.

70. Bowen, *Roots of Modern Conservatism*, 199.

71. Hodgson, *World Turned Right Side Up*, 91–97.

72. Jeff Roche, "Cowboy Conservatism," in *The Conservative Sixties*, ed. David Farber and Jeff Roche (New York: Peter Lang, 2003), 79.

73. Cunningham, *American Politics in the Postwar Sunbelt*, 12.

74. Farber, *Rise and Fall of Modern American Conservatism*, 75.

75. Farber, *Rise and Fall of Modern American Conservatism*, 89–90.

76. Morgan, *Reagan*, 66.

77. Shermer, *Sunbelt Capitalism*, 282–284.

78. Chris Ladd, "How a Sub-Party Captured the GOP," *Forbes*, 4 August 2017.

79. Ladd, "How a Sub-Party Captured the GOP."

CHAPTER ONE. "HE BROUGHT THEM THE GOSPEL"

1. Carl Milliken to Roy Obringer, 6 October 1949 and Carl Milliken to Jerry Wald, 11 October 1949, both in Storm Warning Files: Communication, WBA.

2. "Melodrama Is Taut Film About Klan," *Richmond Times-Dispatch*, 1 February 1951; "Story of Klan Provides Taut, Terrifying Film," *Chicago Tribune*, 9 February 1951.

3. Fairfax Nisbet, "Film Notables Arriving for COMPO Parley," *Dallas Morning News*, 9 June 1952.

4. Billy Graham, *Just as I Am: The Autobiography of Billy Graham* (New York: HarperCollins, 1997), 528–529.

5. Toby Glenn Bates, *The Reagan Rhetoric: History and Memory in 1980s America* (Dekalb: Northern Illinois University Press, 2011), 19.

6. Ronald Reagan, *My Early Life or Where's the Rest of Me?* (London: Sidgwick & Jackson, 1981), 261.

7. "Actor Reagan Due to Visit Here Mar. 20," *Anniston Star*, 3 March 1955.

8. "Reagan to Be Guest of Central Christian," *Lexington Herald-Leader*, 27 March 1955.

9. Bob Ackerman, "Ronald Reagan Says Those Kisses in Movies Don't Bowl You Over," *State*, 21 March 1957.

10. Bates, *The Reagan Rhetoric*, 19.

11. Kurt Ritter, "Ronald Reagan's 1960s Southern Rhetoric: Courting Conservatives for the GOP," *Southern Communication Journal* 64, no. 1 (1998–1999): 334.

12. Reagan, *My Early Life*, 267.

13. Ronald Reagan, *An American Life: The Autobiography* (New York: Threshold, 1990), 129.

14. Lou Cannon, *Governor Reagan: His Rise to Power* (New York: Public Affairs, 2003), 109.

15. Thomas Evans, *The Education of Ronald Reagan: The General Electric Years and the Untold Story of His Conversion to Conservatism* (New York: Columbia University Press, 2006), 111–112.

16. Reagan, *My Early Life*, 267.

17. Ritter, "Reagan's 1960s Southern Rhetoric," 335.

18. Earl Black and Merle Black, *The Rise of Southern Republicans* (Cambridge, MA: Harvard University Press, 2002), 57.

19. Black and Black, *Rise of Southern Republicans*, 59.

20. Anthony Badger, *Why White Liberals Fail: Race and Southern Politics from FDR to Trump* (Cambridge, MA: Harvard University Press, 2022), 112–113.

21. Dewey Grantham, *The Life and Death of the Solid South: A Political History* (Lexington: University Press of Kentucky, 1988), 127–128.

22. Kari Frederickson, *The Dixiecrat Revolt and the End of the Solid South, 1932–1968* (Chapel Hill: University of North Carolina Press, 2001), 231.

23. Black and Black, *Rise of Southern Republicans*, 63.

24. "Republican Party Platform of 1956," The American Presidency Project, UC Santa Barbara, https://www.presidency.ucsb.edu/node/273398.

25. James C. Cobb, *The South and America since World War II* (New York: Oxford University Press, 2012), 46–51.

26. Jason Sokol, *There Goes My Everything: White Southerners in the Age of Civil Rights, 1945–1975* (New York: Knopf, 2006), 116–117.

27. Stephen F. Lawson, *Running for Freedom: Civil Rights and Black Politics in America since 1941* (Malden, MA: Wiley-Blackwell, 2009), 59–61.

28. Ritter, "Reagan's 1960s Southern Rhetoric," 339.

29. Reagan, *An American Life*, 137–139.

30. "Liberalism Lambasted by Reagan," *Dallas Morning News*, 28 February 1962.

31. "Stirring Address," *Dallas Morning News*, 1 March 1962.

32. Eric Pardue, "Kennedyphobia and the Rise of Republicans in Northwest Louisiana, 1960–1962," in *Painting Dixie Red: When, Where, Why, and How the South Became Republican*, ed. Glenn Feldman (Gainesville: University Press of Florida, 2011), 122–126.

33. Gerald Moses, "Reagan Talks on Conservatism at Republican Banquet Here," *Advocate*, 21 January 1964.

34. Ronald Reagan to Charlton Lyons, undated (1964), Series 1, Box 1, CLP.

35. Cannon, *Governor Reagan*, 139.

36. "'Ridicule' and 'Personal Abuse' Charges Raised in N.O. by Lyons," *Advocate*, 20 February 1964.

37. Roy R. Glashan, *American Governors and Gubernatorial Elections, 1775–1978* (London: Meckler, 1979), 116–119.

38. "'Lyons Carpetbagger' Talks About Conservative Beliefs," *Shreveport Times*, 1 March 1964.

39. William A. Link, *Southern Crucible: The Making of an American Region* (New York: Oxford University Press, 2015), 536–537.

40. Gary Donaldson, *Liberalism's Last Hurrah: The Presidential Campaign of 1964* (New York: M. E. Sharpe, 2003), 80–81.

41. Tom Wicker, "Convention Ends; Extremism in Defence of Liberty 'No Vice,' Arizonan Asserts", *New York Times*, 17 July 1964.

42. Lewis L. Gould, *Grand Old Party: The History of the Republicans* (New York: Random House, 2003), 363.

43. Wayne Greenhaw, *Elephants in the Cottonfields: Ronald Reagan and the New Republican South* (New York: Macmillan, 1982), 55.

44. Theodore H. White, *The Making of the President 1964* (London: Jonathan Cape: 1965), 233–234.

45. Donaldson, *Liberalism's Last Hurrah*, 274–276.

46. Greenhaw, *Elephants in the Cottonfields*, 55.

47. Bruce Schulman, *From Cotton Belt to Sunbelt: Federal Policy, Economic Development, and the Transformation of the South, 1938–1980* (Durham, NC: Duke University Press, 1994), 215.

48. David Kraslow, "Dixie Politics Heading for Striking Turnabout," *Los Angeles Times*, 23 September 1964.

49. Donaldson, *Liberalism's Last Hurrah*, 90, 99.

50. Ronald Keith Gaddie, "Realignment," in *The Oxford Handbook of Southern Politics*, ed. Charles Bullock and Mark Rozell (New York: Oxford University Press, 2012), 303–305.

51. Richard H. Rovere, "The Campaign: Goldwater," *New Yorker*, 3 October 1964.

52. Earl Mazo, "Polls Predicting a Johnson Sweep," *New York Times*, 28 October 1964.

53. "1964," The American Presidency Project, UC Santa Barbara, https://www.presidency.ucsb.edu/statistics/elections/1964.

54. White, *Making of the President 1964*, 380.

55. Robert J. Donovan, "The Future of the Republican Party," *Los Angeles Times*, 15 November 1964.

56. White, *Making of the President 1964*, 381.

57. Charles Mohr, "Thurmond Joins Goldwater Drive," *New York Times*, 18 September 1964.

58. David Nordan, "Republicanism Growing Force in Dixie," *Atlanta Constitution*, 15 October 1972.

59. Gould, *Grand Old Party*, 367–368.

60. Ronald Reagan to Charlton Lyons, 29 December 1964, Series 1, Box 1, CLP.

61. Gallup, George, "No Standouts but Nixon Leads GOP Possibilities," *Hartford Courant*, 27 June 1965.

62. James N. Gregory, *The Southern Diaspora: How the Great Migrations of Black and White Southerners Transformed America* (Chapel Hill: University of North Carolina Press, 2005), 18–19.

63. Darren Dochuk, *From Bible Belt to Sunbelt: Plain Folk Religion, Grassroots Politics, and the Rise of Evangelical Conservatism* (New York: W. W. Norton & Company, 2011), 255.

64. James Q. Wilson, "A Guide to Reagan Country: The Political Culture of Southern California," *Commentary*, 1 May 1967.

65. Dochuk, *From Bible Belt to Sunbelt*, 268–269.

66. "Thurmond Says Russia 'Ordered' U.S. Muzzling," *Los Angeles Times*, 30 November 1961.

67. "Major Highlights of Thurmond Talk," *Valley Times*, 17 February 1964.

68. "Brown Assails Prop. 14 as 'Cudgel of Bigotry,'" *Los Angeles Times*, 8 October 1964.

69. "Thurmond Unleashes Attack on Democrats," *Los Angeles Times*, 27 September 1964.

70. Dochuk, *From Bible Belt to Sunbelt*, xvii.

71. Gene Blake, "State Supreme Court Holds Prop. 14 Unconstitutional," *Los Angeles Times*, 11 May 1966.

72. Richard Bergholz, "Reagan Opposes Homeowner Curb," *Los Angeles Times*, 31 October 1966.

73. Alistair Cooke, "Mr. Reagan Touches on Secret Fears," *The Guardian*, 2 November 1966.

74. Carl Greenberg, "Reagan Announces He's Candidate for Governor," *Los Angeles Times*, 5 January 1966.

75. Bergholz, "Reagan Opposes Homeowner Curb."

76. Cooke, "Mr. Reagan Touches on Secret Fears."

77. Matthew Dallek, *The Right Moment: Ronald Reagan's First Victory and the Decisive Turning Point in American Politics* (New York: Oxford University Press, 2000), 226–228.

78. William Buckley, "Ronald Reagan Is Getting Good Start in Race for Governorship," *Los Angeles Times*, 17 December 1965.

79. "California Election Results," US Election Atlas, https://uselectionatlas .org/RESULTS/state.php?fips=6&f=0&off=99.

80. "A Key to the Heart of Columbia," *State*, 30 September 1967.

81. Lee Bandy, "Reagan Warms GOP Hearts," *State*, 30 September 1967.

82. Joseph Crespino, *Strom Thurmond's America* (New York: Hill & Wang, 2012), 197.

83. Remer Tyson, "Reagan's Theme: Safe with GOP," *Atlanta Constitution*, 4 October 1967.

84. Cannon, *Governor Reagan*, 264.

85. Tom Goff, "Reagan-Wallace Differences Blurred, Governor Admits," *Los Angeles Times*, 17 July 1968.

86. Cannon, *Governor Reagan*, 265.

87. Richard M. Nixon, *RN: The Memoirs of Richard Nixon* (New York: Grosset & Dunlap, 1978), 304.

88. Cannon, *Governor Reagan*, 265–266.

89. Jack Nelson, "Reagan Openly Courts 5 Southern Delegations," *Los Angeles Times*, 25 July 1968.

90. Rowland Evans and Robert Novak, "Nixon's Southern Front Is Unravelling," *Boston Globe*, 26 July 1968.

91. Nixon, *RN*, 304.

92. Rick Perlstein, *Nixonland: The Rise of a President and the Fracturing of America* (New York: Scribner, 2008), 283–285.

93. Theodore H. White, *The Making of the President 1968* (London: Jonathan Cape, 1969), 239–240.

94. Ronald Reagan to Charlton Lyons, 3 September 1968, Box 2, 1980 PCP.

95. "The Bellyachers," *State*, 13 August 1968.

96. Numan V. Bartley and Hugh Davis Graham, *Southern Politics and the Second Reconstruction* (Baltimore: Johns Hopkins University Press, 1975), 127.

97. Schulman, *From Cotton Belt to Sunbelt*, 215.

98. Schulman, *From Cotton Belt to Sunbelt*, 180.

99. Sokol, *There Goes My Everything*, 223–227.

100. Kevin M. Kruse, *White Flight: Atlanta and the Making of Modern Conservatism* (Princeton: Princeton University Press, 2005), 251–253.

101. Schulman, *From Cotton Belt to Sunbelt*, 179.

102. Michael A. Cohen, *American Maelstrom: The 1968 Election and the Politics of Division* (New York: Oxford University Press, 2016), 234–236.

103. Sokol, *There Goes My Everything*, 225.

104. Sokol, *There Goes My Everything*, 276.

105. Frederickson, *The Dixiecrat Revolt*, 118–119, 236–237.

106. Lewis L. Gould, *1968: The Election that Changed America* (Chicago: Ivan Dee, 1993), 62.

107. Ray Zeman, "Rumford Act Up to Legislature, Reagan Asserts," *Los Angeles Times*, 30 May 1967.

108. Tom Goff, "Reagan Alters Rumford Stand," *Los Angeles Times*, 3 April 1968.

109. Cannon, *Governor Reagan*, 206.

110. Cannon, *Governor Reagan*, 82.

111. Ronald Reagan Speech to California Republican Assembly, 1 April 1967, Box P17, Series 3, GP; Jerry Gillam, "Governor Signs Law on Abortion," *Los Angeles Times*, 16 June 1967.

112. Jerry Gillam, "Reagan Gets Bill on Loaded Guns," *Los Angeles Times*, 28 July 1967.

113. Dochuk, *From Bible Belt to Sunbelt*, 269.

114. Jack Boettner, "Impact of Graham Crusade Cited After 384,000 Attend," *Los Angeles Times*, 6 October 1969.

115. John Dart, "Graham Launches 10-Day Southland Crusade in Anaheim," *Los Angeles Times*, 27 September 1969.

116. Strom Thurmond to Ronald Reagan, 21 November 1974, Box 4, 1980 PCP.

117. Crespino, *Strom Thurmond's America*, 244.

118. William A. Link, *Righteous Warrior: Jesse Helms and the Rise of Modern Conservatism* (New York: St. Martin's Press, 2008), 146–147.

119. Lou Cannon, "Support for Reagan Grows in South," *Washington Post*, 18 November 1973.

120. "Governor Reagan Made Good Sense," *Mobile Register*, 2 October 1974.

121. Sokol, *There Goes My Everything*, 250–251, 254–262.

122. James Kilpatrick, "The 'New South' Is Rising," *Los Angeles Times*, 19 March 1971; Terry Wooten, "Blacks Finding a 'New South,'" *Chicago Daily Defender*, 18 July 1970.

123. "Old Age Costing South's Democrats Grip on Senate Committees," *Hartford Courant*, 10 April 1972; John Herbers, "Sun of Political Influence Is Rising in the West and Setting in the South," *New York Times*, 20 January 1981.

124. Howell Raines, "George Wallace, Segregation Symbol, Dies at 79," *New York Times*, 14 September 1998.

125. Robert Mason, *Richard Nixon and the Quest for a New Majority* (Chapel Hill: University of North Carolina Press, 2004), 29.

126. Mason, *Richard Nixon and the Quest for a New Majority*, 26.

127. Bartley and Graham, *Southern Politics and the Second Reconstruction*, 127.

128. Greenhaw, *Elephants in the Cotton Fields*, 87.

129. Sean Cunningham, *Cowboy Conservatism: Texas and the Rise of the Modern Right* (Lexington: University Press of Kentucky, 2010), 141.

130. Eugene Risher, "Ford Begs South's Voters to Stop Demo 'Monopoly,'" *Atlanta Constitution*, 20 October 1974.

131. Peter Hannaford Record of Meeting with Ronald Reagan and Barry Goldwater on 5 May 1975, Box 7, PHP.

132. Cannon, *Governor Reagan*, 395–397.

133. Reg Murphy, "Ronald Reagan's Decision Not Easy," *Atlanta Constitution*, 10 July 1975.

134. Arnold Sawislak, "Reagan Tells GOP to Stand Firm," *Boston Globe*, 9 March 1975.

135. Link, *Righteous Warrior*, 148.

136. Link, *Righteous Warrior*, 148; Ferrel Guillory, "Reagan Says Rocky Abused," *News and Observer*, 26 July 1975.

137. Ned Cline, "Reagan Tells Crowd That He'll Be Back," *Greensboro Daily News*, 22 November 1975; Richard Bergholz, "Reagan Returns from Whirlwind 2-Day Trip to Launch Presidential Campaign," *Los Angeles Times*, 22 November 1975.

138. Jesse Helms, "Reagan's Announcement to Seek Presidential Nomination," Record Group 2, Box 229, JHP.

139. Wallace Turner, "Poll Has Ford Losing Ground to Reagan," *New York Times*, 25 November 1975.

140. Helms, "Reagan's Announcement to Seek Presidential Nomination."

CHAPTER TWO. "THIS IS REAGAN COUNTRY"

1. David Nordan, "Republicanism Growing Force in Dixie," *Atlanta Constitution*, 15 October 1972.

2. Sean Cunningham, *Cowboy Conservatism: Texas and the Rise of the Modern Right* (Lexington: University Press of Kentucky, 2010), 153–159; William Lyons, John M. Scheb, Billy Stair, and Joseph G. Jarret, *Government and Politics in Tennessee* (Knoxville: University of Tennessee, 2017), 229–230.

3. "Reagan Strong in South; Ford Said in Trouble," *Hartford Courant*, 14 December 1975.

4. David Nordan, "Ford vs. Reagan: The Dixie Battle," *Atlanta Constitution*, 19 October 1975.

5. Robert Shogan, "Narrow Ford Victory," *Los Angeles Times*, 25 February 1976.

6. David Keene to Tommy Thomas, 19 September 1975, Box 4, CFRC.

7. David Nyhan, "Carter Stuns Wallace; Ford Defeats Reagan," *Boston Globe*, 10 March 1976.

8. Robert Shogan, "Loss Deals Severe Blow to Reagan," *Los Angeles Times*, 10 March 1976.

9. Nyhan, "Carter Stuns Wallace."

10. Jules Witcover, *Marathon: The Pursuit of the Presidency 1972–1976* (New York: Viking Press, 1977), 405–414.

11. Jesse Helms, *Here's Where I Stand: A Memoir* (New York: Random House, 2005), 97.

12. Ernest B. Furgurson, *Hard Right: The Rise of Jesse Helms* (New York: W. W. Norton & Company, 1986), 117.

13. Rob Christensen, *The Paradox of Tar Heel Politics: The Personalities, Elections and Events that Shaped Modern North Carolina* (Chapel Hill: University of North Carolina Press, 2008), 213.

14. Christensen, *Paradox of Tar Heel Politics*, 135–146.

15. Furgurson, *Hard Right*, 64.

16. Furgurson, *Hard Right*, 69–70.

17. Helms, *Here's Where I Stand*, 99.

18. Address by Senator Jesse Helms in Miami, 6 March 1976, Record Group 2, Box 230, JHP.

19. Rob Christensen and Jim Morrill, "Political Kingmaker Tom Ellis Dies," *News and Observer*, 13 July 2018.

20. Christensen, *Paradox of Tar Heel Politics*, 216–223.

21. "Interview with Frank Rouse," 14 November 1996, Southern Oral History Program, University of North Carolina Digital Collections Repository, https://dcr.lib.unc.edu/record/a24a47b6-754c-4d40-9150-86c6f91adc57.

22. "Interview with Frank Rouse."

23. Ned Cline, "Primary's GOP Vote to Test Efforts by Helms, Holshauser," *Greensboro Daily News*, 22 March 1976.

24. William A. Link, *Righteous Warrior: Jesse Helms and the Rise of Modern Conservatism* (New York: St. Martin's Press, 2008), 152–153.

25. Lyn Nofziger, *Nofziger* (Washington DC: Regnery Gateway, 1992), 178–179.

26. James Naughton, "Reagan Suggests Ford Quit the Race," *New York Times*, 19 March 1976.

27. "Reagan 30 minute statement, 16th March 1976," CFRC.

28. Nofziger, *Nofziger*, 178.

29. Jerry Shinn, "7 GOP Governors Ask Reagan to Quit," *Charlotte Observer*, 20 March 1976.

30. Helms speech at Reagan rally, Greenville, 21 February 1976, Record Group 2, Box 230, JHP.

31. Ernest Furgurson, "Ford's Campaign Experts Misread the Real South," *Baltimore Sun*, 28 March 1976.

32. "Interview with Frank Rouse."

33. James Naughton, "Reagan Halts Pamphlet Linking Ford to Brooke," *New York Times*, 21 March 1976.

34. Rick Perlstein, *The Invisible Bridge: The Fall of Nixon and the Rise of Reagan* (New York: Simon & Schuster, 2014), 643.

35. Lou Cannon, *Governor Reagan: His Rise to Power* (New York: Public Affairs, 2003), 142, 423.

36. "Political Advertisement: How Democrats and Republicans Can Help Ronald Reagan. And America," *News and Observer*, 2 February 1976.

37. Link, *Righteous Warrior*, 153.

38. Witcover, *Marathon*, 412.

39. "Back in the Scrap," *Los Angeles Times*, 24 March 1976.

40. "Voter Shifts, TV Spark Reagan Win," *News and Observer*, 25 March 1976.

41. Peter Hannaford, *The Reagans: A Political Portrait* (New York: Coward-McCann, 1983), 85.

42. Furgurson, *Hard Right*, 118–119.

43. Ronald Reagan to Jesse Helms, 18 October 1991, Presidential Letters: Reagan, JHP.

44. Witcover, *Marathon*, 419.

45. Memo from Jeff Bell to Peter Hannaford, 12 April 1976, Box 6, PHP.

46. Rowland Evans and Robert Novak, "In Texas, a Wallace-to-Reagan Switch," *Washington Post*, 21 April 1976.

47. Linda Pavlik, "800 in Attendance at Evening Rally for Reagan in Dallas," *Fort Worth Star-Telegram*, 6 April 1976.

48. Cunningham, *Cowboy Conservatism*, 169–173.

49. Carroll Copelin, "Tower Could Be Big Loser," *Wichita Falls Times*, 26 April 1976.

50. Statement by Reagan state co-chairmen, Ray Barnhardt and Ernest Angelo, April 1976, Box 6, PHP.

51. James Sterba, "Democratic Vote Propels Reagan to Texas Sweep," *New York Times*, 3 May 1976.

52. "An Explanation of the Reagan Victories in Texas and Caucus States," Box 25, JJF.

53. Craig Shirley, *Reagan's Revolution: The Untold Story of the Campaign That Started It All* (Nashville: Nelson Current: 2005), 180, 191.

54. Ferrel Guillory, "Helms Interested in a Cause, but Not G.O.P. Cause," *News and Observer*, 27 June 1976.

55. "Irked Conservatives Look to Third Party," *Chicago Tribune*, 15 February 1975.

56. Kenneth Reich, "Triple Victory for Reagan," *Los Angeles Times*, 5 May 1976; "30,000 vote Republican," *Arkansas Democrat*, 26 May 1976.

57. Witcover, *Marathon*, 427.

58. "Reagan Talks of TVA Sale, but Backs off," *Lexington Herald-Leader*, 22 May 1976.

59. "Ford Rallies . . . " *New York Times*, 27 May 1976.

60. Witcover, *Marathon*, 456–459.

61. Steven Hayward, *The Age of Reagan: The Fall of the Old Liberal Order, 1964–1980* (Roseville, CA: Forum, 2001), 474–475.

62. "Reagan's Dismaying Choice," *Charleston News and Courier*, 28 July 1976.

63. B.E. Quinn to Citizens for Reagan Headquarters, 28 July 1976, Carl Payler to Ronald Reagan, 27 July 1976, C. M. Treppendahl to Ronald Reagan, 27 July 1976, and Edgar Saunders to Ronald Reagan, 28 July 1976, all Box 47, CFRC.

64. Loye Miller, "Schweiker Choice Shakes Conservatives," *Miami Herald*, 27 July 1976.

65. Rowland Evans and Robert Novak, "Miscalculations in the Schweiker ploy," *Greensboro Daily News*, 29 July 1976.

66. Helms, *Here's Where I Stand*, 104.

67. Martin Donsky, "Schweiker Choice Dampens Event," *News and Observer*, 1 August 1976.

68. "Your Move, Ronnie," *Atlanta Constitution*, 29 July 1976.

69. "Schweiker May Alienate La. Reagan Delegates," *Advocate*, 8 August 1976.

70. Larry Neal, "Reagan Move Shocks GOP Leaders in Texas," *Fort Worth Star-Telegram*, 27 July 1976.

71. Levona Page, "Edwards Stands Fast on Reagan Support," *State*, 31 July 1976.

72. "Reagan, Schweiker Grilled," *Atlanta Constitution*, 5 August 1976.

73. Ronald Reagan to Mr. Kiesewetter, 15 November 1979, in *Reagan: A Life in Letters*, ed. Kiron Skinner, Annelise Anderson, and Martin Anderson (New York: Free Press, 2003), 217–218.

74. Jules Witcover, "As Reagan Bid Fades, Strategist Sears Faces Long Knives," *Washington Post*, 19 August 1976.

75. Witcover, *Marathon*, 480–502.

76. John Geddie, "Republicans Nominate Ford, Ending Long, Stormy Race," *Dallas Morning News*, 19 August 1976.

77. Larry Neal, "Viva Reagan Texans May Vote: Si, Work: No," *Fort Worth Star Telegram*, 19 August 1976.

78. Ken Friedlein, "Helms, Reagan Apart at End," *Atlanta Constitution*, 29 August 1976.

79. "Reagan Retrospect," *Atlanta Constitution*, 22 August 1976.

80. Spencer Rich, "GOP Unit Backs Abortion Plank," *Washington Post*, 11 August 1976.

81. Hayward, *Age of Reagan*, 477–478.

82. "Republican Party Platform of 1976," The American Presidency Project, UC Santa Barbara, https://www.presidency.ucsb.edu/node/273415.

83. Gerald Ford, *A Time to Heal: The Autobiography* (New York: Harper & Row, 1979), 398.

84. Roger Simon, "Pulling Apart the Republican Wishbone," *Charlotte News*, 16 August 1976.

85. Jesse Helms to Stanton Evans, 14 September 1976, Record Group 2, Box 1544, JHP.

86. "1976 Presidential Endorsement Speech," 19 August 1976, C-SPAN, https://www.c-span.org/video/?4051-1/1976-presidential-endorsement-speech.

87. Carl Rowan, "Nagging Thoughts from Kansas City," *Atlanta Constitution*, 25 August 1976.

88. "Reagan Pushes Republican Platform on Campaign Swing through State," *Advocate*, 24 September 1976.

89. Linda Pavlik, "Reagan Still Popular," *Fort Worth Star-Telegram*, 15 October 1976.

90. Howard Covington, "Helms Airs Differences in Platforms," *Charlotte Observer*, 29 September 1976.

91. Godfrey Sperling, "South Welcomes Ford, but Hedges on Endorsement," *Christian Science Monitor*, 28 September 1976.

92. William Murchison, "A Breathing 'Corpse,'" *Dallas Morning News*, 11 November 1976.

93. "Reagan Is Stirring Again," *Chicago Tribune*, 5 November 1976.

94. "Could Have Beaten Carter—Reagan," *Los Angeles Times*, 6 December 1976.

95. Cannon, *Governor Reagan*, 434–439.

96. William Martin, *With God on Our Side: The Rise of the Religious Right in America* (New York: Broadway Books, 1996), 77–78.

97. Daniel K. Williams, *God's Own Party: The Making of the Christian Right* (New York: Oxford University Press, 2010), 70–71.

98. Williams, *God's Own Party*, 78–85.

99. Paul Harvey, "Religion, Race, and the Right in the South," in *Politics and Religion in the White South*, ed. Glenn Feldman (Lexington: University of Kentucky Press, 2005), 120.

100. Harvey, "Religion, Race, and the Right in the South," 120.

101. Williams, *God's Own Party*, 85–86.

102. Williams, *God's Own Party*, 163; Martin, *With God on Our Side*, 213.

103. Billie Cheney, "Wanted: A 'Moral Majority,'" *Atlanta Constitution*, 10 November 1979.

104. Randall Balmer, "The Real Origins of the Religious Right," *Politico*, 27 May 2014, https://www.politico.com/magazine/story/2014/05/religious-right-real-origins-107133/.

105. Martin, *With God on Our Side*, 210.

106. Williams, *God's Own Party*, 161.

107. Martin, *With God on Our Side*, 208.

108. Martin, *With God on Our Side*, 209.

109. John Jacobs, "Briggs' Wild Rumors about Gay Teachers," *San Francisco Examiner*, 3 October 1978.

110. Doyle McManus, "Briggs to Try Antigay Move Again in 1980," *Los Angeles Times*, 9 November 1978; Richard West, "Prop. 6 Dangerous, Reagan Believes," *Los Angeles Times*, 23 September 1978.

111. Michael Lopez, "Evangelist Helps Raise a Hope, a Prayer and Money for Prop. 6," *San Diego Union*, 31 October 1978.

112. Ronald Reagan to Robert Mauro, 11 October 1979, in *Reagan: A Life in Letters*, 197–198.

113. Ronald Reagan to Ann King Petroni, 31 July 1980, in *Reagan: A Life in Letters*, 248–250.

114. Ronald Reagan, "State of the Union" Speech, 13 March 1980, in *Reagan:*

In His Own Hand, ed. Kiron Skinner, Annelise Anderson, and Martin Anderson (New York: Touchstone, 2001), 479.

115. David Nyhan, "Falwell Mixes Religion with Politics," *Boston Globe*, 6 July 1980.

116. Martin, *With God on Our Side*, 216–217.

117. Jim Jones and Bill Walker, "Reagan Preaches Ol' Time Religion in His Politics," *Fort Worth Star Telegram*, 23 August 1980.

118. David Rosenbaum, "Conservatives Embrace Reagan on Social Issues," *New York Times*, 21 April 1980.

119. "Speech print—Roundtable National Affairs Briefing," Box 227, 1980 PCP.

120. Jones and Walker, "Reagan Preaches Ol' Time Religion."

121. "Speech Print—Roundtable National Affairs Briefing," Box 227, 1980 PCP.

122. Martin Schram, "George Bush Buried in Southern Voting," *Washington Post*, 12 March 1980.

123. William Endicott, "Reagan Opens Campaign at a Dixie County Fair," *Los Angeles Times*, 4 August 1980.

124. "Ronald Reagan's 1980 Neshoba County Fair Speech," *Neshoba Democrat*, 15 November 2007, https://neshobademocrat.com/stories/ronald -reagans-1980-neshoba-county-fair-speech,49123.

125. Jim Abbott, "The Editor Comments," *The Enterprise-Tocsin*, 7 August 1980.

126. Joseph Crespino, *In Search of Another Country: Mississippi and the Conservative Counterrevolution* (Princeton: Princeton University Press, 2007), 1.

127. Helen Thomas, "Notes on Reagan," *Journal Gazette*, 25 October 1980.

128. Peggy Elam, "Thurmond at Rally: US Needs a Change," *Clarion-Ledger*, 3 November 1980.

129. Earl Black and Merle Black, *The Rise of Southern Republicans* (Cambridge, MA: Harvard University Press, 2002), 218.

130. "1980," The American Presidency Project, UC Santa Barbara, https:// www.presidency.ucsb.edu/statistics/elections/1980.

131. "Election Statistics: 1920-Present," History, Art, and Archives of the US House of Representatives, https://history.house.gov/Institution/Election -Statistics/; "GOP Scores Upsets in 2 Governor Races," *Los Angeles Times*, 6 November 1980.

132. Robert Press, "Southern politics: Can GOP Stay on Top of a Democratic Mountain?" *Christian Science Monitor*, 14 November 1980.

133. Adam Clymer, "Bush Says No Single Group Gave Reagan His Victory," *New York Times*, 18 November 1980.

134. Williams, *God's Own Party*, 144–158.

135. Clymer, "Bush Says No Single Group Gave Reagan His Victory."

CHAPTER THREE. "WE REALLY SEEM TO BE PUTTING A COALITION TOGETHER"

1. Ronald Reagan, *An American Life: The Autobiography* (New York: Threshold, 1990), 229.

2. Reagan, *An American Life*, 230.

3. Ronald Reagan, "Address to the Nation on the Economy," 5 February 1981, PPP-RR (1981), 79–83.

4. Ronald Reagan, "Address before a Joint Session of the Congress on the Program for Economic Recovery," 18 February 1981, PPP-RR (1981), 108–115.

5. Iwan Morgan, *Reagan: American Icon* (London: I.B. Tauris, 2016), 176.

6. Reagan, "Address before a Joint Session of the Congress."

7. Nicol Rae, *Southern Democrats* (Oxford: Oxford University Press, 1994), 89.

8. Richard Lyons, "Conservative Democrats Press for Power in House," *New York Times*, 21 November 1980.

9. Margot Hornblower and T. R. Reid, "After Two Decades, the 'Boll Weevils' Are Back, Whistling Dixie," *Washington Post*, 26 April 1981.

10. Hedrick Smith, "Republican Moderates Won't Be Pushovers," *New York Times*, 20 September 1981.

11. Michael Barone, "The New Boll Weevils Hatch into a Potent Political Force," *Los Angeles Times*, 30 April 1981.

12. Hedrick Smith, "Southern Democrats Discover New Strength in Union with G.O.P.," *New York Times*, 5 May 1981.

13. Steven Roberts "The Importance of Being a Boll Weevil," *New York Times*, 14 June 1981.

14. Hornblower and Reid, "After Two Decades."

15. Members of Congress Historical Voting Records, GovTrack, https://www.govtrack.us/congress/members/all.

16. Rowland Evans and Robert Novak, "'Boll Weevils' Get Revenge," *Richmond Times-Dispatch*, 8 April 1981.

17. Burton Kaufman and Scott Kaufman, *The Presidency of James Earl Carter Jr.* (Lawrence: University Press of Kansas, 2009), 122–131.

18. Evans and Novak, "'Boll Weevils' Get Revenge."

19. Smith, "Southern Democrats Discover New Strength."

20. "Election Statistics: 1920–Present," History, Art, and Archives of the US House of Representatives, https://history.house.gov/Institution/Election -Statistics/.

21. Smith, "Southern Democrats Discover New Strength."

22. Fred Burnes, "GOP Set to Woo Democratic Right to Forge Conservative Majority in House," *Baltimore Sun*, 6 January 1981.

23. Steven Roberts, "New Conservative Coalition," *New York Times*, 7 January 1981.

24. Ronald Reagan, 5 March 1981, *The Reagan Diaries Unabridged, vol. 1* (New York: HarperCollins, 2009).

25. Laurence Barrett, *Gambling with History: Ronald Reagan in the White House* (New York: Doubleday, 1983), 150–151.

26. Henry Eason, "White House Planning Budget Blitz Aimed at Southern Democrats," *Atlanta Constitution*, 17 April 1981.

27. Memo from Lee Atwater to Lyn Nofziger, 22 April 1981, Box 2, MOF.

28. "GOP Mounts 'Southern Blitz' to Sell Reagan Budget," *Charlotte Observer*, 18 April 1981.

29. Eason, "White House Planning Budget Blitz."

30. Lou Cannon, "'Southern Blitz' Set for Economic Plan," *Washington Post*, 18 April 1981.

31. Charles Stenholm et al. to colleagues, 14 April 1981, Box 296, MLP.

32. Reagan, 28 April 1981, *Reagan Diaries Unabridged, vol. 1*.

33. Tom Hamburger, "Appeal from Reagan Gets Anthony's Vote," *Arkansas Gazette*, 6 May 1981.

34. Reagan, 6 May 1981, *Reagan Diaries Unabridged, vol. 1*.

35. House Vote to Agree to an Amendment of H.Con.Res.115, 7 May 1981, GovTrack, https://www.govtrack.us/congress/votes/97-1981/h30.

36. Hedrick Smith, *The Power Game: How Washington Works* (London: Collins, 1988), 472–477.

37. Monroe Karmin and Christopher Bonner, "Democrats' 'Redneck Row' Getting Some Respect," *Miami Herald*, 25 June 1981.

38. Rowland Evans and Robert Novak, "Reagan's Lobbying Technique," *Lexington Herald-Leader*, 28 May 1981.

39. "Editorial," *Advocate*, 10 May 1981.

40. Jack Germond and Jules Witcover, "Weevil Caucus," *Advocate*, 23 June 1981.

41. "Max Friedersdorf Oral History," 24 October 2002, Miller Center, University of Virginia, https://millercenter.org/the-presidency/presidential-oral -histories/max-friedersdorf-oral-history.

42. Joan McKinney, "Breaux and Tauzin Traded Votes for Reagan Aid for Sugar," *Advocate*, 28 June 1981.

43. "Max Friedersdorf Oral History."

44. Smith, *The Power Game*, 478–479.

45. Monroe Karmin, "House Takes Historic Turn to Right," *Miami Herald*, 27 June 1981.

46. Ward Sinclair and Peter Behr, "Horse Trading," *Washington Post*, 27 June 1981.

47. David Stockman, *The Triumph of Politics* (New York: Hodder & Stoughton, 1985), 222.

48. Smith, *The Power Game*, 478.

49. Jim Wright to Marvin Leath, 26 June 1981, Box 296, MLP.

50. House Vote to Pass H.R.3982, 26 June 1981, GovTrack, https://www.govtrack.us/congress/votes/97-1981/h104.

51. Stockman, *Triumph of Politics*, 181.

52. Charles Hatcher to Mr. Gerald Thompson, 8 July 1981, Box 119, CHC.

53. Peter Grier, "Sweeping New Law Has Something for Everyone," *Christian Science Monitor*, 14 August 1981.

54. Roberts, "The Importance of Being a Boll Weevil."

55. Henry Eason, "Georgia Lawmakers Fight for Little Man," *Atlanta Constitution*, 14 June 1981.

56. Steven Roberts, "3 Conservative Democrats Wary on Tax Cut," *New York Times*, 17 May 1981.

57. Memo from Max Friedersdorf to James Baker, Ed Meese, and Michael Deaver, 19 March 1981, Box 2, MOF.

58. Memo from David Gergen to President Reagan, Box 1, PTC.

59. Gene Marlowe, "'Boll Weevil' Faction Ready to Back Tax Cuts," *Richmond Times-Dispatch*, 24 May 1981.

60. Monroe Karmin, "Reagan Hints Tax Plan Deal," *Hartford Courant*, 6 June 1981.

61. Steven Roberts, "Reagan Displays Skill at Crafting Deals," *New York Times*, 30 July 1981.

62. Records of telephone calls to Buddy Roemer, Doug Barnard, and Bill Boner, Box 1, PTC.

63. Jim Wright, *Balance of Power: Presidents and Congress from the Era of McCarthy to the Age of Gingrich* (Atlanta: Turner Publishing, 1996), 367.

64. John Hall and Gene Marlowe, "TV Blitz for Tax Plan Studied," *Richmond Times-Dispatch*, 15 May 1981.

65. "Rep. Fountain Is Angered by Radio Ads on Taxes," *Greensboro Daily News*, 25 June 1981.

66. Record of telephone call to L. H. Fountain, Box 1, PTC.

67. A. L. May, "Alabama's Democratic Governor Pushes Republican Tax Cut in N.C.," *News and Observer*, 28 July 1981.

68. Record of telephone call to Ronnie Flippo, Box 1, PTC.

69. Remarks by Ed Jenkins, CR, 29 July 1981, 18054.

70. Remarks by John Breaux, CR, 29 July 1981, 18236.

71. Remarks by Andy Ireland, CR, 29 July 1981, 18072–18073.

72. Remarks by Buddy Roemer, CR, 29 July 1981, 18065–18066.

73. Memo from Elizabeth Dole to James Baker, 28 July 1981, Box 7, EMF.

74. Michael Mecham, "Rep. Nelson: Reagan Offered a Better Deal," *Florida Today*, 30 July 1981; "Georgians Back Cuts," *Marietta Journal*, 29 July 1981; Bill Neikerk, "Georgia Defection Was for More than Just Peanuts," *Macon News*, 31 July 1981.

75. House Vote to Agree to a Substitute to H.R.4242, 29 July 1981, Gov-Track, https://www.govtrack.us/congress/votes/97-1981/h166.

76. Joan McKinney, "Tax-Cut Fight More Auction than Debate," *Advocate*, 26 July 1981.

77. Barrett, *Gambling with History*, 166–170.

78. Rowland Evans and Robert Novak, "Reagan Compromise Angers Big Business," *Richmond Times-Dispatch*, 9 June 1981.

79. Bill Nichols to Reverend Walker Bynum, 19 August 1981, Accession 82–003, Box 5, WNP.

80. Ed Jenkins to Mr. Joseph Dinatali, 24 March 1982, Box 36, Constituent Services Series, EJP.

81. Art Pine, "'Boll Weevil' Power," *Houston Chronicle*, 5 July 1981.

82. "Bumper Crop," *Fort Worth Star-Telegram*, 15 September 1981.

83. Henry Eason, "Congress' 'Boll Weevils' Don't Get Called on the Carpet, but They May Be Dying Out," *Atlanta Constitution*, 20 September 1981.

84. Monroe Karmin and Christopher Bonner, "House 'Boll Weevil' Democrats Flexing New Muscle," *Macon Telegraph*, 21 June 1981.

85. Office of Policy Development 1982 Election Report, Box 1, JPF.

86. Eason, "Congress' 'Boll Weevils.'"

87. Morgan, *Reagan*, 186.

88. Caroline Atkinson, "The Southern States," *Washington Post*, 10 January 1982.

89. Frank Newport, Jeffrey M. Jones, and Lydia Saad, "Ronald Reagan from the People's Perspective: A Gallup Poll Review," 7 June 2004, Gallup, https://news.gallup.com/poll/11887/ronald-reagan-from-peoples-perspective-gallup-poll-review.

90. William Cotterell, "Reagan Still Rates in the South," *State*, 2 August 1982.

91. Jack Smith, "Hance Defends Record of Boll Weevils," *Fort Worth Star-Telegram*, 26 June 1982.

92. Records of telephone calls to Doug Barnard and Charles Hatcher, Box 2, PTC.

93. Bill Niekirk and Dorothy Collin, "House Oks Budget," *Chicago Tribune*, 11 June 1982.

94. William Eaton and Paul Houston, "House Coalition Gives Reagan Budget Victory," *Los Angeles Times*, 11 June 1982; "Majority Without Control," *Arkansas Gazette*, 12 June 1981.

95. Jim Luther, "Pressures Build in Tax Battle," *Advocate*, 19 August 1982.

96. Kenneth Duberstein memo about meeting with selected House Democrats, 18 August 1982, Box 1, LAF.

97. Luther, "Pressures Build in Tax Battle."

98. Reagan, 18 August 1982, *Reagan Diaries Unabridged, vol. 1.*

99. House Vote to Agree to the Conference Report on H.R.4961, 19 August 1982, GovTrack, https://www.govtrack.us/congress/votes/97-1982/h642.

100. Henry Eason, "'Reaganomics' Critic Fowler Supports President's Tax Hike," *Atlanta Constitution*, 19 August 1982.

101. Cragg Hines, "'Boll Weevils' Split on Reagan Tax Bill," *Houston Chronicle*, 19 August 1982.

102. House Vote to Agree to the Conference Report on H.R.4961, 19 August 1982, GovTrack, https://www.govtrack.us/congress/votes/97-1982/h642.

103. Steven Roberts, "'Boll Weevil' Faces 'Real Democrat' in Florida Runoff Contest," *New York Times*, 3 October, 1982.

104. "Chappell Survives Tough Florida Race," *Atlanta Constitution*, 6 October 1982.

105. Maggie Willis, "The 7th District," *Marietta Journal*, 31 October 1982.

106. Jay Barrow, "Macon's Republican Mayor Supports Billy Evans," *Macon Telegraph*, 3 September 1982; "Evans, Defeated in Runoff, Says He May Try Again," *Augusta Chronicle*, 23 September 1982.

107. Joan McKinney, "Did the Election Kill the Boll Weevils?" *Advocate*, 7 November 1982.

108. David Maraniss, "'Boll Weevil' Winners Feel Lost," *Washington Post*, 21 November 1982.

109. Maraniss, "'Boll Weevil' Winners Feel Lost."

110. Joan McKinney, "Roemer Confirms He Has Discussed Switch to GOP," *Advocate*, 4 January 1983.

111. Joan McKinney, "Roemer Gets Banking," *Advocate*, 5 January 1983.

112. "'Boll Weevils' Get Message," *Richmond Times-Dispatch*, 5 January 1983.

113. Bill Arthur, "Carolinas' Lawmakers Disclaim 'Boll Weevil' Label," *Charlotte Observer*, 10 February 1983.

114. Smith, *The Power Game*, 528.

115. "'Tip' Knifes Doug," *Augusta Chronicle*, 16 January 1983.

116. Nene Foxhall and Cragg Hines, "Unlike Gramm, 2nd 'Boll Weevil' Able to Keep House Assignment," *Houston Chronicle*, 5 January 1983.

117. Maraniss, "'Boll Weevil' Winners Feel Lost."

118. Nene Foxhall, "Gramm Re-Elected to District 6 House Seat," *Houston Chronicle*, 13 February 1983.

119. Dave Montgomery, "Boll Weevils' Sting Less Potent," *Fort Worth Star-Telegram*, 3 October 1982.

120. Mark Thompson, "C'mon Over, Reagan Writes Gramm," *Fort Worth Star-Telegram*, 23 December 1982.

121. "U.S. Rep. Andy Ireland Switches His Allegiance to Republican Party," *Tampa Bay Times*, 18 March 1984.

122. William Murchison, "Meet Kent Hance, Republican," *Dallas Morning News*, 7 May 1985.

123. "Election Statistics: 1920-Present," History, Art, and Archives of the US House of Representatives, https://history.house.gov/Institution/Election-Statistics/.

124. Rae, *Southern Democrats*, 71–72, 90.

125. Roberto Suro, "Louisiana's Governor Shifts to G.O.P. in Career Gamble," *New York Times*, 12 March 1991.

126. Eric Pianin, "GOP Extols Rep. Tauzin's Party Switch," *Washington Post*, 8 August 1995; Christy Hoppe, "Hall on GOP's Roll Now," *Dallas Morning News*, 3 January 2004.

127. "Sonny Montgomery Says Goodbye to Washington," *Commercial Appeal*, 29 December 1996.

128. Mike Christensen, "No Perks for Switch, Deal Says," *Atlanta Constitution*, 11 April 1995.

129. Hornblower and Reid, "After Two Decades."

CHAPTER FOUR. "FREE TRADE WILL DESTROY AMERICA!"

1. David Stockman, *The Triumph of Politics* (New York: Hodder & Stoughton, 1985), 163.

2. Ronald Reagan, *An American Life: The Autobiography* (New York: Threshold, 1990), 343–344.

3. Rob Chambers, "Drought, Tight Credit Hurt Farmer," *Atlanta Constitution*, 11 January 1981.

4. Reagan, *An American Life*, 345.

5. Seth King, "They Lighted Up the Family Farm," *New York Times*, 29 March 1981.

6. Stockman, *Triumph of Politics*, 162.

7. Ronald Reagan to J. C. Galloway, 24 September 1980, Box 67, EMF.

8. "Food Stamps Targeted for Cuts," *Atlanta Constitution*, 31 December 1980.

9. Mary McGrory, "Why Tobacco Subsidies Ride High," *Atlanta Constitution*, 2 March 1981.

10. Stockman, *Triumph of Politics*, 154.

11. Mark Pinsky, "Helms Exhorts Tobacco Bloc to Fight Budget Cuts," *New York Times*, 21 March 1981.

12. Address by Jesse Helms in Raleigh, North Carolina, 20 March 1981, Record Group 2, Box 241, JHP.

13. Helen Dewar, "Spending Cuts Just Fine—in Other Districts," *Washington Post*, 5 February 1981.

14. Spencer Rich, "Ax Poised for Poverty Agency and Anti-Smoking Program," *Washington Post*, 5 March 1981.

15. "Farm Price Support Boost Planned," *Atlanta Constitution*, 1 April 1981; Sonja Hillgren, "Senate Panel Calls for Protection for Farmers against Embargoes," *UPI*, 1 April 1981.

16. Ward Sinclair, "Farm Program Unveiled on Hill," *Washington Post*, 1 April 1981.

17. "Food Stamps Out of the Farm Bill," *Washington Post*, 10 April 1981.

18. Seth King, "Senate Vote Gives Reagan Key Victory on Price Supports," *New York Times*, 26 March 1981.

19. Sonja Hillgren, "House Agriculture Subcommittee Has Rejected an Administration Proposal," *UPI*, 9 April 1981.

20. Henry Eason, "Helms Jousting for Peanut Barons," *Atlanta Constitution*, 16 April 1981.

21. Henry Eason, "Peanut 'Lords' Go to the Barricades," *Atlanta Constitution*, 2 April 1981.

22. Julian Morgan to Bo Ginn, 30 April 1981, Box 215, BGC.

23. Thomas Irvin to Mack Mattingly, 7 May 1981, Box 215, BGC.

24. David Bomar Smith to Strom Thurmond, 3 August 1981, and Strom

Thurmond to David Bomar Smith, 12 August 1981, both in Box 1, Correspondence Management Service Series, STC.

25. Raymond Coffey, "Plumping the Agriculture Budget," *Chicago Tribune*, 7 May 1981.

26. Robert Kaiser, "Senate's Multibillion Farm Bill Still Sprouting," *Washington Post*, 1 May 1981.

27. Seth King, "Not Just Peanuts," *New York Times*, 12 July 1981.

28. Joan McKinney, "Breaux and Tauzin Traded Votes for Reagan Aid for Sugar." *Advocate*, 28 June 1981.

29. Ward Sinclair and Art Harris, "In Tax Crunch, Reagan Flipped for Peanut Bill," *Washington Post*, 1 August 1981.

30. Ward Sinclair, "GOP Senators Argue over Farm Bill," *Washington Post*, 15 September 1981.

31. Remarks by James Exon, CR, 15 September 1981, 20567.

32. Ward Sinclair, "Not a Good Week," *Washington Post*, 22 September 1981.

33. Ernest B. Furgurson, *Hard Right: The Rise of Jesse Helms* (New York: W. W. Norton & Company, 1986), 155–158.

34. Remarks by Jesse Helms, CR, 17 September 1981, 21016.

35. Remarks by Strom Thurmond, CR, 17 September 1981, 21029.

36. William Welch, "Democrats Trying to Even Tobacco Score," *Greensboro Record*, 21 September 1981.

37. Charles Madigan, "Peanut Lobby Wins D.C. Shell Game," *Atlanta Constitution*, 23 September 1981.

38. Remarks by John East, CR, 16 September 1981, 20772; remarks by Howell Heflin, CR, 16 September 1981, 20774.

39. Steven Roberts, "Farm Bloc Facing Unusual Coalition," *New York Times*, 13 October 1981.

40. "House Defeats Peanut, Sugar Price Supports," *Baltimore Sun*, 16 October 1981.

41. Seth King, "Conferees Agree on Keeping Peanut Supports," *New York Times*, 11 November 1981.

42. "Reagan Wins a Squeaker on Farm Bill," *Atlanta Constitution*, 17 December 1981.

43. Remarks by Neal Smith, CR, 16 December 1981, 31801.

44. H. Carlisle Besuden, "Some Legislators Say '81 Farm Bill Partial to South," *Lexington Herald-Leader*, 20 December 1981.

45. Phil Swann, "3 Key Texans Likely to Vote against Farm Bill," *San Antonio Express*, 16 December 1981.

46. Bill Nichols to James Wible, 17 December 1981, Accession 82–003, Box 1, WNP.

47. "Compromise Farm Bill Is Voted by Senate," *Richmond Times-Dispatch*, 11 December 1981.

48. "Reagan Signs Farm Bill," *Chicago Tribune*, 23 December 1981.

49. Ronald Reagan, "Statement on Signing the Agriculture and Food Act of 1981," 22 December 1981, PPP-RR (1981), 1177–1178.

50. Dan Lohwasser, "Pressed Leaf Farmers Study Change," *News and Observer*, 14 December 1981.

51. Remarks by Paul Tsongas, CR, 16 September 1981, 20773.

52. Stockman, *Triumph of Politics*, 164.

53. Larry Schwab, *The Illusion of a Conservative Reagan Revolution* (New Brunswick, NJ: Transaction Publishers, 1991), 86.

54. Ward Sinclair, "Farm Failures Threaten to Reshape Rural U.S.," *Washington Post*, 25 January 1985.

55. Pamela Hollie, "The Sugar Industry's Slide," *New York Times*, 7 December 1984.

56. William Schmidt, "Future of 2 Southern Industries Raises Concern," *New York Times*, 9 December 1984.

57. Ronald Reagan, "The President's News Conference," 21 February 1985, PPP-RR (1985), 197–204.

58. A. L. May, "Block Indicates Leaf Plan Not Final," *News and Observer*, 31 January 1985.

59. A. L. May, "Helms Vows to Use Clout in Leaf Program's Defense," *News and Observer*, 29 January 1985.

60. Ward Sinclair, "Proposal to End Tobacco Program Has Congressional Backers Smoking," *Washington Post*, 5 February 1985.

61. Don Kendall, "Reagan's Farm Plan Draws Fire," *Advocate*, 23 February 1985.

62. "Lawmakers Reluctant to Introduce Farm Bill," *Lexington Herald-Leader*, 13 February 1985.

63. Keith Schneider, "Farm Bill Passes Senate, 61 to 28," *New York Times*, 24 November 1985.

64. Ward Sinclair, "Reagan Signs 5-year Farm Bill," *Washington Post*, 24 December 1985.

65. Ronald Reagan, "Statement on Signing the Food Security Act of 1985," 23 December 1985, PPP-RR (1985), 1502–1503.

66. Schwab, *Illusion of a Conservative Reagan Revolution*, 88.

67. Michael Schulman and Jeffrey Leiter, "Southern Textiles: Contested Puzzles and Continuing Paradoxes," in *Hanging by a Thread: Social Change in Southern Textiles*, ed. Jeffrey Leiter, Michael Schulman, and Rhonda Zingraff (Ithaca, NY: ILR Press, 1991), 3–17.

68. "Textiles Trail in Job Gains," *Atlanta Constitution*, 19 October 1969.

69. Bob Deans, "Have Imported Textiles Become America's New Boll Weevil?" *Atlanta Constitution*, 26 August 1984.

70. Schmidt, "Future of 2 Southern Industries."

71. Timothy Minchin, *Empty Mills: The Fight Against Imports and the Decline of the US Textile Industry* (Lanham, MD: Rowman & Littlefield, 2013), 69–70.

72. Robert Press, "Southern Textile-mill Blues," *Christian Science Monitor*, 31 March 1983.

73. William Schmidt, "Town Built by Textile Mill Faces Future Without It," *New York Times*, 22 December 1984.

74. Robin Toner, "Closing of a Mill Is Like a Funeral," *Atlanta Constitution*, 27 February 1983.

75. Toner, "Closing of a Mill."

76. Minchin, *Empty Mills*, 67–70.

77. Schmidt, "Future of 2 Southern Industries."

78. Craig Hume, "Textile Import Curb Sought," *Atlanta Constitution*, 30 June 1978.

79. Lee Egerstrom, "Carter Vetoes Bills on Imports," *Boston Globe*, 12 November 1978.

80. Ronald Reagan Speech in Columbia, South Carolina, 10 October 1980, Box 434, 1980 PCP.

81. Ronald Reagan to Strom Thurmond, 3 September 1980, Box 3, Legislative Assistant Series, STC; Ronald Reagan to Carroll Campbell, 18 January 1980, OA12242, MDF.

82. James Baker to Carroll Campbell, 11 December 1981, Box 12, MOF.

83. Ronald Reagan to Strom Thurmond, 4 October 1982, Box 3, Legislative Assistant Series, STC.

84. Memo from Malcolm Baldridge to Ronald Reagan, undated 1983, Box 12, MOF.

85. William Klopman to the President, 17 May 1983, OA12242, MDF.

86. Timothy Williams, "Roger Milliken, Conservative Tycoon, Dies at 95," *New York Times*, 31 December 2010.

87. Roger Milliken to Ed Meese, 31 May 1983, Box 66, EMF.

88. Roger Milliken to James Baker, Michael Deaver, and Ed Meese, 27 September 1983, Box 12, MOF.

89. Roger Milliken to James Baker, 3 November 1983; Box 66, EMF.

90. Memo from John Richardson to Kenneth Cribb, 14 November 1983, and Memo from Walter Lenahan to Ed Meese, 17 November 1983, both in Box 66, EMF.

91. Strom Thurmond to Ronald Reagan, 14 October 1983, Box 12, MOF.

92. Carroll Campbell to Ed Meese, 8 November 1983, Box 66, EMF.

93. Ben Thrailkill Jr. to Ronald Reagan, 6 May 1984, Box 29, CCP.

94. James Broyhill to M. B. Oglesby, 7 December 1983, Box 12, MOF.

95. Memo from William Brock to Ed Meese, 17 November 1983, Box 67, EMF.

96. Malcolm Baldrige to Ronald Reagan, undated 1983, Box 66, EMF.

97. Memo from Roger Porter to John Svahn, 10 May 1984, Box 66, EMF.

98. Stephen Roberts, "'Funny Kind of Coalition' on Textiles," *New York Times*, 25 September 1985.

99. James Broyhill et al. to James Baker, 28 June 1985, Series 2, Box 8, EJP.

100. Emily Langer, "Ed Jenkins, Former Democratic Congressman from Georgia, Dies at 78," *Washington Post*, 3 January 2012.

101. Roberts, "'Funny Kind of Coalition.'"

102. Calvin Lawrence, "Championing the Fight against Imports," *Atlanta Constitution*, 20 October 1985.

103. H.R.1562 (99th): Textile and Apparel Trade Enforcement Act of 1985, GovTrack, https://www.govtrack.us/congress/bills/99/hr1562.

104. "Textile Aid Package Introduced, Challenged," *Miami Herald*, 20 March 1985.

105. Sarah Avery, "Bill Limiting Textile Imports Being Offered," *Greensboro Record*, 19 March 1985.

106. Minchin, *Empty Mills*, 97.

107. Art Pine and Ellen Hume, "Protectionist Sentiment Grows in Congress in Face of Inaction by Reagan Administration," *Wall Street Journal*, 29 May 1985.

108. Memo from William Brock and Malcolm Baldrige to the president, 12 March 1985, Box 12, MOF.

109. Pine and Hume, "Protectionist Sentiment."

110. James Baker et al., to Ed Jenkins, 19 June 1985, Box 10, EJP.

111. Memo from "AMK" to "'BK,'" 25 September 1985, Box 9, LAF.

112. Ronald Reagan, "The President's News Conference," 17 September 1985, PPP-RR (1985), 1103–1110.

113. Ronald Reagan, "Remarks at a White House Meeting with Business and Trade Leaders," 23 September 1985, PPP-RR (1985), 1127–1130.

114. Peter Kilborn, "US and 4 Allies Plan Move to Cut Value of Dollar," *New York Times*, 23 September 1985.

115. David Wilman, "Despite Plea from Japan, Reagan Sets New Tariffs," *Boston Globe*, 18 April 1987.

116. "Textile Executives Express Disappointment with Reagan," *Greensboro News and Record*, 23 September 1985.

117. House Vote to Approve H.R.1562, 10 October 1985, GovTrack, https://www.govtrack.us/congress/votes/99-1985/h320.

118. "Senate Defies Veto Threat with Approval of Trade Bill," *Houston Chronicle*, 14 November 1985.

119. Roger Milliken to Strom Thurmond, 14 November 1985, Box 75, Correspondence Management Service Series, STC.

120. Bill Arthur, "Textile Bill OK'D in Senate," *Charlotte Observer*, 14 November 1985.

121. David Pace, "Southern Republicans Plead Textile Bill's Case," *Macon Telegraph*, 6 December 1985.

122. Ronald Reagan, 5 December 1985, *The Reagan Diaries Unabridged, vol. 2* (New York: HarperCollins, 2009).

123. Ronald Reagan, "Message to the House of Representatives Returning without Approval the Textile and Apparel Industries Bill," 17 December 1985, PPP-RR (1985), 1486–1487.

124. Robert Rosenblatt, "Congressmen Pledge to Attempt Textile Veto Override in August," *Los Angeles Times*, 19 December 1985.

125. Memo from Haley Barbour to Mitchell Daniels Jr., 31 January 1986, Box 3, WLF.

126. Talking points for James Broyhill meeting with James Baker, 16 January 1986, Box 3, WLF.

127. Memo from Edward Stucky to Haley Barbour, 15 May 1986, Box 11, ESF.

128. Stuart Auerbach, "New Textile Pact Entangled in Veto Battle," *Washington Post*, 2 August 1986.

129. Carroll Campbell to Tom DeLay, 22 July 1986, Box 32, CCP.

130. Records of telephone calls to Buddy Roemer and Charles Stenholm, both 4 August 1986, Box 9, PTC.

131. "Override of Import Bill Veto Will Shatter Global Markets, Reagan Warns," *Arkansas Gazette*, 6 August 1986.

132. Carroll Campbell to Republican Colleagues, 23 July 1986, Box 32, CCP.

133. Remarks by Newt Gingrich, CR, 6 August 1986, 19341.

134. Remarks by Thomas Hartnett, CR, 6 August 1986, 19342.

135. Remarks by Sonny Montgomery, CR, 6 August 1986, 19378.

136. Nolan Walters, "House Vote Sustains Reagan's Veto on Textile Imports," *Fort Worth Star-Telegram*, 7 August 1986.

137. Minchin, *Empty Mills*, 116.

138. Minchin, *Empty Mills*, 132.

139. "Reagan Vetoes Textile Bill," *Arkansas Gazette*, 29 September 1988.

140. House Vote to Pass H.R.1154, 4 October 1988, GovTrack, https://www.govtrack.us/congress/votes/100-1988/h900.

141. Minchin, *Empty Mills*, 138.

142. "Textile Executives Express Disappointment," *Greensboro News and Record.*

143. Lenahan to Meese, 17 November 1983, EMF.

144. Lee Bandy, "Reagan Ready to Veto Import Limits," *State*, 18 December 1985.

CHAPTER FIVE. "IT WAS JESUS THAT GAVE US THIS VICTORY"

1. Jim Jones, "Robison Says Evangelicals Deserve Some of the Credit for Reagan's Win," *Fort Worth Star-Telegram*, 5 November 1980.

2. Adam Clymer, "Bush Says No Single Group Gave Reagan His Victory," *New York Times*, 18 November 1980.

3. "No Advice for Reagan, Falwell Says," *Richmond Times-Dispatch*, 7 November 1980.

4. Mark Rozell and Mark Caleb Smith, "Religious Conservatives and the Transformation of Southern Politics," in *The Oxford Handbook of Southern Politics*, ed. Charles Bullock and Mark Rozell (New York: Oxford University Press, 2012), 135–137.

5. "Falwell Says Effort Paid Off," *Richmond Times-Dispatch*, 5 November 1980.

6. David Nyhan, "New Right Leaders Warn Reagan," *Boston Globe*, 7 November 1980.

7. Bruce Buursma, "Moral Majority: Crusade Has Just Begun," *Chicago Tribune*, 6 November 1980.

8. Marjorie Hyer, "Evangelical Christians Meet to Develop Strategy for 1980s," *Washington Post*, 30 January 1981.

9. George Skelton, "Reagan Names First Woman to High Court," *Los Angeles Times*, 8 July 1981.

10. "O'Connor: Long on Experience," *Boston Globe*, 8 July 1981.

11. Drummond Ayres, "'A Reputation for Excelling,'" *New York Times*, 8 July 1981.

12. "Reagan Draws Criticism on Justice Choice," *Atlanta Constitution*, 8 July 1981.

13. Adam Clymer, "Nomination of Judge O'Connor Protested by Abortion Foes at Rally," *New York Times*, 4 September 1981.

14. Jim Jones, "Robison Denies Backing O'Connor," *Fort Worth Star-Telegram*, 17 July 1981.

15. William Martin, *With God on Our Side: The Rise of the Religious Right in America* (New York: Broadway Books, 1996), 228.

16. "2 Church Papers Criticize Reagan over Falwell Call," *Houston Chronicle*, 15 July 1981.

17. Jon Margolis, "The 2 Faces of American Conservatives," *Chicago Tribune*, 12 July 1981.

18. "Reagan Pushing O'Connor," *Charlotte Observer*, 9 July 1981.

19. Saul Friedman, "O'Connor Seen as Political Plus," *Miami Herald*, 9 July 1981.

20. Memo from Morton Blackwell to Elizabeth Dole, 8 July 1981, Box 20, EDF.

21. L. G. Graham to President Reagan, 8 July 1981 and Mary Jane Kimball to President Reagan, 8 July 1981, both in Box 70, AHF.

22. E. Wayne Wall to Strom Thurmond, 13 July 1981, Box 10, Volume Mail Series, STC.

23. Sam Thielman to Jesse Helms, 7 July 1981, Record Group 2, Box 2084, JHP.

24. Memo from Ed Thomas to Ed Meese, 27 July 1981, Box 7, EMF.

25. Margolis, "The 2 Faces of American Conservatives."

26. Memo from Max Friedersdorf to Jim Baker, Ed Meese et al., 14 July 1981, Box 7, EMF.

27. Carol Giacomo, "O'Connor, Calling on Congressmen, Hears Assurances of Confirmation," *Hartford Courant*, 15 July 1981.

28. Fred Barbash, "O'Connor, Helms Meet 40 Minutes," *Washington Post*, 17 July 1981.

29. Rob Christensen, "Helms Troubled about O'Connor," *News and Observer*, 22 September 1981.

30. "O'Connor Ends Testimony on Nomination," *Boston Globe*, 11 September 1981.

31. Record of telephone call to Jeremiah Denton, 16 September 1981, Box 7, EMF.

32. Jim Mann, "O'Connor OK'd by Unanimous Vote in Senate," *Los Angeles Times*, 22 September 1981.

33. Charles Madigan, "Abortion, O'Connor on Agenda of Christian Right Convention," *Chicago Tribune*, 4 September 1981; "National Sin Is Abortion, Falwell Tells Dallas Audience," *Arkansas Gazette*, 6 September 1981.

34. "Falwell Says Goldwater Has Chosen Not to Run," *Houston Chronicle*, 17 September 1981.

35. "Neutral Stance Slated," *Advocate*, 18 September 1981.

36. Fred Barbash, "Abortion Vote Called Mistake by O'Connor," *Washington Post*, 10 September 1981.

37. William Branigin, Fred Barbash, and Daniela Deane, "Supreme Court Justice O'Connor Resigns," *Washington Post*, 1 July 2005.

38. Memo from Elizabeth Dole to Michael Deaver, 16 December 1981, Box 20, EDF.

39. Cal Thomas to James Baker, 9 October 1981, Box 13, MBF.

40. Dole to Deaver, Box 20, EDF.

41. Benjamin Taylor, "Social Issues Come Center Stage," *Boston Globe*, 10 January 1982.

42. "'Jilted' Conservatives Plotting Course to Regain Reagan's Ear," *State*, 22 January 1982.

43. Cal Thomas to Morton Blackwell, 1 March 1982, Box 13, MBF.

44. Morton Blackwell to Cal Thomas, 25 March 1982, Box 13, MBF.

45. Neil Young, *We Gather Together: The Religious Right and the Problem of Interfaith Politics* (New York: Oxford University Press, 2016), 211–214.

46. Vera Glaser, "Senators Push for Legislation Defining Embryo as Person," *Lexington Herald-Leader*, 15 April 1981.

47. "New Anti-Abortion Proposal Would Leave Policy to States," *Fort Worth Star-Telegram*, 3 September 1981.

48. Marjorie Hyer, "Catholics Criticized for Supporting Hatch Antiabortion Amendments," *Washington Post*, 17 November 1981.

49. "Reagan Reaffirms His Opposition to Abortion," *Atlanta Constitution*, 23 January 1982.

50. David Zerhusen to Larry Hopkins, 26 January 1982, Box 154, LHP.

51. President Reagan to Jesse Helms, 5 April 1982, Presidential Letters, JHP.

52. Memo from Richard Doerflinger to Pro-Life Coordinators, 17 September 1982, Box 20, EDF.

53. Ernest Furgurson, "Senator May Filibuster Antiabortion Measure," *Baltimore Sun*, 22 April 1981.

54. Carol Giacomo, "Pro-Lifers' Squabbling Jeopardizes Legislative Drive," *Hartford Courant*, 22 January 1982.

55. Bill Peterson, "In the Administration, a Pattern Develops on Conservatives' Agenda," *Washington Post*, 22 February 1982.

56. Bill Peterson, "Parliamentary Jockeys Maneuver for Lead on Anti-Abortion Bill," *Washington Post*, 18 August 1982.

57. Memo from Morton Blackwell to Elizabeth Dole, 20 August 1982, Box 25, SGF.

58. White House "Talking Points" memo, undated 1982, Box 1, JEJF.

59. Memo from Michael Uhlmann and Stephen Galebach to Edwin Harper, 23 August 1982, Box 25, SGF.

60. Howell Raines, "Reagan Harks Back to the Campaign," *New York Times*, 13 September 1982.

61. Charles Austin, "Religious Right Begins Losing Faith in Reagan," *Atlanta Constitution*, 22 August 1982.

62. Memo, "Administration Efforts in Behalf of the Abortion Amendment," 24 September 1982, and President Reagan letter to senators, 7 September 1982, both in Box 2, FMF.

63. "Abortion Filibuster Survives Senate Vote," *Advocate*, 10 September 1982.

64. "Senate Kills Helms Proposal Restricting Right to Abortion," *Charlotte Observer*, 16 September 1982.

65. Tom Seppy, "Senate Defeats Abortion Issue," *Advocate*, 29 June 1983.

66. Seppy, "Senate Defeats Abortion Issue."

67. "Falwell Expects Reshaped Court Would Outlaw Most Abortions," *Boston Globe*, 11 October 1984.

68. Phil Gailey, "Conservative Study Gives Reagan a Mixed Rating," *New York Times*, 25 November 1983.

69. Steven K. Green, "Evangelicals and the Becker Amendment: A Lesson in Church-State Moderation," *Journal of Church and State* 33, no. 3 (Summer 1991): 548–549.

70. Max Baucus, "Court-Stripping Bill Must Be Defeated," *Atlanta Constitution*, 9 September 1982.

71. Steven Weisman, "Reagan Neutral on Bid to Curb Court on Prayer," *New York Times*, 9 September 1982; David Rogers, "Helms Loses His Fight on School Prayer Bill," *Boston Globe*, 24 September 1982.

72. Ronald Reagan, "Remarks at a White House Ceremony in Observance of National Day of Prayer," 6 May 1982, PPP-RR (1982), 573–575.

73. George Skelton, "Reagan Urges School Prayer Amendment," *Los Angeles Times*, 7 May 1982.

74. Memo from Gary Bauer to Edwin Harper, 8 March 1982, Box 44, EMF.

75. George Gallup, "People Favor Prayers in Public Schools," *Washington Post*, 16 May 1980.

76. School Prayer Polling Summary, 1982, Box 44, EMF.

77. Kenneth Briggs, "Doubts on School Prayer," *New York Times*, 8 May 1982.

78. Daniel K. Williams, *God's Own Party: The Making of the Christian Right* (New York: Oxford University Press, 2010), 200–201.

79. *Statistical Abstract of the United States: 1982–1983 (103rd Edition)*, 54–55.

80. George Vecsey, "Southern Baptists Choose a Conservative President," *New York Times*, 13 June 1979.

81. Young, *We Gather Together*, 217–218.

82. Williams, *God's Own Party*, 200–202.

83. "McAteer Had White House Backing to Seek SBC Act," *Baptist Press*, 1 July 1982.

84. Jim Jones, "Prayers in School Endorsed," *Fort Worth Star Telegram*, 18 June 1982.

85. Tom Wicker, "The Baptist Switch," *New York Times*, 22 June 1982.

86. Adrian Rogers to Morton Blackwell, 13 July 1982, Box 18, MBF.

87. Morton Blackwell to Reverend Richard Bridges, 21 July 1982, Box 19, MBF.

88. Memo from Gary Bauer to Edwin Harper, 22 June 1982, Box 2, WHORM.

89. Wicker, "The Baptist Switch."

90. Gary Jarmin to Morton Blackwell, 20 July 1982, Box 18, MBF.

91. Matthew Moen, *The Christian Right and Congress* (Tuscaloosa: University of Alabama Press, 1989), 102.

92. "Support from Moral Majority Not Automatic, President Told," *Arkansas Gazette*, 8 August 1982.

93. Ronald Reagan, "Radio Address to the Nation on Domestic Social Issues," 22 January 1983, PPP-RR (1983), 94–95.

94. Ronald Reagan, "Address Before a Joint Session of the Congress on the State of the Union," 25 January 1983, PPP-RR (1983), 102–110.

95. Memo from Ken Duberstein to Faith Whittlesey, 20 June 1983, Box 19, MBF; Memo from Faith Whittlesey to James Baker and Ed Meese, 11 October 1983, Box 11, MOF.

96. Bill Stall, "Prayer Proposal Defeated," *Hartford Courant*, 21 March 1984.

97. Martin Tolchin, "Amendment Drive on School Prayer Loses Senate Vote," *New York Times*, 21 March 1984.

98. Martin, *With God on Our Side*, 234.

99. "Republican Party Platform of 1984," The American Presidency Project, UC Santa Barbara, https://www.presidency.ucsb.edu/node/273427.

100. "This Time on Tipping Toes, Religion Heads to Schools," *Philadelphia Inquirer*, 27 April 1984.

101. "Poll Shows Moral Majority Whites Give Reagan Southern Advantage," *Atlanta Constitution*, 3 October 1984.

102. Tom Barnes, "South's Leaders Not Optimistic About Mondale," *Hartford Courant*, 31 July 1984.

103. Ben Bradlee Jr., "Southern Baptist Preachers Mix Religion, Campaigning for Reagan," *Boston Globe*, 19 October 1984.

104. Helen Dewar, "Senate Kills Measure on School Prayer," *Washington Post*, 11 September 1985.

105. "Role of Moral Majority in Conservative Victories Significant, Falwell Says," *Arkansas Gazette*, 9 November 1984.

106. Kevin Mirada, "Right Claims Results," *Dallas Morning News*, 10 November 1984.

107. "U.S. Exploring Stronger Ties to Vatican," *Houston Chronicle*, 9 December 1983.

108. Bob Jones Jr. to Ronald Reagan, 30 December 1983, Box 1, CSF.

109. "U.S., Vatican Reopen Relations," *Advocate*, 11 January 1984.

110. "Scandals Bring Hard Times for Nation's TV Evangelists," *New York Times*, 6 October 1989.

111. Ruth Marcus, "Judge a Favorite with Conservative Lawyers, Activists," *Washington Post*, 18 June 1986.

112. Stuart Taylor, "Bork Could Tilt Law at Once if Seated," *New York Times*, 6 July 1987.

113. Ruth Marcus, "Groups Unlimber Media Campaigns over Bork," *Washington Post*, 4 August 1987.

114. Senate Vote to Confirm the Nomination of Robert H. Bork, 23 October 1987, GovTrack, https://www.govtrack.us/congress/votes/100-1987/s348.

115. Edward Walsh, "Bork's Foes Build Strategy on South," *Washington Post*, 4 October 1987.

116. Jeffrey Giles to J. Bennett Johnston, 1 October 1987, Box 161, JBJP.

117. J. Bennett Johnston to Robert Boh, 15 October 1987, Box 161, JBJP.

118. Kevin Mirada, "Senate Rejects Bork," *Dallas Morning News*, 24 October 1987.

119. Robert Barnes, "Justice Kennedy to Retire from Supreme Court," *Washington Post*, 27 June 2018.

120. "Bork Nomination Sparks Debate on Place of Religion in Politics," *St. Petersburg Times*, 15 August 1987.

121. Williams, *God's Own Party*, 204.

122. Gary Geipel, "5,000 Rally in Capital to Urge Nuclear Freeze," *Los Angeles Times*, 9 March 1983.

123. Williams, *God's Own Party*, 211.

124. Rich Jaroslovsky, "Politics '84—Bible Is Battle Cry," *Wall Street Journal*, 18 September 1984.

125. Barbara White, "Falwell Will Fold Group," *Augusta Chronicle*, 12 June 1989.

126. Terry Mattingly, "Reagan Boosted Political, Religious Conservatives," *Knoxville News-Sentinel*, 12 June 2004.

CHAPTER SIX. "AFFIRMATIVE ACTION IS UN-AMERICAN"

1. E. R. Shipp, "Across the Rural South, Segregation as Usual," *New York Times*, 27 April 1985.
2. E. R. Shipp, "The Races in Mississippi," *New York Times*, 2 April 1985.
3. Roy Reed, "Little Rock a Symbol Again," *New York Times*, 23 March 1985.
4. William Schmidt, "Selma, 20 Years After the Rights March," *New York Times*, 1 March 1985.
5. William Schmidt, "Jim Crow Is Gone, but White Resistance Remains," *New York Times*, 6 April 1985.
6. Art Harris, "Three White Men Arrested in Slaying of Black Youth," *Washington Post*, 26 March 1981.
7. Judith Paterson, "The 'New Republican' South," *Christian Science Monitor*, 23 July 1982.
8. Shipp, "Across the Rural South."
9. Rachelle Patterson, "Reagan Calls Busing Failure," *Boston Globe*, 19 November 1980.
10. "Republican Party Platform of 1980," The American Presidency Project, UC Santa Barbara, https://www.presidency.ucsb.edu/node/273420.
11. "US Hearing on UNC System Will Resume," *Charlotte Observer*, 24 February 1981.
12. Spencer Rich, "Califano Acts to Cut N.C. University Aid over Bias," *Washington Post*, 27 March 1979.
13. Steven Roberts, "What Is the Difference Between Califano and Carolina? Plenty!," *New York Times*, 15 April 1979.
14. "Education Nominee to Discuss UNC Case," *Charlotte Observer*, 17 January 1981.
15. Rob Christensen, "UNC Desegregation Agreement Signed," *News and Observer*, 3 July 1981.
16. "NAACP Fight Is Expected in UNC Case," *Greensboro Daily News*, 22 June 1981; Charles Babcock, "U.S. Accepted Desegregation Plan Once Rejected for N.C. Colleges," *Washington Post*, 11 July 1981.
17. "Praise, Criticism Greet Accord," *News and Observer*, 21 June 1981; "East Gives Credit to Administration," *Greensboro Record*, 4 July 1981.
18. Ronald Reagan, *An American Life: The Autobiography* (New York: Threshold, 1990), 198.

19. Fred Hechinger, "The Department That Would Not Die," *New York Times*, 14 November 1982.

20. "Push Is on for Further University System Integration," *Atlanta Constitution*, 7 June 1981.

21. Hugh Davis Graham, "Nixon and Civil Rights: Explaining an Enigma," *Presidential Studies Quarterly* 26, no. 1 (Winter 1996): 93–106.

22. Christensen, "Bell Vows Less Federal Intervention," *News and Observer*, 16 January 1981.

23. "Remarks by William Bradford Reynolds to The Fourth Annual Conference on Equal Employment Opportunity," 20 October 1981, Education Resources Information Center (ERIC), Institute of Education Sciences, https://files.eric.ed.gov/fulltext/ED208160.pdf.

24. "Reagan Fires Chief of Civil Rights Board," *Atlanta Constitution*, 17 November 1981.

25. Vernon Jordan, "Reagan Hurting Civil Rights Program," *Atlanta Constitution*, 16 December 1981.

26. "House Heads Toward Voting Rights Showdown, Certain to Affect the South," *Arkansas Gazette*, 27 July 1981.

27. William A. Link, *Righteous Warrior: Jesse Helms and the Rise of Modern Conservatism* (New York: St. Martin's Press, 2008), 259.

28. Joseph Crespino, *Strom Thurmond's America* (New York: Hill & Wang, 2012), 291.

29. Steven Roberts, "House Vote Backs Keeping Key Parts of 1965 Voting Act," *New York Times*, 6 October 1981.

30. Lou Cannon, "Reagan Dodges Voting Rights Issue," *Washington Post*, 30 June 1981.

31. Laurence Barrett, "An Interview with Ronald Reagan," *Time Magazine*, 5 January 1981.

32. Lou Cannon, *President Reagan: The Role of a Lifetime* (New York: Public Affairs, 2000), 458.

33. Memo from Diana Lozano to Elizabeth Dole, 10 June 1981, Box 60, EDF.

34. House Vote to Pass H.R.3112, 5 October 1981, GovTrack, https://www.govtrack.us/congress/votes/97-1981/h228.

35. Memo from Elizabeth Dole to Richard Darman, 7 October 1981, Box 60, EDF.

36. Richard Barrett to Jesse Helms, 30 April 1982, Box 2152, Record Group 2, JHP.

37. Marjorie Gervin to Jesse Helms, 6 May 1982, Box 2152, Record Group 2, JHP.

38. J. H. Killebrew, to Bill Nichols, 11 September 1981, Box 5, WNP.

39. H. O. Cochran to Ed Jenkins, 11 November 1981, Box 30, EJP.

40. Gene L. Howard to Bill Nichols, 3 December 1981, Box 5, WNP.

41. William Perdue to Bill Nichols, 14 October 1981, Box 5, WNP.

42. Memo from Mel Bradley to Martin Anderson, 4 November 1981, Box 15, MLBF.

43. Ronald Reagan, "Statement about Extension of the Voting Rights Act," 6 November 1981, PPP-RR (1981), 1018.

44. "A Strong Voting Shield for Blacks?" *Boston Globe*, 2 March 1982.

45. Aaron Epstein, "Administration Would Weaken Voting Act," *Hartford Courant*, 28 January 1982; Reginald Stuart, "March Is Begun in Alabama to Back Voting Rights Law," *New York Times*, 7 February 1982.

46. Senate Vote to Pass H.R.3112, 18 June 1982, GovTrack, https://www.gov track.us/congress/votes/97-1982/s687.

47. Claude Sitton, "Helms' Filibuster Gives State a Black Eye," *News and Observer*, 20 June 1982.

48. Crespino, *Strom Thurmond's America*, 296.

49. Herbert Denton, "Reagan Signs Voting Rights Act Extension," *Washington Post*, 30 June 1982.

50. Memo from Edwin Harper to the President, 5 March 1982, Box 18, EDF.

51. Clyde Penn, "Holiday for King: Shall It Overcome?" *Los Angeles Times*, 11 August 1981.

52. "Voting: The New Black Power," *New York Times*, 27 November 1983.

53. Crespino, *Strom Thurmond's America*, 296.

54. "Helms Set to Filibuster King Holiday Bill," *Boston Globe*, 3 October 1983.

55. Remarks by Jesse Helms, 3 October 1983, CR, 26866–26878.

56. Steven Roberts, "Senators Are Firm on King Holiday," *New York Times*, 19 October 1983.

57. Helen Dewar, "Solemn Senate Votes for National Holiday Honoring Rev. King," *Washington Post*, 20 October 1983.

58. Link, *Righteous Warrior*, 265–269.

59. Larry Greene to Jesse Helms, 24 October 1983, and Donald Buck to Jesse Helms, 23 October 1983, both in Box 2171, Record Group 2, JHP.

60. John Boswell to Strom Thurmond, 18 September 1983, and Chester Kirkevold to Strom Thurmond, 19 September 1983, both in Box 11, Volume Mail Series, STC.

61. Bob Dart, "Maddox Virulently Fights King Holiday," *Atlanta Constitution*, 6 October 1983.

62. "Reagan Sympathetic, but Cautious on a King Holiday," *New York Times*, 11 May 1982.

63. Gladwyn Hill, "Reagan Not Sure Johnson Has Quit," *New York Times*, 10 April 1968.

64. Ronald Reagan to Meldrim Thompson, 3 October 1983, *Reagan: A Life in Letters*, ed. Kiron Skinner, Annelise Anderson, and Martin Anderson (New York: Free Press, 2003), 634.

65. Ronald Reagan, "The President's News Conference," 19 October 1983, PPP-RR (1983), 1486–1493.

66. Ronald Reagan, "Remarks on Signing the Bill Making the Birthday of Martin Luther King, Jr., a National Holiday," 2 November 1983, PPP-RR (1983), 1529–1530.

67. Ronald Reagan, "The President's News Conference," 11 February 1986, PPP-RR (1986), 200–208.

68. "Bob Jones University Apologizes for its Racist Past," *Journal of Blacks in Higher Education*, no. 62 (Winter 2008/2009): 22–23.

69. David Whitman, "Ronald Reagan and Tax Exemptions for Racist Schools," John F. Kennedy School of Government, Harvard University, 1984, Box 60, MDF.

70. Robert Lindsey, "Reagan to Debate His G.O.P. Rivals in South Carolina," *New York Times*, 31 January 1980.

71. Whitman, "Ronald Reagan and Tax Exemptions."

72. James Guth, "South Carolina: The Christian Right Wins One," *PS: Political Science and Politics* 28, no. 1 (March 1995): 8–9.

73. "Republican Party Platform of 1980."

74. "Trent Lott to Donald Regan, 30 October 1981" and "Trent Lott to Rex Lee, 30 October 1981" in *Legislation to Deny Tax Exemption to Racially Discriminatory Private Schools: Hearing Before the Committee on Finance*, United States Senate, 97th Congress, 1 February 1982.

75. "Talking Points: Meeting with Senator Thurmond, 17 December 1981" in *Administration's Change in Federal Policy Regarding the Tax Status of Racially Discriminatory Private Schools: Hearing Before the Committee on Ways and Means*, House of Representatives, 97th Congress, 4 February 1982.

76. Whitman, "Ronald Reagan and Tax Exemptions."

77. "Memo from Peter Wallison to Donald Regan, 17 December 1981," in *Administration's Change in Federal Policy*.

78. "Presidential Log of Selected House Mail," December 1981, Box 1, DNF.

79. "Memo from Ann Dore McLaughlin to Dave Gergen, 7 January 1982," in *Legislation to Deny Tax Exemption*.

80. Eliot Brenner, "Democrats, Liberals Assail Tax Decision on Biased Schools," *Hartford Courant*, 10 January 1982

81. "Biased Schools' Tax Breaks OK'd," *Chicago Tribune*, 9 January 1982.

82. "Reagan's Reversal on Racism," *Baltimore Sun*, 12 January 1982.

83. "The Rewarding of Bias," *Los Angeles Times*, 12 January 1982.

84. Robert A. Jordan, "Tax-Exempt Decision Gives a Wrong Signal to School Segregationists," *Boston Globe*, 12 January 1982.

85. Jordan, "Tax-Exempt Decision."

86. Hal Gulliver, "Trying to Turn Back the Clock," *Atlanta Constitution*, 12 January 1982.

87. "Exemption from IRS Restored," *Atlanta Constitution*, 9 January 1982.

88. Ronald Reagan, "The President's News Conference," 19 January 1982, PPP-RR (1982), 36–43.

89. Laurence Barrett, *Gambling with History: Ronald Reagan in the White House* (New York: Doubleday, 1983), 415–420.

90. Mark Pinsky, "Publicity Has Left Some at Christian Schools 'Gun Shy,'" *Boston Globe*, 10 February 1982.

91. "Students Asked to Lobby for Tax Policy," *Charlotte Observer*, 16 January 1982.

92. "Bob Jones Says Reagan's Change on Tax Exemptions Was 'A Sell-Out,'" *Columbia Record*, 27 January 1982.

93. Delbert Rose to Larry Hopkins, 26 February 1982, Box 151, LHP.

94. Steve and Gwen Jones to Ed Jenkins, 8 February 1982, Box 38, EJP; Betty Ferguson to Morton Blackwell, 9 February 1982, Box 64, MBF.

95. Emmett Dickens to Jesse Helms, 19 February 1982, Box 2121, Record Group 2, JHP; John J. Bourn to President Reagan, 6 February 1982, Box 64, MBF.

96. Rowland Evans and Robert Novak, "The Private School Fiasco Raises Friends' Ire," *Augusta Chronicle*, 30 January 1982.

97. "Summary of House Calls Regarding Tax Exemption Bill," 18 January 1982, Box 4, MOF.

98. Memo from Nancy Risque to M. B. Oglesby, 16 February 1982, Box 4, MOF.

99. "Bob Jones: We're Guinea Pigs," *Atlanta Constitution*, 10 October 1982.

100. Jim Mann, "Court Upholds Tax on Biased Schools," *Los Angeles Times*, 25 May 1983.

101. Phil Gailey, "Bob Jones, in Sermon, Assails Supreme Court," *New York Times*, 25 May 1983; "Bob Jones 'Mourning,'" *Baltimore Sun*, 25 May 1983; Glen Elsasser, "Racially Biased Schools Lose Tax-Exemption Case," *Chicago Tribune*, 25 May 1983.

102. Bob Jones III to Ronald Reagan, 30 December 1983, Box 1, CSF.

103. Memo from John Roberts to Fred Fielding, 4 January 1984, Box 6, JRF.

104. John Crewdson, "Judge's Stand on Busing Divides Louisiana Town on Racial Lines," *New York Times*, 9 January 1981.

105. Crewdson, "Judge's Stand"; Art Harris, "Louisiana Busing Face-Off Defused as State Judge Accepts U.S. Plan," *Washington Post*, 16 January 1981.

106. "Dueling Judges Show No Sign of Relenting in La. Busing Case," *Baltimore Sun*, 13 January 1981.

107. Harris, "Louisiana Busing Face-Off."

108. "3 in Busing Dispute Join Private School," *New York Times*, 22 January 1981.

109. "McDonald Move Called Meddling," *Atlanta Constitution*, 7 February 1981.

110. Charles Waite to Ronald Reagan, 19 January 1981, Box 55, JBJP.

111. Carolyn and Harold Boblitt to Larry Hopkins, 28 January 1982, Box 154, LHP.

112. "Half of Blacks in a Poll Question Busing's Value," *New York Times*, 2 March 1981.

113. "Busing Issue Forecast" memo, 28 September 1981, Box 16, EDF.

114. Lawrence J. McAndrews, *The Era of Education: The Presidents and the Schools, 1965–2001* (Chicago: University of Illinois Press, 2006), 168–170.

115. Mark White to President Reagan, 6 May 1981, Box 1, DWF.

116. Robert Hodierne, "New Day for Anti-Busing Bill," *Charlotte Observer*, 28 April 1981.

117. Joan McKinney, "Bills Aim at Limit on Busing," *Advocate*, 25 February 1981.

118. "Statement by J. Bennett Johnston on 'The Neighborhood School Act,'" Box 55, JBJP.

119. Richard E. Lee to J. Bennett Johnston, 25 February 1981, and Lawrence Derthick Jr. to J. Bennett Johnston, 23 March 1981, both in Box 55, JBJP.

120. Wesley Pippert, "Anti-Busing Legislation Passes Senate," *UPI*, 2 March 1982.

121. Memo from Morton Blackwell to Elizabeth Dole, 22 July 1982, Box 16, EDF.

122. "House Prohibits Spending for School Busing Litigation," *Atlanta Constitution*, 10 December 1982.

123. "Issues to Rebuild the Winning Reagan Coalition of 1980," Jerry Falwell to Ronald Reagan, 13 November 1983, Box 28, EMF.

124. Ronald Reagan, "Remarks at a Reagan-Bush Rally in Charlotte, North Carolina," 8 October 1984, PPP-RR (1984), 1465–1468.

125. "You Were Wrong, Mr. President," *Charlotte Observer*, 9 October 1984.

126. McAndrews, *Era of Education*, 173–174.

127. Martin Weil, "Wm. French Smith, Attorney General Under Reagan, Dies," *Washington Post*, 30 October 1990.

128. "Meese Doubts Value of Busing," *Hartford Courant*, 16 March 1985.

129. Ashley Halsey, "A Crucial Court Case Challenges School Busing," *Philadelphia Inquirer*, 7 January 1985; Stephen Engelberg, "Norfolk Busing Case Viewed as Key to Keeping U.S. Schools Integrated," *New York Times*, 3 February 1985.

130. Stuart Taylor, "The Court Sees No Evil in Ending a Busing Plan," *New York Times*, 9 November 1986.

131. McAndrews, *Era of Education*, 175.

132. Sheldon Goldman, "Reagan's Judicial Legacy: Completing the Puzzle and Summing Up," *Judicature* 72, no. 6 (April–May 1989): 327–329.

133. McAndrews, *Era of Education*, 168.

134. Shipp, "The Races in Mississippi."

135. David Cook, "'State of Black America' Paints Grim Picture," *Christian Science Monitor*, 24 January 1986.

136. Schmidt, "Jim Crow Is Gone."

137. Ronald Smothers, "Election Results Troubling Blacks," *New York Times*, 9 November 1984.

138. Sanford J. Ungar and Peter Vale, "South Africa: Why Constructive Engagement Failed," *Foreign Affairs*, Winter 1985/86.

139. Lou Cannon, "Reagan Expected to Veto South African Sanctions but Adopt Other Action," *Washington Post*, 22 August 1985.

140. Bob Secter, "Helms Stalls Vote on Anti-Apartheid Moves," *Los Angeles Times*, 9 July 1985.

141. "How Congress Voted," *Morning Call*, 14 July 1985.

142. "Back from South Africa, Falwell Called Part of 'Immoral Minority,'" *Hartford Courant*, 21 August 1985.

143. Mary McGrory, "Falwell, Reagan stumbling on S. Africa," *Boston Globe*, 28 August 1985.

144. Ronald Reagan, "Message to the House of Representatives Returning Without Approval a Bill Concerning Apartheid in South Africa," 26 September 1986, PPP-RR (1986), 1278–1280.

145. David Shribman and Robert Greenberger, "Senate, Joining House, Overrides Veto by Reagan of South Africa Sanctions," *Wall Street Journal*, 3 October 1986; Senate Vote to Adopt, over the President's Veto, HR.4868, 2 October 1986, GovTrack, https://www.govtrack.us/congress/votes/99-1986/s692.

146. Remarks by Jesse Helms, CR, 2 October 1986, 27849.

147. Nancy Schwerzler, "Senate, 78–21, Overrides Veto on Sanctions," *Baltimore Sun*, 3 October 1986.

148. Lou Cannon, *President Reagan*, 462–463.

149. Ronald Reagan, "Message to the Senate Returning without Approval the Civil Rights Restoration Act of 1987 and Transmitting Alternative Legislation," 16 March 1988, PPP-RR (1988), 345–346.

150. "An Indecent Veto," *St. Petersburg Times*, 20 March 1988.

151. George Curry, "Civil Rights Veto Overridden," *Chicago Tribune*, 23 March 1988.

152. Milton Coleman, "Reagan Rating Falls in Poll of Blacks," *Washington Post*, 18 January 1986.

153. Juan Williams, "The Reagan Era Ends with Our Nation Even More Racially Divided," *St. Petersburg Times*, 27 November 1988.

EPILOGUE

1. Joseph Crespino, *Strom Thurmond's America* (New York: Hill & Wang, 2012), 289.

2. Jerry Hagstrom, *Beyond Reagan: The New Landscape of American Politics* (New York: W. W. Norton, 1988), 202–207; 241–243.

3. Guy Gugliotta, "Hill Conferees Clear Major Farm Changes," *Washington Post*, 22 March 1996; Senate Vote to Pass H.R. 2854: Federal Agriculture Improvement and Reform Act of 1996, 28 March 1996, GovTrack, https://www.govtrack.us/congress/votes/104-1996/s57.

4. Llewellyn Rockwell, "Freedom to Farm—Thanks to the Taxpayer," *Los Angeles Times*, 9 April 1996.

5. Michael Grunwald, "Record Farm Bailout Nears Hill Approval," *Washington Post*, 13 October 1999.

6. Timothy Minchin, *Empty Mills: The Fight Against Imports and the Decline of the US Textile Industry* (Lanham, MD: Rowman & Littlefield, 2013), 140–150.

7. Senate Vote to Pass H.R.3450: North American Free Trade Agreement Implementation Act, 20 November 1993, GovTrack, https://www.govtrack.us/congress/votes/103-1993/s395.

8. "State of the South 2002: Shadows in the Sunbelt Revisited," MDC Inc., Chapel Hill, NC, September 2002, https://www.mdcinc.org/wp-content/uploads/2017/11/sos_02.pdf.

9. Reginald Stuart, "Democrats Resurging in South?" *Philadelphia Daily News*, 2 March 1988.

10. Tom Baxter, "Ronald Reagan, 1911–2004," *Atlanta Journal-Constitution*, 10 June 2004.

11. James C. Cobb, *The South and America Since World War II* (New York: Oxford University Press, 2012), 179.

12. Wayne Flint, "The Transformation of Southern Politics, 1954 to the Present," in *A Companion to the American South*, ed. John B. Boles (Malden, MA: Blackwell Publishers, 2002), 499.

13. Michael Lind, "The Southern Coup," *New Republic*, 19 June 1995.

14. Christopher Caldwell, "The Southern Captivity of the GOP," *The Atlantic*, June 1998.

15. Doug Rossinow, *The Reagan Era: A History of the 1980s* (New York: Columbia University Press, 2015), 242–244.

16. John Dillin, "As Dust Settles, Campaigns Take Shape," *Christian Science Monitor*, 10 March 1988.

17. Rossinow, *Reagan Era*, 244–247.

18. Roger Simon, "How a Murderer and Rapist Became Bush's Most Valuable Player," *Baltimore Sun*, 11 November 1990.

19. Rossinow, *Reagan Era*, 247.

20. Thomas Edsall, "New GOP Chief Renowned for Dividing Foes," *Washington Post*, 20 January 1989.

21. Peter Applebome, "Subtly and Not, Race Bubbles Up as Issue in North Carolina Contest," *New York Times*, 2 November 1990.

22. David Lauter, "Affirmative Action Poised to Become Political Divide," *Los Angeles Times*, 21 February 1995.

23. Adam Nagourney, "Dole Sees Failure of Three Decades in Anti-Bias Fight," *New York Times*, 29 October 1996.

24. Neil Young, "How George H. W. Bush Enabled the Rise of the Religious Right," *Washington Post*, 6 December 2018.

25. Pat Buchanan, "Why Do They Hate Dixie?" *The American Conservative*, 1 December 2003.

26. "Pat Buchanan 1992 Republican Convention Address," 17 August 1992, C-SPAN, https://www.c-span.org/video/?31255-1/pat-buchanan-1992-republican-convention-address.

27. R. W. Apple, "Behind Bush's Mixed Abortion Signals," *New York Times*, 15 August 1992.

28. Flint, "Transformation of Southern Politics," 499.

29. Frances FitzGerald, *The Evangelicals: The Struggle to Shape America* (New York: Simon & Schuster, 2017), 422.

30. John F. Persinos, "Has the Christian Right Taken Over the Republican Party?" *Campaigns and Elections* 15, no. 9 (September 1994): 20–24.

31. Jim Wooten, "The South Is Back: Oh, Happy Day," *Atlanta Journal*, 4 January 1995.

32. Wooten, "The South Is Back."

33. "In Their Own Words: The Republican Promises," *New York Times*, 11 November 1994; Nicole Hemmer, *Partisans: The Conservative Revolutionaries Who Remade American Politics in the 1990s* (New York: Basic Books, 2022), 9.

34. "Gingrich: Don't Rush on Abortion," *Chicago Tribune*, 8 May 1995.

35. David Broder, "When Unity Becomes Division," *Washington Post*, 1 March 1996.

36. Hemmer, *Partisans*, 8.

37. Broder, "When Unity Becomes Division."

38. Godfrey Hodgson, *The World Turned Right Side Up: A History of the Conservative Ascendancy in America* (London: Houghton Mifflin, 1996), 286.

39. Caldwell, "Southern Captivity of the GOP."

40. "Gingrich Sees Passage of Multiyear Tax Cut," *Atlanta Constitution*, 13 May 1981.

41. Kevin Merida, "Sen. Trent Lott and a Troublesome Tie," *Washington Post*, 29 March 1999.

42. John Nichols, "Trent Lott's 'Uptown Klan,'" *The Nation*, 12 December 2002.

43. Sheryl Gay Stolberg, "Under Fire, Lott Apologizes for His Comments at Thurmond's Party," *New York Times*, 10 December 2002.

44. Adam Clymer, "30-Year Dream of Leadership Is Undone by a Lack of Allies," *New York Times*, 21 December 2002.

45. Neil Lewis, "Trent Lott," *New York Times*, 3 December 1994.

46. Joseph A. Aistrup, *The Southern Strategy Revisited: Republican Top-Down Advancement in the South* (Lexington: University of Kentucky Press, 1996), 51.

47. Anthony Badger, *Why White Liberals Fail: Race and Southern Politics from FDR to Trump* (Cambridge, MA: Harvard University Press, 2022), 156.

48. Earl Black and Merle Black, *The Rise of Southern Republicans* (Cambridge, MA: Harvard University Press, 2002), 205.

AFTERWORD: REPUBLICAN CIVIL WAR IN THE AGE
OF TRUMP

1. Susan Glasser, "Is Trump the Second Coming of Reagan?" *New Yorker*, 18 May 2018; Daniel Drezner, "How Donald Trump is like Ronald Reagan," *Washington Post*, 8 February 2018.

2. Emma Margolin, "'Make America Great Again'—Who Said It First?"

NBC News, 9 September 2016, https://www.nbcnews.com/politics/2016-elec tion/make-america-great-again-who-said-it-first-n645716.

3. Nicole Hemmer, *Partisans: The Conservative Revolutionaries Who Remade American Politics in the 1990s* (New York: Basic Books, 2022), 253–254, 267–270; Martin Walker, "Bush as Reagan's Heir," *UPI*, 9 June 2004.

4. Chris Good, "On Social Issues, Tea Partiers Are Not Libertarians," *The Atlantic*, 6 October 2010.

5. Vanessa Williamson, Theda Skocpol, and John Coggin, "The Tea Party and the Remaking of Republican Conservatism," *Perspectives on Politics* 9, no. 1 (March 2011): 26, 32–35.

6. Tim Alberta, *American Carnage: On the Front Lines of the Republican Civil War and the Rise of President Trump* (New York: Harper, 2019), 345–346.

7. Alberta, *American Carnage*, 202, 242, 255.

8. Drew DeSilver, "Freedom Caucus Districts Look Much Like Other GOP-Held Districts," Pew Research Center, 22 October 2015, https://www .pewresearch.org/short-reads/2015/10/22/freedom-caucus-districts-look -much-like-other-gop-held-districts/.

9. Michael Lind, "How the South Skews America," *Politico*, 3 July 2015, https://www.politico.com/magazine/story/2015/07/how-the-south-skews -america-119725/.

10. "Tracking Trump: Approval by State," Morning Consult, https://morn ingconsult.com/tracking-trump-2/.

11. David Jackson, "Why the South likes Donald Trump," *USA Today*, 29 February 2016.

12. Josh Hafner, "Donald Trump Loves the 'Poorly Educated'—and They Love Him," *USA Today*, 24 February 2016; Dan Carter, "What Donald Trump Owes George Wallace," *New York Times*, 10 January 2016.

13. Stuart Stevens, "Trump Chooses Open Racism. What Does His Party Choose?" *Washington Post*, 18 July 2019.

14. Ewan Palmer, "More People See the Confederate Flag as a Sign of Southern Pride Than as a Symbol of Racism," *Newsweek*, 10 June 2020.

15. Alberta, *American Carnage*, 457–458.

16. Alberta, *American Carnage*, 495–504.

17. Jeremy Peters, *Insurgency: How Republicans Lost Their Party and Got Everything They Ever Wanted* (New York: Crown, 2022), 196–200, 255–260.

18. Katie Reilly, "Here Are All the Times Donald Trump Insulted Mexico," *Time*, 31 August 2016.

19. Charlie Savage, "Justice Dept. to Take on Affirmative Action in College Admissions," *New York Times*, 1 August 2017.

20. Erica L. Green, "Trump Officials Reverse Obama's Policy on Affirmative Action in Schools," *New York Times*, 3 July 2018.

21. Raymond Hernandez, "After Challenges, House Approves Renewal of Voting Act," *New York Times*, 14 July 2006.

22. Sean Sullivan, "Everything You Need to Know about the Supreme Court Voting Rights Act Decision," *Washington Post*, 25 June 2013.

23. Matt Ford, "The Entirely Preventable Battles Raging over Voting Rights," *The Atlantic*, 14 April 2017.

24. Sheryl Gay Stolberg, "House Passes Voting Rights Bill Despite Near Unanimous Republican Opposition," *New York Times*, 6 December 2019.

25. Chris Kromm, "South Rising: Region's Political Clout Growing under Trump," *Facing South*, 21 April 2017, https://www.facingsouth.org/2017/04/south-rising-regions-political-clout-growing-under-trump.

26. Matt Ford, "The Incredible Shrinking GOP," *New Republic*, 5 August 2019.

27. Alberta, *American Carnage*, 596.

28. Anthony Badger, *Why White Liberals Fail: Race and Southern Politics from FDR to Trump* (Cambridge, MA: Harvard University Press, 2022), 186.

29. Ross Baker, "Trump Is Right: Mitch McConnell Is One of the Greatest Senate Leaders of All Time," *Washington Post*, 25 October 2018.

30. Badger, *Why White Liberals Fail*, 175.

31. Karen Yourish, Larry Buchanan, and Denise Lu, "The 147 Republicans Who Voted to Overturn Election Results," *New York Times*, 7 January 2021.

32. "Scalise Should Step Down," *Chicago Tribune*, 31 December 2014.

33. Jonathan Chait, "The Future of Trumpism," *New York Magazine*, 29 March 2022.

34. Robert Barnes and Ann Marimow, "Supreme Court Ruling Leaves States Free to Outlaw Abortion," *Washington Post*, 24 June 2022.

35. "Tracking the States Where Abortion Is Now Banned," *New York Times*, 10 February 2023.

36. "A Nation of Immigrants? Diverging Perceptions of Immigrants Increasingly Marking Partisan Divides," Public Religion Research Institute, 12 March 2020, https://www.prri.org/research/a-nation-of-immigrants-diverging-perceptions-of-immigrants-increasingly-marking-partisan-divides/.

37. Jonathan Rauch, "It's George Wallace's World Now," *The Atlantic*, 26 April 2020.

Select Bibliography

Administration's Change in Federal Policy Regarding the Tax Status of Racially Discriminatory Private Schools: Hearing Before the Committee on Ways and Means, House of Representatives, 97th Congress, 4 February 1982. Washington, DC: US Government Printing Office, 1982.

Aistrup, Joseph A. *The Southern Strategy Revisited: Republican Top-Down Advancement in the South.* Lexington: University of Kentucky Press, 1996.

Alberta, Tim. *American Carnage: On the Front Lines of the Republican Civil War and the Rise of President Trump.* New York: Harper, 2019.

Badger, Anthony. *Why White Liberals Fail: Race and Southern Politics from FDR to Trump.* Cambridge, MA: Harvard University Press, 2022.

Barrett, Laurence. *Gambling with History: Ronald Reagan in the White House.* New York: Doubleday, 1983.

Bartley, Numan V. *The New South: 1945–1980.* Baton Rouge: Louisiana State University Press, 1995.

Bartley, Numan V., and Hugh Davis Graham. *Southern Politics and the Second Reconstruction.* Baltimore: Johns Hopkins University Press, 1975.

Bates, Toby Glenn. *The Reagan Rhetoric: History and Memory in 1980s America.* Dekalb: Northern Illinois University Press, 2011.

Black, Earl, and Merle Black. *The Rise of Southern Republicans.* Cambridge, MA: Harvard University Press, 2002.

"Bob Jones University Apologizes for its Racist Past." *Journal of Blacks in Higher Education,* no. 62 (Winter 2008/2009): 22–23.

Bowen, Michael. *The Roots of Modern Conservatism: Dewey, Taft, and the Battle for the Soul of the Republican Party.* Chapel Hill: University of North Carolina Press, 2011.

Cannon, Lou. *Governor Reagan: His Rise to Power.* New York: Public Affairs, 2003.

———. *President Reagan: The Role of a Lifetime.* New York: Public Affairs, 2000.

Christensen, Rob. *The Paradox of Tar Heel Politics: The Personalities, Elections and Events That Shaped Modern North Carolina.* Chapel Hill: University of North Carolina Press, 2008.

Cobb, James C. *The Selling of the South: The Southern Crusade for Industrial Development, 1936–1980.* Baton Rouge: Louisiana State University Press, 1982.

———. *The South and America Since World War II*. New York: Oxford University Press, 2010.

Cohen, Michael A. *American Maelstrom: The 1968 Election and the Politics of Division*. New York: Oxford University Press, 2016.

Crespino, Joseph. *In Search of Another Country: Mississippi and the Conservative Counterrevolution*. Princeton: Princeton University Press, 2007.

———. *Strom Thurmond's America*. New York: Hill & Wang, 2012.

Cunningham, Sean. *American Politics in the Postwar Sunbelt*. New York: Cambridge University Press, 2014.

———. *Cowboy Conservatism: Texas and the Rise of the Modern Right*. Lexington: University Press of Kentucky, 2010.

Dallek, Matthew. *The Right Moment: Ronald Reagan's First Victory and the Decisive Turning Point in American Politics*. New York: Oxford University Press, 2000.

Dochuk, Darren. *From Bible Belt to Sunbelt: Plain Folk Religion, Grassroots Politics, and the Rise of Evangelical Conservatism*. New York: W. W. Norton & Company, 2011.

Donaldson, Gary. *Liberalism's Last Hurrah: The Presidential Campaign of 1964*. New York: M. E. Sharpe, 2003.

Edwards, Lee. *Goldwater: The Man Who Made a Revolution*. Washington, DC: Regnery History, 1995.

Evans, Thomas. *The Education of Ronald Reagan: The General Electric Years and the Untold Story of His Conversion to Conservatism*. New York: Columbia University Press, 2006.

Farber, David. *The Rise and Fall of Modern American Conservatism: A Short History*. Princeton: Princeton University Press, 2010.

FitzGerald, Frances. *The Evangelicals: The Struggle to Shape America*. New York: Simon & Schuster, 2017.

Flint, Wayne. "The Transformation of Southern Politics, 1954 to the Present." In *A Companion to the American South*, edited by John B. Boles, 494–505. Malden, MA: Blackwell Publishers, 2002.

Ford, Gerald R. *A Time to Heal: The Autobiography*. New York: Harper & Row, 1979.

Frederickson, Kari. *The Dixiecrat Revolt and the End of the Solid South, 1932–1968*. Chapel Hill: University of North Carolina Press, 2001.

Freeman, Curtis W. "'Never Had I Been So Blind': W. A. Criswell's 'Change' on Racial Segregation." *Journal of Southern Religion* 10 (2007): 1–12.

Furgurson, Ernest B. *Hard Right: The Rise of Jesse Helms*. New York: W. W. Norton & Company, 1986.

Gaddie, Ronald Keith. "Realignment." In *The Oxford Handbook of Southern Politics*, edited by Charles Bullock and Mark Rozell, 289–313. New York: Oxford University Press, 2012.

Glashan, Roy R. *American Governors and Gubernatorial Elections, 1775–1978*. London: Meckler, 1979.

Goldman, Sheldon. "Reagan's Judicial Legacy: Completing the Puzzle and Summing Up." *Judicature* 72, no. 6 (April–May 1989): 318–330.

Gould, Lewis L. *1968: The Election that Changed America*. Chicago: Ivan Dee, 1993.

———. *Grand Old Party: The History of the Republicans*. New York: Random House, 2003.

Graham, Billy. *Just As I Am: The Autobiography of Billy Graham*. New York: HarperCollins, 1997.

Graham, Hugh Davis. "Nixon and Civil Rights: Explaining an Enigma." *Presidential Studies Quarterly* 26, no. 1 (Winter 1996): 93–106.

Grantham, Dewey. *The Life and Death of the Solid South: A Political History*. Lexington: University Press of Kentucky, 1988.

Green, Steven K. "Evangelicals and the Becker Amendment: A Lesson in Church-State Moderation." *Journal of Church and State* 33, no. 3 (Summer 1991): 541–567.

Greenhaw, Wayne. *Elephants in the Cottonfields: Ronald Reagan and the New Republican South*. New York: Macmillan, 1982.

Gregory, James N. *The Southern Diaspora: How the Great Migrations of Black and White Southerners Transformed America*. Chapel Hill: University of North Carolina Press, 2005.

Guth, James. "South Carolina: The Christian Right Wins One." *PS: Political Science and Politics* 28, no. 1 (March 1995): 8–11.

Hagstrom, Jerry. *Beyond Reagan: The New Landscape of American Politics*. New York: W. W. Norton, 1988.

Hannaford, Peter. *The Reagans: A Political Portrait*. New York: Coward-McCann, 1983.

Harvey, Paul. "Religion, Race, and the Right in the South." In *Politics and Religion in the White South*, edited by Glenn Feldman, 101–124. Lexington: University of Kentucky Press, 2005.

Hayward, Steven. *The Age of Reagan: The Fall of the Old Liberal Order, 1964–1980*. Roseville, CA: Forum, 2001.

Helms, Jesse. *Here's Where I Stand: A Memoir*. New York: Random House, 2005.

Hemmer, Nicole. *Partisans: The Conservative Revolutionaries Who Remade American Politics in the 1990s*. New York: Basic Books, 2022.

Hodgson, Godfrey. *World Turned Right Side Up: A History of the Conservative Ascendancy in America*. London: Houghton Mifflin, 1996.

Honey, Michael. "Operation Dixie: Labor and Civil Rights in the Postwar South." *The Mississippi Quarterly* 45, no. 4 (Fall 1992): 439–452.

Katznelson, Ira. *Fear Itself: The New Deal and the Origins of Our Time*. New York: Liveright, 2013.

Kaufman, Burton, and Scott Kaufman. *The Presidency of James Earl Carter Jr.* Lawrence: University Press of Kansas, 2009.

Kruse, Kevin M. *White Flight: Atlanta and the Making of Modern Conservatism*. Princeton: Princeton University Press, 2005.

Lassiter, Matthew. "Big Government and Family Values: Political Culture in the Metropolitan Sunbelt." In *The Myth of Southern Exceptionalism*, edited by Matthew Lassiter and Joseph Crespino, 82–109. Philadelphia: University of Pennsylvania Press, 2011.

Lawson, Stephen F. *Running for Freedom: Civil Rights and Black Politics in America Since 1941*. Malden, MA: Wiley-Blackwell, 2009.

Legislation to Deny Tax Exemption to Racially Discriminatory Private Schools: Hearing Before the Committee on Finance, United States Senate, 97th Congress, 1 February 1982. Washington, DC: US Government Printing Office, 1982.

Lewis, George. *The White South and the Red Menace: Segregationists, Anticommunism, and Massive Resistance, 1945–1965*. Gainesville: University Press of Florida, 2004.

Link, William A. *Righteous Warrior: Jesse Helms and the Rise of Modern Conservatism*. New York: St. Martin's Press, 2008.

———. *Southern Crucible: The Making of an American Region*. New York: Oxford University Press, 2015.

Lyons, William, John M. Scheb, Billy Stair, and Joseph G. Jarret. *Government and Politics in Tennessee*. Knoxville: University of Tennessee, 2017.

Martin, William. *With God on Our Side: The Rise of the Religious Right in America*. New York: Broadway Books, 1996.

Mason, Robert. *The Republican Party and American Politics from Hoover to Reagan*. New York: Cambridge University Press, 2012.

———. *Richard Nixon and the Quest for a New Majority*. Chapel Hill: University of North Carolina Press, 2004.

McAndrews, Lawrence J. *The Era of Education: The Presidents and the Schools, 1965–2001*. Chicago: University of Illinois Press, 2006.

McGirr, Lisa. *Suburban Warriors: The Origins of the New American Right*. Princeton, NJ: Princeton University Press, 2001.

Miller, Edward H. *Nut Country: Right-Wing Dallas and the Birth of the Southern Strategy*. Chicago: University of Chicago Press, 2015.

Minchin, Timothy. *Empty Mills: The Fight Against Imports and the Decline of the US Textile Industry*. Lanham, MD: Rowman and Littlefield, 2013.

Moen, Matthew. *The Christian Right and Congress*. Tuscaloosa: University of Alabama Press, 1989.

Morgan, Iwan. *Reagan: American Icon*. London: I. B. Tauris, 2016.

Nixon, Richard M. *RN: The Memoirs of Richard Nixon*. New York: Grosset & Dunlap, 1978.

Nofziger, Lyn. *Nofziger*. Washington: Regnery Gateway, 1992.

Pardue, Eric. "Kennedyphobia and the Rise of Republicans in Northwest Louisiana, 1960–1962." In *Painting Dixie Red: When, Where, Why, and How the South Became Republican*, edited by Glenn Feldman, 122–137. Gainesville: University Press of Florida, 2011.

Perlstein, Rick. *The Invisible Bridge: The Fall of Nixon and the Rise of Reagan*. New York: Simon & Schuster, 2014.

———. *Nixonland: The Rise of a President and the Fracturing of America*. New York: Scribner, 2008.

Persinos, John F. "Has the Christian Right taken over the Republican Party?" *Campaigns and Elections* 15, no. 9 (September 1994): 20–24.

Peters, Jeremy. *Insurgency: How Republicans Lost Their Party and Got Everything They Ever Wanted*. New York: Crown, 2022.

Rae, Nicol. *Southern Democrats*. Oxford: Oxford University Press, 1994.

Reagan, Ronald. *An American Life: The Autobiography*. New York: Threshold, 1990.

———. *My Early Life or Where's The Rest of Me?* London: Sidgwick & Jackson, 1981.

———. *The Reagan Diaries Unabridged: Vol. 1*. New York: HarperCollins, 2009.

———. *The Reagan Diaries Unabridged: Vol. 2*. New York: HarperCollins, 2009.

Ritter, Kurt. "Ronald Reagan's 1960's Southern Rhetoric: Courting Conservatives for the GOP." *Southern Communication Journal* 64, no. 1 (1998–1999): 333–345.

Roche, Jeff. "Cowboy Conservatism." In *The Conservative Sixties*, edited by David Farber and Jeff Roche, 79–92. New York: Peter Lang, 2003.

Rossinow, Doug. *The Reagan Era: A History of the 1980s*. New York: Columbia University Press, 2015.

Rozell, Mark, and Mark Caleb Smith. "Religious Conservatives and the Transformation of Southern Politics." In *The Oxford Handbook of Southern Politics*, edited by Charles Bullock and Mark Rozell, 133–152. New York: Oxford University Press, 2012.

Salt, James. "Sunbelt Capital and Conservative Political Realignment in the 1970s and 1980s." *Critical Sociology* 16, no. 2–3 (May 1989): 145–163.

Schulman, Bruce. *From Cotton Belt to Sunbelt: Federal Policy, Economic Development and the Transformation of the South, 1938–1980.* Durham, NC: Duke University Press, 1994.

Schulman, Michael, and Jeffrey Leiter. "Southern Textiles: Contested Puzzles and Continuing Paradoxes." In *Hanging by a Thread: Social Change in Southern Textiles*, edited by Jeffrey Leiter, Michael Schulman, and Rhonda Zingraff, 3–20. Ithaca, NY: ILR Press, 1991.

Schwab, Larry. *The Illusion of a Conservative Reagan Revolution.* New Brunswick, NJ: Transaction Publishers, 1991.

Shermer, Elizabeth Tandy. *Sunbelt Capitalism: Phoenix and the Transformation of American Politics.* Philadelphia: University of Pennsylvania Press, 2013.

Shirley, Craig. *Reagan's Revolution: The Untold Story of the Campaign That Started It All.* Nashville: Nelson Current: 2005.

Skinner, Kiron, Annelise Anderson, and Martin Anderson, eds. *Reagan: A Life in Letters.* New York: Free Press, 2003.

———, eds. *Reagan: In His Own Hand.* New York: Touchstone, 2001.

Smith, Hedrick. *The Power Game: How Washington Works.* London: Collins, 1988.

Sokol, Jason. *There Goes My Everything: White Southerners in the Age of Civil Rights, 1945–1975.* New York: Knopf, 2006.

Statistical Abstract of the United States: 1982–1983 (103rd Edition). Washington, DC: US Census Bureau, 1982.

Stockman, David. *The Triumph of Politics.* New York: Hodder & Stoughton, 1985.

Warren, Robert Penn. *Segregation: The Inner Conflict in the South.* London: Eyre & Spottiswoode, 1957.

White, Theodore H. *The Making of the President 1964.* London: Jonathan Cape: 1965.

———. *The Making of the President 1968.* London: Jonathan Cape, 1969.

Williams, Daniel K. *God's Own Party: The Making of the Christian Right.* New York: Oxford University Press, 2010.

Williamson, Vanessa, Theda Skocpol, and John Coggin. "The Tea Party and the Remaking of Republican Conservatism." *Perspectives on Politics* 9, no. 1 (March 2011): 25–43.

Witcover, Jules. *Marathon: The Pursuit of the Presidency 1972–1976*. New York: Viking Press, 1977.

Wright, Jim. *Balance of Power: Presidents and Congress from the Era of McCarthy to the Age of Gingrich*. Atlanta: Turner Publishing, 1996.

Young, Neil. *We Gather Together: The Religious Right and the Problem of Interfaith Politics*. New York: Oxford University Press, 2016.

Index

www.ingramcontent.com/pod-product-compliance
Lightning Source LLC
Chambersburg PA
CBHW020335100426
42812CB00029B/3136/J